Better Homes
& Gardens.

Annual
Recipes 2020

Meredith, Consumer Marketing
Des Moines, Iowa

CHERRY-ORANGE COBBLER
Recipe on page 147

from the editor

This year has been challenging in many ways, but there has been one bright spot—most of us are spending more time at home cooking in the kitchen and learning new skills. That feeling of being happy at home has always been part of our mission at *Better Homes & Gardens.*

For years now I've had my go-to recipes, the ones I return to again and again. Over the past year, however, I started to bore myself while cooking three meals a day. So I dove back into my bookshelves to find some old favorites.

We all remember our first experience cooking from a cookbook. Like many of our readers, mine was with the *Better Homes & Gardens New Cook Book* (also known as the Red Plaid) first published in 1930. I have distinct memories of baking with Mom while its flour-stained, ring-bound pages lay splayed on the countertop. As the years went by, I accumulated a large library of cookery books on whatever new cuisine or author caught my interest.

However, in the daily rush of my pre-quarantine life, I found I rarely cracked open my cookbooks anymore. I was too busy or at least that's what I told myself. Now with more time spent at home, I enjoy thumbing through the pages of favorites old and new to see where they are stained or naturally fall open. I'll be armed with an even broader repertoire of go-tos and classics sporting their own dog-eared pages. Finding an internet recipe on the fly is undeniably convenient, but I'll always have a spot for my old paper-bound friends loyally waiting for me on the shelf whenever I need them. We hope this book someday means the same to you.

Stephen Orr, Editor in Chief
Better Homes & Gardens. magazine

Better Homes & Gardens.

Annual Recipes 2020

Our seal assures you that
every recipe in *Better Homes &
Gardens. Annual Recipes 2020*
has been tested in the Better
Homes & Gardens. Test Kitchen.
This means that each recipe
is practical and reliable, and
it meets our high standards of
taste appeal. We guarantee
your satisfaction with this book
for as long as you own it.

All of us at Meredith Consumer
Marketing are dedicated to
providing you with information
and ideas to enhance your
home. We welcome your
comments and suggestions.
Write to us at: Meredith
Consumer Marketing,
1716 Locust St., Des Moines, IA
50309-3023.

Pictured on front cover:
Triple-Chocolate Shortcut Mousse,
recipe on page 99.

MEREDITH CONSUMER MARKETING
Consumer Marketing Product Director: Daniel Fagan
Consumer Marketing Product Manager: Max Daily
Consumer Products Marketing Manager: Kylie Dazzo
Senior Production Manager: Liza Ward

WATERBURY PUBLICATIONS, INC.
Editorial Director: Lisa Kingsley
Associate Editor: Tricia Bergman
Creative Director: Ken Carlson
Associate Design Director: Doug Samuelson
Production Assistant: Mindy Samuelson
Contributing Copy Editors: Peg Smith, Carrie Truesdell
Contributing Indexer: Mary Williams

BETTER HOMES & GARDENS® MAGAZINE
Editor in Chief: Stephen Orr
Food Editor: Jan Miller

MEREDITH CORPORATION
Chairman: Stephen M. Lacy
Vice Chairman: Mell Meredith Frazier

In Memoriam: E.T. Meredith III (1933–2003)

**CORN & POTATO STEW
WITH CORNMEAL
DUMPLINGS**
Recipe on page 227

"HEARTBEET" COOLER
Recipe on page 214

COMFORT Everyone relates to food that recalls memories. Occasion, locale, those present—all contribute to nostalgic memories of taste and aroma. If you've cooked and baked often this year and found making familiar recipes comforting, perhaps you've also tried a few new recipes from *Better Homes & Gardens* magazine. And perhaps some have now become part of your repertoire.

In this cookbook you'll find an entire year's collection of delicious, tried and tested recipes—all achievable, with step-by-step instructions, plus many that call for fresh, seasonal ingredients. Expert BH&G food specialists, popular and respected chefs, cookbook authors, and food bloggers inspire homecooking—for breakfast, lunch, dinner, snacks, and special occasions. We're convinced that this collection of recipes will reinvigorate your assurance in creative, healthful cooking.

LOOK FOR

MONTHLY FEATURES Food pros share recipes, techniques, and tips to inspire and guide cooking success. You'll learn how to pile on healthful veggies—on a pizza! Hummus and Lamb Pizza with Romaine (page 19) is just one tempting combination. In February, the beauty of chicories in Chicken, Escarole, & Orecchiette Soup (page 52) as well as Braised Belgian Endive (page 50) warm body and soul, while pan-wiches feed a crowd, and big-batch sippers quench thirst.

March centers on the power of sour, from Lemon Tiramisu (page 63) to Chicken Adobo with Coconut Rice (page 66). A culinary journey with experts explains how to explore new cuisines: Huevos con Migos (page 112), Lamb Chops with Potatoes & Herb-Brown Butter Vinaigrette (page 109), and Priya's Dal (page 114). Come summer, fresh produce is center stage in Sweet & Sour Cherry Slab Pie (page 148), juicy melons in Lemondrop Melon & Chile Granita (page 165), and Grilled Zucchini & Goat Cheese Toasts (page 176).

In September, Zoë François bakes bread from her recipes for no-knead yeast dough (page 191). Cast-iron cookware has made a resurgence, and we have innovative recipes for this versatile kitchen tool. With hints of autumn chills, warm stews are welcomed—along with recipes for fresh earthy beets: Pork & Squash Stew with Ginger-Red Cabbage Slaw (page 227) and Beet & Onion Jam Galette (page 220). Thanksgiving dinner (beginning page 230) boasts Glazed Roast Turkey; a creative array of sides; and delectable desserts, such as Orange-Almond Cake with Cranberry Curd (page 240) as well as Pear Tarts with Caramelized Pastry Cream (page 254).

BREAKFAST Productive days begin with breakfast. Fortunately, the meal appears in sizes, shapes, and plans to please. Options include Cream Cheese Danishes (page 167) for a brunch spread, Fire-Roasted Tomato Strata (page 259) to serve family or guests, healthful and savory Breakfast Salad with Avocado & Eggs (page 184), and Sheet-Pan Eggy Bagels (page 157)—a fun and updated take on toad-in-a-hole.

FAST & FRESH Because weeknight meals create challenges for managing time, ingredients, and freshness, we offer time-saving recipes that call for lean protein, seasonal fruits and vegetables, leafy greens, and ultra-nutritious grains. Selections include Grain Salad with Greens, Cherries, and Crispy Bacon (page 37); Thai Shrimp & Cucumber Lettuce Wraps (page 59); Veggie Farfalle with Mediterranean Meatballs (page 188); Shortcut Pho (page 212); and many more.

POACHED VEGGIES
WITH WALNUT RELISH
Recipe on page 101

contents

33   117   165

**NO-KNEAD DOUGH
LOAF**
Recipe on page 191

11

CRISPY SALMON
WITH VEGGIES
& PESTO
Recipe on page 28

january

Begin the year by piling crisp salads on home-baked pizzas, assembling and stocking healthful to-go breakfasts, and putting cookers to work to get dinner on the table.

19 21 23

SALAD & PIZZA

Revamp weekly pizza night: Bake fresh crusts, layer on quick and satisfying toppings, then crown with colorful and crunchy salads. It's pizza as the ultimate budget-friendly one-dish meal.

CHICKEN & PEPPER PIZZA WITH KALE

When you have less than 30 minutes to get dinner in the oven, this pie—made with step-saving ingredients—will be your hero.

HANDS-ON TIME 25 min.
TOTAL TIME 45 min.

½   cup white vinegar
1   Tbsp. sugar
1   clove garlic, minced
1   cup thinly sliced red onion
1   12- to 16-oz. pkg. fresh white or whole wheat pizza dough
3   Tbsp. plus 1 tsp. olive oil
½   cup sliced red bell pepper
8   oz. shredded cooked chicken
½   cup purchased pizza sauce
2   oil-packed dried tomatoes, finely chopped
2   Tbsp. finely chopped toasted hazelnuts*
1   Tbsp. lemon juice
1   6-oz. bunch Tuscan or curly kale, stemmed and thinly sliced

1. For pickled onion: In a small saucepan bring vinegar, sugar, garlic, and ½ tsp. salt just to boiling, stirring to dissolve sugar. Add ½ cup of the onion. Return to boiling; reduce heat. Simmer 2 minutes; let cool.

2. Preheat oven to 425°F. On a lightly floured surface roll dough to a 12- to 14-inch circle. Place on a greased baking sheet; brush edges with 1 tsp. oil. Bake 10 minutes. Remove from oven.

3. Meanwhile, in a 10-inch skillet cook bell pepper and remaining ½ cup onion in 1 Tbsp. hot oil over medium 5 minutes or until tender. Add chicken; cook to warm through.

4. Spread crust with pizza sauce; top with chicken mixture. Carefully slide pizza onto oven rack; bake 10 minutes or until edges are browned.

5. Meanwhile, for salad: In a large bowl whisk together remaining 2 Tbsp. oil, the dried tomatoes, hazelnuts, lemon juice, ¼ tsp. salt, and ⅛ tsp. black pepper. Add kale; toss to coat, gently massaging to soften. Drain pickled onion, discarding liquid. Toss with kale mixture. Top pizza with salad. Serves 4.

EACH SERVING *508 cal, 22 g fat (3 g sat fat), 50 mg chol, 623 mg sodium, 51 g carb, 5 g fiber, 8 g sugars, 27 g pro*

THE CRUST A big time-saver is purchased dough, available in the refrigerated section at major grocery and specialty stores. For maximum crispiness, brush rolled-out dough with olive oil then parbake before topping. (Extra time? Try food processor dough from Potato & Leek Pizza with Arugula, page 16).

THE TOPPINGS Shredded deli chicken, combined with sautéed veggies, is a hearty and convenient topper for pizza.

THE GREENS Deep green kale provides vitamins, flavor, and glossy color. To tenderize Tuscan or curly kale, gently massage the leaves with a little olive oil. Then combine the greens with hazelnuts, sun-dried tomatoes, and pickled red onions.

*TO TOAST HAZELNUTS: SPREAD THEM IN A SHALLOW BAKING PAN. TOAST IN A 350°F OVEN 8 TO 10 MINUTES OR UNTIL LIGHTLY BROWNED. COOL SLIGHTLY, THEN PLACE IN A CLEAN KITCHEN TOWEL AND RUB OFF LOOSE SKINS.

A GENEROUS SPRINKLE OF CORNMEAL KEEPS THE DOUGH FROM STICKING TO THE BAKING SHEET AND EASES TRANSFER TO A CUTTING BOARD.

THE CRUST No kneading is required for this homemade pizza dough. Whirl everything together in the food processor and let it rise. It freezes well, too.

THE TOPPINGS Sliced potatoes on pizza add heartiness and flavor. Sauté potatoes with leeks and rosemary to soften them a bit before baking. As they bake on the pizza, potato slices crisp. This pie could be considered a sophisticated play on a French pizza.

THE GREENS The pepperiness of arugula calls for a simple vinaigrette of olive oil, lemon juice, and Dijon mustard—a minimal flavor enhancer. Finely grated Parmesan cheese is the final topping.

POTATO & LEEK PIZZA WITH ARUGULA

Removing sandy grit from leeks is tedious but necessary. Here's how: Thinly slice the leeks lengthwise, then swish thoroughly in a bowl of water, letting sand and grit sink to the bottom. Then drain the leeks on paper towels, patting them dry before adding to a recipe.

HANDS-ON TIME 25 min.
TOTAL TIME 1 hr. 25 min.

2	cups all-purpose flour
1	pkg. active dry yeast
1	tsp. sugar
5	Tbsp. olive oil, plus more for brushing dough and coating bowl
⅔	cup warm water (105°F to 115°F)
8	oz. Yukon Gold or red potatoes, sliced ⅛ inch thick
2	medium leeks, halved and thinly sliced (2 cups)
⅓	cup thinly sliced onion
1	tsp. chopped fresh rosemary Cornmeal
1	lemon (1 tsp. zest, 1 Tbsp. juice)
¼	tsp. Dijon mustard
1	5-oz. pkg. baby arugula
¼	cup grated Parmesan cheese

1. Coat a medium bowl with olive oil. In a food processor combine flour, yeast, sugar, and ½ tsp. salt. With food processor running, add 1 Tbsp. olive oil and the warm water. Process until dough forms. Shape into a smooth ball. Place in prepared bowl; turn once to coat dough surface. Cover bowl with plastic wrap. Let stand in a warm place 45 to 60 minutes or until double in size.

2. Meanwhile, in a 10-inch skillet cook potatoes, leeks, and onion in 1 Tbsp. olive oil. Sprinkle with rosemary, ¼ tsp. salt, and ¼ tsp. black pepper. Cook over medium-high 5 to 6 minutes or until potatoes are light brown and leeks and onion are tender, turning occasionally.

3. Preheat oven to 450°F. Lightly grease a baking sheet; sprinkle with cornmeal. On a lightly floured surface roll and stretch dough into a 12×8-inch rectangle. Place on prepared baking sheet. Lightly brush with olive oil. Top with potato-leek mixture. Sprinkle with salt. Bake 15 minutes or until crust is golden.

4. Meanwhile, for salad: In a medium bowl whisk together lemon zest and juice, 3 Tbsp. oil, the mustard, ¼ tsp. salt, and ¼ tsp. black pepper. Add arugula; toss to coat. Top pizza with salad. Sprinkle with Parmesan and additional black pepper. Serves 4.

EACH SERVING *511 cal, 20 g fat (3 g sat fat), 4 mg chol, 560 mg sodium, 72 g carb, 5 g fiber, 5 g sugars, 12 g pro*

PICKLED SWEET PEPPERS, SLICED OR WHOLE, ARE ON-TARGET INGREDIENTS FOR ANY GREEK SALAD. IN THIS RECIPE, GROUND BEEF OR TURKEY CAN STAND IN FOR THE GROUND LAMB.

HUMMUS & LAMB PIZZA WITH ROMAINE

Jarred sweet piquanté peppers (Peppadew is a popular brand) are mildly zesty—just the right amount to complement the sweetness. Whole pickled peppers, stuffed with goat cheese or whipped feta, are delicious as simple appetizers.

HANDS-ON TIME 15 min.
TOTAL TIME 25 min.

8	oz. ground lamb, beef, or turkey
½	cup chopped onion
1	large clove garlic, minced
1	Tbsp. chopped fresh oregano
1	8.8-oz. pkg. purchased naan (two 8½×7-inch naan breads)
2	Tbsp. plus 2 tsp. olive oil
1	10-oz. container hummus
2	Tbsp. cider vinegar
2	tsp. Dijon mustard
6	cups thinly sliced romaine lettuce
1	cup cherry tomatoes, halved
½	cup sliced sweet piquanté, cherry, or Italian sweet peppers
½	cup crumbled feta cheese

1. Preheat oven to 450°F. In a 10-inch skillet cook ground lamb, onion, and garlic over medium-high until meat is browned. Drain off fat. Stir in oregano and ½ tsp. each salt and black pepper.
2. Place naan on a large baking sheet;* brush each with 1 tsp. of the oil. Spread with hummus. Top with lamb mixture. Bake 10 to 15 minutes or until naan edges are lightly browned and crisp.
3. Meanwhile, for salad: In a large bowl whisk together remaining 2 Tbsp. oil, the vinegar, and mustard. Season with salt and pepper. Add lettuce, tomatoes, and peppers; toss. Top pizza with salad; sprinkle with feta. Serves 4.
*Tip For a crispier crust, bake pizza directly on the oven rack.
EACH SERVING *619 cal, 34 g fat (10 g sat fat), 55 mg chol, 1,163 mg sodium, 56 g carb, 7 g fiber, 8 g sugars, 23 g pro*

THE CRUST Naan is the traditional puffed flatbread of Indian cuisine. In this recipe, naan makes assembly easy for a weeknight meal. Pita bread could also substitute as the pizza base. For crisp crusts, bake the flatbreads directly on an oven rack.

THE TOPPINGS Spiced lamb is a typical Greek gyro filling. For this pizza, the lamb is combined with hummus, another common Mediterranean food.

THE SALAD Top the pie with romaine tossed with tart vinaigrette, crumbled feta, and pickled peppers.

TAKE IT TO GO

Stock up on breakfast sandwiches and fruit pops over the weekend to prepare for busy weekday mornings. These shortcuts call for frozen waffles, PB&J, fresh fruits, and pantry items to satisfy morning hunger.

FREEZER SANDWICHES

To customize these sandwiches, substitute a variety of herbs, cheeses, or greens to suit your taste.

HANDS-ON TIME 10 min.
TOTAL TIME 20 min.

Nonstick cooking spray
8   eggs
⅓   cup milk
1   Tbsp. snipped fresh chives
1   Tbsp. Dijon mustard
2   Tbsp. chopped fresh basil
6   English muffins, split and toasted
6   slices bacon, crisp-cooked
6   slices cheddar cheese
   Baby spinach (optional)

1. Preheat oven to 350°F. Line a 13×9-inch baking pan with foil, extending foil over pan edges; coat with cooking spray. In a bowl whisk together eggs, milk, chives, mustard, basil, ½ tsp. salt, and ¼ tsp. black pepper. Pour egg mixture into pan.
2. Bake 8 to 10 minutes or until eggs are set. Using foil, lift out eggs; cut into six rectangles, then halve each rectangle.
3. For each sandwich, layer two rectangles on one English muffin bottom; top with 1 slice bacon, 1 slice cheese, and muffin top. Wrap sandwiches in plastic wrap. Freeze in a resealable plastic bag up to 1 month. To serve or pack, remove plastic then wrap in paper towel. Microwave 1½ to 2 minutes, turning once. If desired, add baby spinach leaves. Makes 6 sandwiches.

SMOOTHIE POPS

HANDS-ON TIME 10 min.
TOTAL TIME 4 h hr. 10 min.

1   cup frozen raspberries
1   cup cran-apple juice
1   frozen banana, sliced
½   cup plain Greek Yogurt
1   tsp. honey

Place all ingredients in a high-speed blender. Cover and process until smooth. Pour into 12 ice pop molds. Freeze at least 4 hours. Makes 12 pops.
For orange version: Substitute 1 cup carrot slices and/or apple chunks for the berries and orange juice for the cran-apple; add ¼ tsp. orange zest.

WAFFLE TARTINES

Toast frozen whole wheat waffles then spread with a variety of toppers:
Avocado smashed avocado, cucumber, red onion, crumbled feta.
Lox cream cheese, lox, capers, snipped fresh dill
Chive-Mushroom garlic and herb cheese spread, sautéed mushrooms, snipped fresh chives

SWEET ROLLS

Spread flour, whole grain, or whole wheat tortillas with nut butter, chocolate-hazelnut spread, jam, and/or yogurt. Top with banana slices, berries, granola, chocolate chips, and/or nuts. Roll up and secure with picks, or enjoy open-face.

DINNER MAKEOVER

Apply these strategies—from slow to quick cooking and making a couple dishes to serve multiple ways—to serve delicious weeknight dinners that exceed expectations.

BEEF & BROCCOLI

BUTTER CHICKEN

STRATEGY #1
PICK A COOKER

Low and slow, or hot and fast? Take your choice of cooking dinner during the day while you're home or away, or having ingredients ready to add to a pressure cooker minutes before mealtime.

BUTTER CHICKEN

Worldly popular, this Indian-style chicken dish has a creamy tomato-base sauce. Serve it over rice along with slices of naan; both will soak up delicious flavors.

HANDS-ON TIME 20 min.
TOTAL TIME 8 hr. 30 min. (slow cooker); 1 hr. (pressure cooker)

6   Tbsp. butter
3½   to 4 lb. bone-in chicken thighs, skinned (6 to 8)
1   Tbsp. grated fresh ginger
1   Tbsp. garam masala
3   cloves garlic, minced
1   tsp. ground cumin
½   tsp. ground turmeric
¼   tsp. cayenne pepper
1   14.5-oz. can diced tomatoes
1   cup chopped yellow onion
½   cup heavy cream

SLOW COOKER In a large skillet heat 3 Tbsp. butter over medium. Add chicken half at a time; cook 4 minutes or until lightly browned, turning once. Transfer to a 4- to 5-qt. slow cooker. Add ginger, garam masala, garlic, cumin, ½ tsp. salt, the turmeric, and cayenne; toss to coat. Stir in drained tomatoes and onion. Cover; cook on low 8 to 9 hours. Stir in cream and remaining 3 Tbsp. butter. For a thicker sauce, transfer chicken to a dish; cover to keep warm. Use the browning setting, or transfer cooking liquid to a large skillet. Bring to boiling. Boil gently, uncovered, 7 to 10 minutes or until slightly thickened. Serves 6.

PRESSURE COOKER In a 6-qt. electric pressure cooker use the sauté setting to heat 3 Tbsp. butter. Add chicken half at a time; cook 4 minutes or until lightly browned, turning once. Add ginger, garam masala, garlic, cumin, ½ tsp. salt, the turmeric, cayenne, undrained tomatoes, and onion. Lock lid. Set cooker on high pressure to cook 10 minutes. Let stand 15 minutes to release pressure naturally. Release any remaining pressure. Open lid carefully. Stir in cream and remaining 3 Tbsp. butter. For a thicker sauce, transfer chicken to a serving dish; cover to keep warm. Use sauté setting to bring cooking liquid to boiling. Boil, uncovered, 7 to 10 minutes or until slightly thickened.

EACH SERVING *409 cal, 25 g fat (13 g sat fat), 213 mg chol, 542 mg sodium, 7 g carb, 1 g fiber, 3 g sugars, 25 g pro*

BEEF & BROCCOLI

Flank and bottom round steaks are inexpensive cuts that become deliciously tender in cookers.

HANDS-ON TIME 15 min.
TOTAL TIME 8 hr. 45 min. (slow cooker); 30 min. (pressure cooker)

2   cups sliced yellow onion
1   1½- to 1¾-lb. beef flank steak or beef bottom round steak, cut across the grain into 4 to 6 portions
½   cup reduced-sodium beef broth
½   cup reduced-sodium soy sauce
3   Tbsp. hoisin sauce
2   Tbsp. packed dark brown sugar
1   Tbsp. rice wine vinegar or cider vinegar
1   Tbsp. grated fresh ginger
5   cloves garlic, minced
1   Tbsp. cornstarch
4   cups fresh broccoli florets
     Toasted sesame seeds (optional)
     Rice noodles or rice

SLOW COOKER Place onion and beef in a 3½- or 4-qt. slow cooker. In a small bowl combine broth, soy sauce, hoisin, brown sugar, vinegar, ginger, and garlic; pour over meat mixture. Cover; cook on low 8 to 10 hours. Remove meat, reserving onion and cooking liquid in cooker. Cover meat to keep warm. In a small bowl combine 3 Tbsp. water and the cornstarch. Turn heat setting to high. Stir into cooking liquid. Add broccoli. Cover; cook 15 minutes or until cooking liquid is thickened and bubbly and broccoli is crisp-tender. Slice meat thinly across the grain. Stir into broccoli mixture. If desired, top with sesame seeds. Serve over rice noodles or rice. Serves 6.

PRESSURE COOKER Place onion and meat in a 6-qt. electric pressure cooker. In a small bowl combine broth, soy sauce, hoisin, brown sugar, vinegar, ginger, and garlic; pour over meat mixture. Lock lid. Set on high pressure. Cook 15 minutes. Immediately release pressure. Remove meat; cover to keep warm. In a small bowl combine 3 Tbsp. water and the cornstarch. Stir into cooking liquid in cooker. Add broccoli. Using the sauté setting, cook and stir until cooking liquid is thickened and bubbly and broccoli is crisp-tender. Slice meat thinly across the grain. Stir into broccoli mixture. If desired, top with sesame seeds. Serve over rice noodles or rice.

EACH SERVING *273 cal, 8 g fat (3 g sat fat), 43 mg chol, 843 mg sodium, 23 g carb, 3 g fiber, 11 g sugars, 28 g pro*

STRATEGY #2
COOK ONCE FOR THREE MEALS

Here's a compelling case for the much-appreciated Sunday roast and the meals that stem from it during the following week. Roast an ample-size piece of meat, enjoy a meal from it one day, then pack away the remainder in the fridge or freezer to shortcut meals days later. This recipe serves as a base that takes on various flavors and styles of dishes, so it tastes and looks different each meal.

ITALIAN PORK ROAST

Seasoned with Italian seasoning, rosemary, fennel seeds, and garlic, the result is a moist, tender, and flavorful roast. The versatile ragu comes about with tomatoes and mushrooms added during the last hour of cooking.

HANDS-ON TIME 20 min.
TOTAL TIME 4 hr. 50 min.

- 1 4- to 5-lb. boneless pork shoulder roast
- 2 Tbsp. dried Italian seasoning, crushed
- 2 Tbsp. dried rosemary, crushed
- 2 Tbsp. minced fresh garlic
- 2 tsp. fennel seeds, crushed
- 1 tsp. crushed red pepper
- 2 lb. cherry tomatoes
- 1 8-oz. pkg. sliced fresh cremini or button mushrooms
- 2 cups chopped yellow onion
- ½ cup dry red wine or beef broth
- ½ of a 6-oz. can tomato paste (⅓ cup)

1. Preheat oven to 325°F. Place roast fat side up in a 6- to 8-qt. Dutch oven. In a small bowl stir together Italian seasoning, rosemary, garlic, fennel seeds, 2 tsp. black pepper, 1½ tsp. salt, and crushed red pepper. Rub all over pork.
2. Roast, covered, 3½ hours. Add tomatoes, mushrooms, and onion. Whisk together wine and tomato paste. Pour over pork and tomato mixture. Continue roasting, uncovered, 1 hour more or until tender and a thermometer inserted in meat registers at least 190°F.
3. Remove and shred meat. Return meat to cooking liquid in pot. Store in an airtight container. Refrigerate up to 4 days or freeze up to 3 months. Makes 11 cups.
SLOW COOKER VARIATION Prepare pork as directed, except place meat in a 6- to 7-qt. slow cooker. Cover; cook on low 8 to 10 hours. Add tomatoes, mushrooms, onion, and wine mixture. (Cooker will be full.) Cover; increase heat to high. Cook 1 hour more. Continue as directed in Step 3.
EACH 1 CUP *131 cal, 3 g fat (1 g sat fat), 49 mg chol, 238 mg sodium, 5 g carb, 1 g fiber, 2 g sugars, 20 g pro*

Pork Ragu & Pasta Choose a hearty pasta, such as rigatoni, penne, or pappardelle, to capture the thick, meaty sauce of the ragu. When 15 minutes roasting or reheating time remains, bring a pot of water to boiling to cook pasta.

Cheesy Calzone Divide 1 pound of pizza dough into four portions. On a floured surface roll each into a 6-inch circle. Mix 1 cup pork ragu with enough jarred marinara to be saucy. Top each circle with 1 slice provolone cheese, some ragu, and, if desired, pickled banana peppers. Fold dough over filling; seal edges with a fork. Prick tops, brush with egg wash, and sprinkle with Parmesan. Bake at 425°F for 15 minutes or until golden.

Italian Pork on Ciabatta This chewy Italian-style bread is a natural for barbecue-style pulled pork. The dense texture of the bread will absorb the rich tomato sauce. Top with fresh basil and/or spinach.

ITALIAN
PORK ROAST

CUBAN
PORK ROAST

TRADITIONALLY, CUBAN PORK IS GENEROUSLY FLAVORED WITH GARLIC, OREGANO, CUMIN, AND SOUR ORANGES. THIS VERSION HAS A COMBO OF ORANGES AND LIMES.

CUBAN PORK ROAST

Serve Cubanos from the first serving of the roast, then reserve leftovers for the Pork & Sweets Bowl and the Quesadillas recipes. The roast is delicious shredded directly from cooking, especially with the citrus juices squeezed over.

HANDS-ON TIME 20 min.
TOTAL TIME 4 hr. 50 min.

- 1   4- to 5-lb. boneless pork shoulder roast
- ¼   cup chopped flat-leaf parsley
- 2   Tbsp. minced fresh garlic
- 2   Tbsp. dried oregano, crushed
- 4   tsp. onion powder
- 4   tsp. ground cumin
- 1   orange, quartered
- 1   lime, quartered
- 1   medium onion, quartered

1. Preheat oven to 325°F. Place pork fat side up in a 5- to 6-qt. Dutch oven. In a small bowl stir together parsley, garlic, oregano, onion powder, cumin, 2 tsp. black pepper, and 1½ tsp. salt. Rub all over pork.
2. Roast, covered, 3½ hours. Add orange, lime, and onion wedges. Roast, uncovered, 1 hour more or until tender and an instant-read thermometer inserted in meat registers at least 190°F.
3. Transfer meat to a cutting board, reserving citrus, onion, and cooking liquid. Shred meat. In a large bowl toss meat with enough cooking liquid to moisten. Once cool, squeeze citrus over meat to release juices; stir into meat. Store meat mixture in an airtight container in refrigerator up to 4 days or freeze up to 3 months. Makes about 7 cups.
SLOW COOKER VARIATION Prepare as directed, except place meat in a 6- to 7-qt. slow cooker. Cover; cook on low 8 to 10 hours, adding citrus and onion the last 1 hour of cooking.
EACH 1 CUP *145 cal, 6 g fat (2 g sat fat), 61 mg chol, 347 mg sodium, 3 g carb, 1 g fiber, 1 g sugars, 20 g pro*

Pork & Black Bean Quesadillas Layer pork, shredded Monterey Jack cheese, black beans, and jalapeño peppers on flour tortillas. Cook in hot oil until browned and cheese is melted.

Pork & Sweets Bowl Roast sweet potato slices (drizzled with maple syrup, if desired). In a bowl arrange pork, sweet potato slices, romaine, avocado, and purchased fresh pico de gallo. To make a quick garlic-citrus sauce (aka mojo) to spoon over, cook 4 cloves minced garlic in 2 Tbsp. hot oil. Add ⅓ cup each orange and lime juice and ½ tsp. each cumin and salt. Simmer 5 minutes.

Cubanos On Cuban bread or hoagie buns layer mustard, dill pickles, sliced Swiss cheese, deli ham, and shredded pork. Toast sandwiches in a panini press (or in a skillet, weighted with a second skillet and cans of food) until cheese is melted.

STRATEGY #3
COOK STRAIGHT FROM THE FREEZER

The next time your dinner plans are still frozen solid, try one of these 30-minute, one-pan recipes that call for frozen chicken or salmon. No thawing required.

GREEK CHICKEN SKILLET

Let's set expectations. When frozen chicken is cooked, ice crystals melt and add moisture, steaming or poaching the chicken. But the chicken will not brown. Lack of browning is only one reason to add a vibrant lemon-dill-olive sauce—the best reason is the excellent enticing flavor the sauce contributes.

HANDS-ON TIME 15 min.
TOTAL TIME 40 min. plus freezing

2   lemons
2   Tbsp. sliced fresh or pickled
    jalapeño,* drained
1   Tbsp. olive oil
2   cloves garlic, minced
1   tsp. dried dill weed
2   8-oz. skinless, boneless chicken
    breast halves, halved horizontally
1   14-oz. can reduced-sodium chicken
    broth
1   Tbsp. butter
¾   cup dried orzo pasta
1   9-oz. pkg. sliced fresh Brussels
    sprouts
¼   cup pitted green olives
¼   cup crumbled feta cheese

1. Zest and juice one lemon. In a 1-gallon resealable plastic freezer bag mix together the zest and juice, jalapeño pepper, oil, garlic, dill, ½ tsp. salt, and ¼ tsp. black pepper. Place chicken in bag. Slice remaining lemon; add to bag. Turn to coat. Remove air from bag; seal. Lay flat on a baking sheet. Freeze up to 3 months. (To use fresh chicken, in a skillet combine all ingredients through butter. Bring to boiling, then add orzo. Simmer, covered, 10 minutes. Add

Brussels sprouts and olives; simmer, covered, 5 minutes more or until orzo is tender and chicken is done (165°F.)
2. Remove frozen chicken from bag; place in an extra-large skillet. Add chicken broth and butter. Bring to boiling; reduce heat. Simmer, covered, 7 minutes. Add orzo. Return to boiling; reduce heat. Simmer, covered, 10 minutes more. Add Brussels sprouts and olives. Return to boiling; reduce heat. Simmer, covered, 5 minutes more or until orzo is tender and chicken is done (165°F) Top with feta. Serves 4.
***Tip** Chile peppers contain oils that can irritate skin and eyes. Wear plastic or latex gloves when working with them.
EACH SERVING *349 cal, 13 g fat (4 g sat fat), 99 mg chol, 859 mg sodium, 27 g carb, 5 g fiber, 3 g sugars, 33 g pro*

CRISPY SALMON WITH VEGGIES & PESTO

Photo on page 12.

Not all frozen fish will remain tender and moist during roasting. The fish must have healthy fat, such as salmon. Reserve delicate white fish to cook when it's thawed.

HANDS-ON TIME 10 min.
TOTAL TIME 35 min.

4   4- to 5-oz. frozen* salmon fillets,
    about 1 inch thick
1   pint cherry tomatoes
8   oz. fresh green beans, trimmed
4   oz. sugar snap peas, trimmed
2   Tbsp. olive oil
⅓   cup purchased garlic croutons,
    coarsely crushed
2   Tbsp. purchased basil pesto
3   to 4 tsp. red wine vinegar

1. Preheat oven to 400°F. Line a 15×10-inch baking pan with foil. Place frozen salmon in pan. Arrange tomatoes, beans, and peas around salmon. Drizzle all with oil. Sprinkle with ½ tsp. salt and ¼ tsp. black pepper.
2. Bake 20 minutes or until fish flakes easily when tested with fork, stirring vegetables once. Remove from oven.
3. Preheat broiler. Arrange rack 4 to 5 inches from heat. Sprinkle fish with crushed croutons. Broil 1 to 2 minutes or until browned. In a small bowl stir together pesto and vinegar. Drizzle over fish and vegetables. Serves 4.
***Tip** If using thawed or fresh salmon, prepare as directed in Step 1. Bake 15 minutes or until fish flakes easily when tested with a fork. Continue as directed in Step 3.
EACH SERVING *308 cal, 17 g fat (2 g sat fat), 63 mg chol, 480 mg sodium, 12 g carb, 3 g fiber, 5 g sugars, 26 g pro*

GREEK CHICKEN
SKILLET

HEART CUTOUTS
Recipe on page 33

february

Let your creativity show with cookies for your valentine. Plus, score with party snacks for winter gatherings, and discover healthful smoothies, fresh main dishes, and the beauty of chicories.

36

42

47

Cookies,
A LOVE STORY

This Valentine's Day give a gift from the heart. One sugar cookie dough and simple techniques yield endless ways to say "I love you."

HEART CUTOUTS

HANDS-ON TIME 25 min.
TOTAL TIME 45 min.

1½	cups butter, softened
1	cup sugar
¼	tsp. baking powder
1	egg
1	tsp. vanilla
1	tsp. almond extract (optional)
¾	tsp. salt
3½	cups all-purpose flour
	Red and/or pink food coloring (optional)
	Egg white (optional)
1	Tbsp. water (optional)
	Colored sugars (optional)
½	tsp. edible luster dust (optional)
1	tsp. vodka (optional)

1. Preheat oven to 375°F. In a large bowl beat butter with a mixer on medium to high 30 seconds. Add sugar and baking powder. Beat until combined, scraping sides of bowl occasionally. Beat in egg, vanilla, and, if desired, almond extract until combined. Beat in salt and flour. Divide dough into two or three portions; tint each with food coloring as desired. On a lightly floured surface roll out dough to ⅛- to ¼-inch thickness.
2. For Striped and Patchwork Cookies, see how-to, right. For Painted Cookies, combine egg white, water, and a few drops of red or pink food coloring. Using a small brush, brush dough with swipes of color. If using colored sugars, brush dough with egg white; sprinkle with colored sugar.
3. Cut out hearts using 2- to 3-inch cookie cutters. Place cutouts 1 inch apart on ungreased cookie sheets. Bake 6 to 8 minutes or until edges are firm but not browned. (Adjust timing for smaller and larger cookies.) Let cool on a wire rack. If desired, mix luster dust and vodka; brush onto cooled cookies. Makes 48 (2- to 3-inch) cookies.
EACH COOKIE *102 cal, 6 g fat (4 g sat fat), 19 mg chol, 86 mg sodium, 11 g carb, 4 g sugars, 1 g pro*

HOW-TO

STRIPED COOKIES Cut rolled dough into strips of various widths and arrange in stripes. Use a rolling pin to gently press the seams together before cutting out cookies.

PATCHWORK COOKIES Cut out hearts from doughs of different colors and swap them into cutouts of the same size. Cut out larger hearts; bake as directed.

party food
SUPER SNACKS

Surprise fans gathered for the big game with drinks and eats that have clever, tempting, and delicious takes on the usual fare.

VEGGIE REUBEN PAN-WICHES

These sandwiches have a classic Reuben's flavor hallmarks— sauerkraut and Swiss cheese—plus a mustard-caraway butter mixture poured over top.

HANDS-ON TIME 35 min.
TOTAL TIME 1 hr.

12　3-inch pretzel rolls, split
2　cups fresh baby spinach
1　cup drained and thinly sliced roasted red bell peppers
½　cup thinly sliced red onion
½　cup thinly sliced cucumber
1　cup well-drained sauerkraut
6　oz. thinly sliced Swiss cheese
½　cup Thousand Island dressing
6　Tbsp. butter, melted
1　Tbsp. coarse-ground mustard
1　tsp. caraway seeds, crushed
½　tsp. minced dried onion

1. Preheat oven to 350°F. Line a 13×9-inch pan with foil. Coat with nonstick cooking spray. Arrange roll bottoms in prepared pan.
2. Layer spinach, peppers, onion, cucumber, sauerkraut, and Swiss cheese on roll bottoms. Spread dressing on cut side of roll tops. Add roll tops to sandwiches. Stir together butter, mustard, caraway seeds, and dried onion; drizzle over rolls. Cover with foil.
3. Bake 15 minutes. Uncover; bake 10 to 15 minutes more or until cheese is melted and rolls are lightly browned. Serves 12.
EACH SERVING *300 cal, 19 g fat (7 g sat fat), 31 mg chol, 647 mg sodium, 31 g carb, 2 g fiber, 7 g sugars, 9 g pro*

STOUT & STORMY

This is a riff on the Dark and Stormy (a rum-ginger beer cocktail) by adding ginger to a simple syrup and swapping ginger beer for milk stout.

TOTAL TIME 1 hr. 10 min.

¾　cup chopped fresh ginger
¾　cup sugar
¾　cup water
1　cup dark rum
¾　cup lime juice
4　12-oz. bottles milk stout, chilled

1. For ginger simple syrup: In a small saucepan combine ginger, sugar, and water. Bring to boiling, stirring to dissolve the sugar. Remove from heat. Cover and chill at least 1 hour or up 8 hours. Strain to remove ginger. Discard ginger.
2. In a pitcher combine simple syrup, rum, lime juice, and milk stout. Serves 8.
EACH SERVING *197 cal, 12 mg sodium, 22 g carb, 22 g sugars, 1 g pro*

PICKLED MICHELADA

A zesty take on the popular Bloody Mary.

TOTAL TIME 10 min.

　　8　lime wedges
　　Chile-lime seasoning
2　cups clam-tomato juice cocktail or vegetable juice
½　cup brine from a jar of pickled jalapeño peppers
½　cup lime juice
2　Tbsp. Worcestershire sauce
4　12-oz. bottles Mexican lager, chilled

Rub rims of 8 pint glasses with a lime wedge; dip rims in seasoning. In a pitcher combine clam-tomato cocktail, brine, lime juice, and Worcestershire sauce. Add lager. Serve over ice. Serves 8.
EACH SERVING *300 cal, 19 g fat (7 g sat fat), 31 mg chol, 647 mg sodium, 31 g carb, 2 g fiber, 7 g sugars, 9 g pro*

STOUT & STORMY

PICKLED MICHELADA

VEGGIE REUBEN
PAN-WICHES

TURKEY MUFFULETTA PAN-WICHES

The sandwiches can be made well before kickoff—minus the butter drizzle. Covered and refrigerated, they're ready to drizzle and bake in time for the game.

HANDS-ON TIME 25 min.
TOTAL TIME 50 min.

Nonstick cooking spray
12 3-inch ciabatta rolls, split
1 16-oz. jar pickled mixed vegetables (giardiniera), drained and chopped
1 cup drained and chopped roasted red bell peppers
½ cup coarsely chopped pimiento-stuffed green olives
2 Tbsp. olive oil
12 oz. thinly sliced deli turkey
6 oz. thinly sliced mozzarella cheese
¼ cup butter, melted
2 cloves garlic, minced
1 tsp. dried Italian seasoning, crushed

1. Preheat oven to 350°F. Line a 13×9-inch baking pan with foil. Coat foil with nonstick cooking spray. Arrange roll bottoms in prepared pan.
2. In a bowl combine pickled mixed vegetables, peppers, olives, and olive oil. Layer roll bottoms with turkey, vegetable mixture, and cheese. Add roll tops to sandwiches. Stir together butter, garlic, and Italian seasoning; drizzle over rolls. Cover with foil.
3. Bake 15 minutes. Uncover; bake 10 to 15 minutes more or until cheese is melted and rolls are lightly browned. Serves 12.
EACH SERVING *345 cal, 12 g fat (4 g sat fat), 33 mg chol, 1,086 mg sodium, 41 g carb, 1 g fiber, 2 g sugars, 16 g pro*

THESE ZESTY SLIDERS, INSPIRED BY THE FAMOUS NEW ORLEANS SANDWICH AND ENHANCED WITH EXTRA FLAVOR, WILL HAVE FANS CHEERING.

FAST & FRESH

Easy, delicious recipes for a better dinner tonight.

GRAIN SALAD WITH GREENS, CHERRIES & CRISPY BACON

Any tender greens, including baby kale, spinach, or mustard greens, work in this recipe. If you can't find fresh cherries, substitute frozen and thaw before using.

HANDS-ON TIME 10 min.
TOTAL TIME 40 min.

1   cup farro, rinsed and drained
4   slices bacon
1   5 oz. pkg. baby kale
1½ cups sweet cherries, pitted
¼   cup red wine vinegar
3   Tbsp. olive oil
1   tsp. coarse-grain mustard
2   oz. blue cheese, sliced or crumbled

1. In a medium saucepan bring 3 cups water and the farro to boiling; reduce heat. Cover; simmer 30 minutes or until tender. Drain off excess liquid.

2. Meanwhile, in a large skillet cook bacon over medium until browned and crisp. Transfer to paper towels to drain, reserving drippings in skillet. Add kale to skillet by the handful, cooking and stirring until each addition is wilted. Remove skillet from heat; stir in farro, bacon, cherries, ½ tsp. salt, and ¼ tsp. black pepper.

3. For dressing: In a small bowl whisk together vinegar, oil, mustard, ½ tsp. salt, and ¼ tsp. black pepper. Add to farro mixture; toss to coat. Top with blue cheese. Serves 4.

EACH SERVING *417 cal, 24 g fat (8 g sat fat), 25 mg chol, 930 mg sodium, 41 g carb, 5 g fiber, 8 g sugars, 11 g pro*

SHEET-PAN MEATBALLS WITH RED ONIONS & ARTICHOKES

Serve meatballs over spinach for extra color and nutrients, or over couscous or pasta.

HANDS-ON TIME 30 min.
TOTAL TIME 50 min.

- 1   Tbsp. olive oil plus more for coating pan
- ¼   cup fresh bread crumbs
- 1   egg, lightly beaten
- 1¼   lb. ground pork
- 1   lemon, zested and juiced
- ½   cup chopped flat-leaf parsley, fresh mint, and/or fresh chives
- ¼   cup finely chopped shallot
- 2   red onions, cut into ½-inch-thick wedges
- 1   14-oz. can artichoke hearts, drained, rinsed, halved, and patted dry

1. Preheat oven to 400°F. Brush two 15×10-inch baking pans with olive oil. In a large bowl combine bread crumbs and 2 Tbsp. water; let stand 5 minutes. Stir in egg, pork, lemon zest, herbs, shallot, and ½ tsp. each salt and black pepper until well-combined (do not overmix). Gently shape mixture into 2-inch balls. Place in one prepared pan.
2. Place onions and artichoke hearts in second prepared pan; drizzle with 1 Tbsp. olive oil. Sprinkle with salt and black pepper; toss to coat. Bake on separate oven racks 15 minutes. Remove from oven. Turn oven to broil. Broil vegetables 4 to 5 inches from heat 5 to 7 minutes or until tender and browned, stirring halfway through. Repeat for meatballs, broiling until done (165°F) and browned, turning halfway through.
3. Transfer meatballs and vegetables to a platter. Pour half the lemon juice into each hot pan; scrape up browned bits. Drizzle lemon juice mixture over meatballs and vegetables. Serves 4.
EACH SERVING *440 cal, 31 g fat (8 g sat fat), 143 mg chol, 753 mg sodium, 13 g carb, 2 g fiber, 4 g sugars, 29 g pro*

SHRIMP & HOMINY STEW

Soft, chewy hominy is dried corn that's been soaked and puffed to twice its size and had its hull and germ removed.

TOTAL TIME 30 min.

1   Tbsp. vegetable oil
4   cloves garlic, minced
2   tsp. ground mild chile pepper

1   14.5-oz. can diced tomatoes, undrained
1   15-oz. can hominy, rinsed and drained
1   lb. uncooked shrimp, peeled and deveined
1   to 2 Tbsp. chopped fresh oregano

1. In a 4- to 5-qt. pot heat vegetable oil over medium. Add garlic and chile pepper; cook 1 to 2 minutes or until fragrant, stirring frequently (do not let garlic brown). Add tomatoes, 3 cups water, the hominy, and ½ tsp. salt. Bring to boiling; reduce heat. Simmer, uncovered, 5 minutes.

2. Add shrimp; cook 3 to 4 minutes or until shrimp are opaque. Stir in oregano. Serves 4.

EACH SERVING *188 cal, 5 g fat (1 g sat fat), 159 mg chol, 735 mg sodium, 16 g carb, 4 g fiber, 4 g sugars, 22 g pro*

immune-boosting SMOOTHIES

Each of these concoctions is packed with nutrition that will help you stay healthy any time of the year.

GREAT GREENS ELIXIR

Start your morning on a nutrition high note with this apple-sweetened drink.

TOTAL TIME 20 min.

2   Granny Smith apples, cored and chopped
1   cup baby spinach
1   cup coarsely torn romaine lettuce
2   cups unsweetened coconut water or filtered water
1½ cups coarsely chopped cucumber
1   stalk celery, trimmed and cut up
⅓   cup flat-leaf parsley leaves
3   Tbsp. lemon juice

In a blender combine all ingredients. Cover and blend on high until nearly smooth. Pour mixture, half at a time, through a fine-mesh sieve set over a bowl. Let stand 5 minutes, stirring solids occasionally. Transfer pulp to a bowl. Discard pulp or reserve for another use. Cover and chill up to 24 hours or serve over ice. Serves 2.

EACH SERVING *165 cal, 1 g fat (0 g sat fat), 0 mg chol, 98 mg sodium, 40 g carb, 7 g fiber, 27 g sugars, 2 g pro*

VANILLA TAHINI SHAKE

Sip this shake about an hour before bedtime to promote good sleep, which is key to keep your immune system at top performance.

TOTAL TIME 15 min.

3   bananas, peeled, cut into 1-inch chunks, and frozen
2   to 2½ cups unsweetened vanilla almond milk
6   Medjool dates, pitted
½   cup steamed cauliflower, cooled
¼   to ⅓ cup tahini
1   tsp. honey
1   tsp. vanilla
¼   tsp. ground cinnamon
3   cinnamon sticks (optional)

In a blender combine bananas, 2 cups of the milk, and the dates. Blend on high until dates are incorporated. Add remaining ingredients and blend until smooth, about 1 minute. Add additional milk, if needed, to reach desired consistency. If desired, serve with additional cinnamon or a cinnamon stick. Serves 3.

EACH SERVING *399 cal, 13 g fat (2 g sat fat), 0 mg chol, 134 mg sodium, 72 g carb, 8 g fiber, 49 g sugars, 7 g pro*

TROPICAL GOLDEN SMOOTHIE

Refresh with pineapple and mango, protein-rich kefir, and a hint of coconut.

TOTAL TIME 10 min.

1   cup frozen cubed pineapple
1   cup frozen cubed mango
2   cups plain kefir
½   cup unsweetened coconut water
1   Tbsp. chia seeds
1   Tbsp. lime juice
1   tsp. chopped fresh ginger

In a blender combine all ingredients. Cover and blend on high until smooth. Serves 3.

EACH SERVING *232 cal, 4 g fat (2 g sat fat), 13 mg chol, 112 mg sodium, 44 g carb, 3 g fiber, 39 g sugars, 9 g pro*

BLUEBERRY ALMOND BUTTER SMOOTHIE

Packed with vitamin E and antioxidants, this smoothie is an energizer to counter a 3 p.m. slump. Bonus: 7 g fiber and 267 mg calcium— more than a third of the daily recommendation.

TOTAL TIME 10 min.

1½ cups frozen blueberries
1   banana, peeled, cut into 1-inch chunks, and frozen
2   cups unsweetened almond milk
2   Tbsp. almond butter

In a blender combine all ingredients. Cover and blend on high until smooth. Serves 2.

EACH SERVING *250 cal, 13 g fat (1 g sat fat), 0 mg chol, 218 mg sodium, 33 g carb, 7 g fiber, 18 g sugars, 5 g pro*

GUT HEALTH IS LINKED TO IMMUNITY: UP TO 70% OF IMMUNE SYSTEM CELLS ARE LOCATED IN THE GUT.

VITAMIN C from spinach, romaine, and lemon stimulates infection-fighting antibodies. Spinach is also a good source of folate and zinc, both crucial to a strong immune system.

TROPICAL GOLDEN SMOOTHIE

GREAT GREENS ELIXIR

KEFIR is a fermented drink that supplies probiotics (good bacteria to help boost the immune system). Pineapple and mango give women nearly 100% and men 80% of their daily vitamin C needs.

BANANAS supply magnesium and potassium, which help relax muscles. Tahini has B6, a vitamin that's key to producing infection-fighting T cells, and selenium, which helps reduce inflammation.

ALMONDS are rich in vitamin E, which plays an important role in immune cell function. Blueberries have chemicals called flavonoids that reduce cell damage.

VANILLA TAHINI SHAKE

BLUEBERRY ALMOND BUTTER SMOOTHIE

SUGAR AND SPICE

Top healthful breakfast bowls with lightly sweetened and roasted fruit, taking advantage of fruit at peak season or to enhance the sweetness of fruit that's just beyond its peak.

SPICED ROASTED FRUIT

Because sweetness varies depending on type and ripeness of fruit, adjust the amount of sugar accordingly. To serve a breakfast version of fruit crumble, sprinkle some Crispy Oats over each bowlful of goodness.

HANDS-ON TIME 10 min.
TOTAL TIME 20 min.

- ¼ to ½ cup packed brown sugar
- ½ tsp. ground cardamom or cinnamon
- 6 cups fresh fruit, such as grapes, berries, and/or sliced pears
- 3 Tbsp. butter, melted
  Ricotta cheese, yogurt, or oatmeal (optional)
  Crispy Oats (optional)

Preheat oven to 450°F. In a small bowl combine brown sugar and cardamom. Line a 15×10-inch sheet pan with parchment paper. Spread fruit in prepared pan. Drizzle with butter then sprinkle with sugar mixture. Bake, uncovered, 10 to 15 minutes or until fruit is soft and starting to brown. Let cool slightly. If desired, serve over ricotta, yogurt, or oatmeal; top with Crispy Oats. Makes 4 servings.

EACH SERVING *273 cal, 9 g fat (6 g sat fat), 23 mg chol, 75 mg sodium, 50 g carb, 7 g fiber, 35 g sugars, 2 g pro*

Crispy Oats Combine 1 cup regular or quick-cooking oats and 3 Tbsp. each brown sugar and melted butter. Spread evenly in a baking pan and bake at 350°F for 15 minutes, stirring once.

Sledding
PARTY SNACKS

Make-ahead snacks, big-batch warm drinks, and a few extra layers ensure the success of a neighborhood sledding party that's chill in all the right ways.

MAPLE-ROSEMARY MIXED NUTS

Photo on page 44.

Lightly sweetened and herbed, this snack-worthy mix renews energy to return to cold-weather adventures—or to nibble while huddled close to the fire.

HANDS-ON TIME 15 min.
TOTAL TIME 35 min.

1   cup pecan halves
1   cup walnut pieces
1   cup blanched hazelnuts
1   cup raw cashews
¼   cup pure maple syrup
2   Tbsp. olive or canola oil
1   Tbsp. finely chopped fresh rosemary
1   Tbsp. finely chopped fresh thyme
1   large clove garlic, minced
¼   tsp. cayenne pepper (optional)
1   Tbsp. sea salt flakes

1. Preheat oven to 350°F. Line a shallow pan with foil. Spread nuts in an even layer in pan. Bake 10 to 12 minutes or until lightly toasted.
2. Meanwhile, in a small bowl stir together maple syrup, oil, herbs, garlic, and, if desired, cayenne. Remove nuts from oven. Drizzle syrup mixture over nuts; toss well. Bake 10 minutes more, stirring once.
3. Sprinkle with sea salt; stir. Let cool completely in pan on a wire rack. Store covered at room temperature up to 5 days. If desired, warm in a skillet over medium-low to serve. Serves 16.
EACH SERVING *204 cal, 18 g fat (2 g sat fat), 437 mg sodium, 9 g carb, 2 g fiber, 4 g sugars, 4 g pro*

SMOKY POPCORN MIX

Photo on page 44.

Paprika gives this baked snack mix a taste of smoke. Cones rolled from scrapbooking paper are easy to fill, hold, and snack from.

HANDS-ON TIME 10 min.
TOTAL TIME 35 min.

½   cup butter
2   Tbsp. Worcestershire sauce
2   tsp. smoked paprika
1   to 2 tsp. chili powder
1   tsp. onion powder
½   tsp. garlic powder
½   tsp. ground cumin
½   tsp. dried thyme, crushed
8   cups popped unsalted popcorn
1½ cups corn chips
1½ cups bite-size cheese crackers
1   cup sesame sticks
1   cup plain crunchy corn kernel snacks

1. Preheat oven to 275° F. In a small saucepan melt butter over medium-low. Stir in Worcestershire, paprika, chili powder, onion powder, garlic powder, cumin, and thyme. In a roasting pan combine popcorn, corn chips, crackers, sesame sticks, and crunchy corn kernel snacks. Pour butter mixture over popcorn mixture. Stir to coat.
2. Bake 25 to 30 minutes or until lightly toasted, stirring every 10 minutes. Transfer to a large piece of foil. Let cool completely. Store in an airtight container up to 2 days or freeze up to 1 month. Serves 12.
EACH SERVING *267 cal, 18 g fat (7 g sat fat), 20 mg chol, 397 mg sodium, 24 g carb, 2 g fiber, 1 g sugars, 4 g pro*

DANISH-STYLE MULLED WINE

Photo on page 44.

Choose a fruity red wine, such as a Malbec or Côtes du Rhône, for this adults-only warming winter drink.

HANDS-ON TIME 10 min.
TOTAL TIME 8 hr. 25 min.

In a large pitcher combine 1 bottle (750 ml.) wine, ½ cup vodka, ½ cup dark brown sugar, 1 cinnamon stick (3 inches), 4 slices fresh ginger, 1 Tbsp. green cardamom pods, 2 tsp. orange zest, and 8 whole cloves. Cover; let stand at room temperature 8 hours or overnight. Strain; discard solids. To serve, warm mixture over medium-low 15 to 20 minutes or until steaming (do not boil); strain. If desired, serve with additional cinnamon sticks. Serves 8.
EACH SERVING *165 cal, 8 mg sodium, 16 g carb, 14 g sugars*

GINGER-PEAR CIDER

Photo on page 44.

For an all-ages winter warmer, heat apple cider with pear wedges, orange slices, and fresh ginger.

HANDS-ON TIME 15 min.
TOTAL TIME 1 hr. 15 min.

Pour 2 qt. fresh apple cider into a 4- to 5-qt. pot. Add 1 large Bosc pear, cored and cut into thin wedges; ½ of a medium orange, sliced; 1 stick cinnamon (3 inches); 1-inch piece fresh ginger, sliced; and 1½ tsp. vanilla. Cover; heat over low 1 hour. Strain; discard solids. If desired, add bourbon or spiced rum, and serve with additional orange slices. Serves 12.
EACH SERVING *107 cal, 17 mg sodium, 26 g carb, 1 g fiber, 22 g sugars*

MAPLE-ROSEMARY
MIXED NUTS
Recipe on page 43

SMOKY
POPCORN MIX
Recipe on page 43

GINGER-PEAR CIDER
Recipe on page 43

DANISH-STYLE
MULLED WINE
Recipe on page 43

CHOCOLATE SPICE CAKE

Pumpkin pie spice and a splash of root beer play up the rich cocoa flavor in this brownie-like snack cake.

HANDS-ON TIME 25 min.
TOTAL TIME 2 hr., includes cooling

1	cup unsalted butter (2 sticks)
¾	cup unsweetened cocoa powder
1	Tbsp. pumpkin pie spice
1	cup root beer or stout beer
½	cup sour cream or plain yogurt
2	eggs
1	tsp. vanilla
2	cups all-purpose flour
1¾	cups sugar
1½	tsp. baking powder

1. Preheat oven to 350°F. Grease a 13×9-inch pan. In a medium saucepan melt butter over medium. Whisk in cocoa and pumpkin pie spice. Add the root beer. Whisk sour cream, eggs, and vanilla into root beer mixture.

2. In a large bowl whisk together flour, sugar, baking powder, and ¾ tsp. salt. Make a well in center of flour mixture. Stir root beer mixture into flour mixture just until combined. Spread evenly into prepared pan.

3. Bake 30 to 35 minutes or until a toothpick inserted in center comes out clean. Cool in pan on a wire rack. If desired, cut cake into cubes and thread onto skewers. Dust with powdered sugar. Serves 16.

EACH SERVING *284 cal, 14 g fat (8 g sat fat), 57 mg chol, 170 mg sodium, 39 g carb, 2 g fiber, 24 g sugars, 3 g pro*

BISTRO
SALAD

THE BETTER SIDE OF BITTER

Chicories, a family of bitter leafy greens, are well known for vibrant color and complex flavor. These winter beauties promise seasonal food adventures.

Bitter flavors tend to polarize. Perhaps that's why chicories—relatives of the lettuce family that includes escarole, frisée, and radicchio—are less popular than their mild cousins.

Fans of the chicory family recognize that the greens are in season during winter months. Now is the time to scoop up a variety from produce aisles or local farmers markets, watching for lesser-known types that offer a wide and versatile range of exceptional tastes.

BISTRO SALAD

TOTAL TIME 25 min.

4	slices bacon, chopped
½	cup coarse bread crumbs* or panko
4	cloves garlic, minced
2	Tbsp. chopped flat-leaf parsley
¼	cup olive oil
1	shallot, finely chopped
¼	cup red wine vinegar
1	Tbsp. Dijon mustard
1	small head escarole, trimmed and leaves separated
	Lemon wedges

1. In a large skillet cook bacon over medium until browned and crisp; transfer to paper towels to drain, reserving drippings. Add bread crumbs and 2 cloves garlic to skillet. Cook and stir 2 minutes or until bread crumbs are browned. Transfer to a small bowl; stir in bacon and parsley.

2. Add 1 Tbsp. olive oil to large skillet. Heat over medium. Add remaining garlic and the shallot, stirring to scrape up any browned bits. Cook and stir 2 minutes. Remove from heat. Stir in vinegar, mustard, ½ tsp. salt, and ¼ tsp. black pepper until combined. Whisk in remaining olive oil.

3. Arrange escarole on a platter; spoon dressing over escarole. Top with crumb mixture and, if desired, additional parsley. Serve with lemon wedges. Serves 4.

*Tip In a food processor process one slice artisanal bread until coarse crumbs form.

EACH SERVING *230 cal, 18 g fat (3 g sat fat), 12 mg chol, 536 mg sodium, 12 g carb, 4 g fiber, 1 g sugars, 7 g pro*

KNOW YOUR CHICORIES

Get acquainted with the wide variety of chicories and how to serve them.

SPECKLED RADICCHIO Tender, freckled leaves are best eaten raw in salads or cooked gently.

ESCAROLE At first glance it could be mistaken for lettuce; it's a good choice for salads and soups.

ENDIVE Available in Belgian and red varieties, endive has densely packed leaves with a juicy crunch.

ROSA DI PADOVA This has the deep crimson from radicchio with a texture more like romaine.

FRISÉE These exuberantly curly greens are often included in mesclun salad blends.

ROSSO TARDIVO Identify this green by its pointed spearlike leaves and mild flavor.

CHIOGGIA Round heads of Chioggia radicchio are easy to find among the bitter brethren.

LA ROSA DI VENETO This variety has a mild flavor and tender, rosy leaves similar to head lettuce.

CURLY ENDIVE Eat ruffle-edge endive raw in a salad, and reserve the larger leaves for a sauté or soup.

**BRAISED
BELGIAN ENDIVE**
Recipe on page 50

**GRILLED RADICCHIO
WITH CHEESE**
Recipe on page 50

BRAISED BELGIAN ENDIVE

Photo on page 48.

You've likely eaten Belgian endive leaves as part of fancy appetizers. This dish takes them into comfort-food territory. Braise endive wedges in apple cider vinegar just until softened, then top with crisp prosciutto, toasted walnuts, and Gruyère.

HANDS-ON TIME 10 min.
TOTAL TIME 35 min.

4   thin slices prosciutto
2   Tbsp. butter
1   Tbsp. olive oil
2   cloves garlic, minced
4   heads Belgian endive, halved
¼   cup apple cider vinegar
½   cup shredded Gruyère cheese (2 oz.)
½   cup chopped walnuts, toasted*
1   Tbsp. chopped fresh rosemary

1. Heat an extra-large skillet over medium. Add prosciutto; cook 3 to 4 minutes or until crisp, turning once. Remove; crumble when cool. In same skillet melt butter and heat oil over medium-high. Add garlic; cook and stir 1 minute. Add endive; cook 3 to 5 minutes or until browned, turning occasionally. Add vinegar, ¼ tsp. salt, and ¼ tsp. black pepper.
2. Cover; reduce heat. Cook 10 to 15 minutes or until the tip of a knife inserts easily into endive. Uncover; sprinkle with cheese. Turn off heat. Let stand, covered, 5 minutes or until is cheese melted. Sprinkle prosciutto, walnuts, and rosemary over endive. Serves 8.
*Tip Toast small amounts of nuts or seeds in a dry skillet over medium heat 3 to 5 minutes, stirring frequently. For larger amounts, preheat oven to 350°F. Spread nuts or seeds in a shallow baking pan. Bake 5 to 10 minutes or until lightly browned, shaking pan once or twice.
EACH SERVING *172 cal, 13 g fat (4 g sat fat), 19 mg chol, 309 mg sodium, 10 g carb, 9 g fiber, 1 g sugars, 8 g pro*

GRILLED RADICCHIO WITH CHEESE

Photo on page 49.

Soaked in a sweet-sour balsamic marinade, grilled to bring out mellow smokiness, and topped with salty, robust blue cheese, this side is designed to tempt all your taste buds.

HANDS-ON TIME 10 min.
TOTAL TIME 1 hr. 20 min., includes chilling

2   heads radicchio, trimmed and quartered, leaving stem ends intact
⅓   cup white balsamic vinegar
¼   cup olive oil
4   cloves garlic, minced
½   cup crumbled blue cheese or feta cheese (2 oz.)

1. Place radicchio in a large resealable plastic bag set in a shallow dish. For marinade: In a small bowl whisk together vinegar, oil, garlic, ¼ tsp. salt, and ¼ tsp. black pepper. Pour over radicchio. Seal bag, turning to coat. Chill 1 to 2 hours. Drain, reserving marinade.
2. Grill radicchio on the rack of a covered grill directly over medium 8 to 10 minutes, turning occasionally until each side is lightly charred. Turn wedges cut sides up; sprinkle with cheese. Grill 2 to 3 minutes more or until cheese is softened. Drizzle with reserved marinade. Serves 8.
EACH SERVING *123 cal, 9 g fat (2 g sat fat), 5 mg chol, 162 mg sodium, 5 g carb, 7 g sugars, 3 g pro*

ROAST BEEF WITH BEETS & CHICORIES

With a colorful tumble of beets and chicories and slices of peppercorn-crusted roast, this dish is as impressive looking as it is delicious. Its true appeal is the simple technique that richly flavors the greens. While the beef rests, chicories are tossed into the same pan for a quick roast in the pan juices.

HANDS-ON TIME 10 min.
TOTAL TIME 1 hr. 40 min.

1   2-lb. beef eye of round roast
1   Tbsp. cracked black peppercorns
¼   cup olive oil
6   to 8 small red and/or golden beets, trimmed, scrubbed, and quartered
8   cups torn mixed chicories, such as radicchio, escarole, frisée, and/or Belgian endive
1   medium onion, halved and thinly sliced (1⅓ cups)
4   cloves garlic, sliced
½   of an 8-oz. container crème fraîche
2   Tbsp. prepared horseradish

1. Preheat oven to 325°F. Place a rack in a roasting pan. Sprinkle beef with peppercorns and ½ tsp. salt, pressing in peppercorns. In a large skillet heat 1 Tbsp. oil over medium-high. Add beef; brown on all sides. Set beef on rack in roasting pan. Arrange beets around beef in pan. Drizzle with 1 Tbsp. oil. Sprinkle with ¼ tsp. salt; turn to coat. Roast, uncovered, 1¼ to 1½ hours or until beef reaches 135°F and beets are tender. Transfer beets and beef to a platter. Let stand, covered, 15 minutes.
2. Meanwhile, increase oven to 425°F. Remove rack from pan. Add chicories, onion, and garlic to pan. Drizzle with remaining olive oil. Sprinkle with ¼ tsp. salt; toss to coat. Roast, uncovered, 10 minutes or until tender, stirring once.
3. In a small bowl stir together crème fraîche and horseradish. Slice beef. Serve with beets, chicories, and horseradish sauce. Serves 6 to 8.
EACH SERVING *379 cal, 19 g fat (6 g sat fat), 98 mg chol, 598 mg sodium, 18 g carb, 5 g fiber, 10 g sugars, 34 g pro*

ROAST BEEF
WITH BEETS
& CHICORIES

STUFFED
RADICCHIO

CHICKEN, ESCAROLE & ORECCHIETTE SOUP

Homemade chicken noodle soup goes Italian. A rich broth results from bone-in chicken pieces, pasta "little ears" replace egg noodles, and escarole—the traditional green in Italian wedding soup—melts into silky, flavorful ribbons.

HANDS-ON TIME 30 min.
TOTAL TIME 2 hr.

3   lb. meaty bone-in chicken pieces
1   large onion, cut into thin wedges
1   tsp. dried thyme, crushed
4   cloves garlic, sliced
2   bay leaves
10   cups torn escarole and/or frisée
1   cup thinly bias-sliced carrots
1   cup thinly sliced celery
2   cups dried orecchiette pasta
½   cup chopped fresh basil
    Parmesan cheese

1. In a 6- to 8-qt. pot combine chicken pieces, onion, 2 tsp. salt, the thyme, ½ tsp. black pepper, the garlic, and bay leaves. Add 8 cups water. Bring to boiling; reduce heat. Simmer, covered, 1 hour or until chicken is very tender and falls off the bones.
2. Remove chicken from broth. When cool enough to handle, remove meat from bones. Discard bones and skin. Cut meat into bite-size pieces. Discard bay leaves. Return chicken to broth. Add 8 cups escarole, the carrots, and celery. Return to boiling; reduce heat. Simmer, covered, 15 minutes. Stir in pasta; return to a simmer. Cook 7 to 9 minutes or until pasta and escarole are tender. Stir in basil and remaining escarole. Top each serving with grated Parmesan cheese. Serves 8.
EACH SERVING *332 cal, 11 g fat (3 g sat fat), 79 mg chol, 713 mg sodium, 29 g carb, 4 g fiber, 3 g sugars, 30 g pro*

STUFFED RADICCHIO

Wrap sturdy radicchio leaves around a mix of ground meat, orzo, raisins, and almonds in this spin on cabbage rolls. Roasting mellows the radicchio's bitter edge, while enough bite remains to balance a bit of sweetness from the cherry tomato sauce.

HANDS-ON TIME 25 min.
TOTAL TIME 1 hr.

½   cup dried orzo pasta
2   Tbsp. olive oil
1   cup cherry tomatoes, halved
1   14.5-oz. can crushed tomatoes
2   Tbsp. packed brown sugar
1   Tbsp. lemon juice
4   cloves garlic, minced
8   oz. ground beef
8   oz. ground pork sausage
½   cup finely chopped fresh fennel, fronds reserved
¼   cup raisins
¼   cup slivered almonds, toasted
2   Tbsp. chopped flat-leaf parsley
⅛   tsp. ground cloves
12   radicchio leaves

1. Preheat oven to 400°F. In a medium saucepan cook orzo in boiling salted water 5 minutes; drain. Rinse with cold water; drain again.
2. For sauce: In a large skillet heat 1 Tbsp. olive oil over medium-high. Add cherry tomatoes; cook and stir 3 to 4 minutes or until softened and charred. Add crushed tomatoes, brown sugar, lemon juice, 2 cloves garlic, ½ tsp. salt, and ¼ tsp. black pepper. Bring to boiling; reduce heat. Simmer, uncovered, 5 minutes. Spoon into a 3-qt. baking dish.
3. For filling: In a large bowl combine orzo, beef, pork, fennel, raisins, almonds, parsley, remaining 2 cloves garlic, ½ tsp. salt, ¼ tsp. black pepper, and the cloves.
4. Divide filling among radicchio leaves. Roll each leaf around filling and arrange seam sides down on sauce. Brush with remaining 1 Tbsp. olive oil.
5. Bake, uncovered, 25 to 30 minutes or until filling registers 160°F. Let stand 10 minutes. Top with fennel fronds. Serves 6.
EACH SERVING *340 cal, 19 g fat (5 g sat fat), 49 mg chol, 762 mg sodium, 26 g carb, 4 g fiber, 13 g sugars, 17 g pro*

CHICKEN, ESCAROLE
& ORECCHIETTE SOUP

**MOZZARELLA-STUFFED
KIMCHI MEATBALLS**
Recipe on page 66

march

Layer flavor with veggies in an Irish pie, a quiche, lettuce wraps, a Middle Eastern lasagna, and more. Discover tart ingredients. Plus, satisfy your curiosity and taste buds with plant-based "meat."

57 61 63

VEGGIE SHEPHERD'S PIE

This month we celebrate St. Patrick's Day with a vegetarian refresh of an Irish favorite.

VEGGIE SHEPHERD'S PIE

Cauliflower and parsnips lighten the traditional mashed potato topper. For the shamrock detail, after baking the pies, lightly press a cookie cutter into the topper to outline the shape, then sprinkle in chopped herbs.

HANDS-ON TIME 25 min.
TOTAL TIME 1 hr. 15 min.

- 2   Tbsp. olive oil
- 6   Tbsp. butter
- 2   lb. sliced cremini and/or button mushrooms
- 1   large leek, washed, trimmed, halved, and sliced (1 cup)
- 4   cloves garlic, minced
- 4   carrots, cut into 1-inch chunks
- 1   lb. parsnips, peeled and cut into 1-inch chunks
- 1   cup dried brown lentils, rinsed and drained
- 2½   cups vegetable broth
- 12   oz. Yukon Gold potatoes, peeled and chopped
- 3   cups cauliflower florets
- ½   cup sour cream
- 2   Tbsp. all-purpose flour
- 1   12-oz. bottle stout beer
- 3   Tbsp. tomato paste
- 1   cup frozen peas
- 2   Tbsp. finely chopped fresh herbs, such as flat-leaf parsley, thyme, oregano, and/or rosemary

1. In a 5- to 6-qt. pot or Dutch oven heat oil and 2 Tbsp. butter over medium-high. Add mushrooms, leek, garlic, 1 tsp. salt, and ¼ tsp. black pepper. Cook 8 to 10 minutes or until tender (liquid will not be evaporated). Stir in carrots, half the parsnips, the lentils, and broth. Bring to boiling; reduce heat. Simmer, covered, 25 to 30 minutes or until lentils are tender.

2. Meanwhile, in a 3- to 4-qt. saucepan cook potatoes, cauliflower, and remaining parsnips in enough salted water to cover 20 minutes or until potatoes are tender. Drain; return to pot. Add remaining butter, ½ tsp. salt, and ¼ tsp. pepper. Let stand, covered, 5 minutes. Mash; stir in sour cream.

3. Preheat oven to 425°F. In a small bowl stir together flour and ½ cup stout. Stir into lentil mixture with remaining stout, tomato paste, and peas. Cook and stir until thickened and bubbly. Stir in herbs. Divide among eight 10- to 12-oz. casserole dishes. Place dishes on a rimmed baking sheet.

4. Spread or pipe mashed potato mixture onto pies. Bake 15 minutes or until browned and bubbly. Let stand 10 minutes. Serves 8.

EACH SERVING *378 cal, 15 g fat (8 g sat fat), 30 mg chol, 398 mg sodium, 49 g carb, 9 g fiber, 11 g sugars, 14 g pro*

A HEARTY MIX OF MUSHROOMS, LEEKS, CARROTS, PARSNIPS, AND LENTILS SIMMERED WITH STOUT REPLACES THE TRADITIONAL GROUND MEAT IN THESE SINGLE-SERVING MINI SHEPHERD'S PIES. LUCKY FOR YOU, LENTILS ARE A HARBINGER OF GOOD FORTUNE AND PROSPERITY.

SHEET-PAN QUICHE

Skip the fuss of rolling and crimping pastry. Instead, pull out a trusty sheet pan. This press-in-the-pan dough makes quick work of brunch.

SWEET POTATO, ONION, SPINACH & BACON QUICHE

HANDS-ON TIME 15 min.
TOTAL TIME 1 hr. 5 min.

- 2½ cups all-purpose flour
- 1 cup butter, cut up
- ¼ to ⅓ cup ice water
- 6 slices bacon
- 2 medium sweet potatoes (about 8 oz. each), peeled and coarsely chopped
- 1 cup chopped onion
- 2 cloves garlic, minced
- 6 cups fresh baby spinach
- 10 eggs
- 2½ cups milk
- 1 Tbsp. chopped fresh herbs, such as flat-leaf parsley, basil, and/or thyme

1. Preheat oven to 375°F. Grease a 15×10-inch baking pan. In a food processor pulse to combine flour and 2 tsp. salt. Add butter; pulse until mixture resembles fine crumbs. Add ice water, 1 Tbsp. at a time, until dough just starts to come together.

2. Transfer dough to prepared pan. No rolling required: Press dough firmly and evenly into the bottom of the pan. (Egg mixture will completely cover.) Bake 10 minutes.

3. Meanwhile, in an extra-large skillet cook bacon over medium until crisp. Drain bacon on paper towels, reserving drippings in skillet. Chop or crumble bacon.

4. Add potatoes, onion, and garlic to skillet. Cook and stir 5 to 6 minutes or just until potatoes are just tender. Gradually add spinach, stirring just until wilted. Spread on hot crust.

5. In a large bowl whisk together eggs, milk, ½ tsp. salt, and ¼ tsp. black pepper. Stir in herbs. Pour egg mixture over spinach mixture. Sprinkle with bacon.

6. Bake 40 to 45 minutes or until quiche appears set. Cool 10 minutes. Serves 12.
EACH SERVING *433 cal, 28 g fat (14 g sat fat), 212 mg chol, 846 mg sodium, 32 g carb, 2 g fiber, 5 g sugars, 13 g pro*
Make Ahead The night before brunch, prepare as directed, let cool 30 minutes, then cover and refrigerate overnight. Reheat in a 375°F oven 15 minutes or until an instant-read thermometer registers 165°F.

FAST & FRESH

Easy, delicious recipes for a better dinner tonight.

THAI SHRIMP & CUCUMBER LETTUCE WRAPS

Jasmine rice is an aromatic long grain rice from Thailand—Indian basmati is a comparable substitute. To save time, look for microwavable packs of either variety.

TOTAL TIME 20 min.

2   limes
1   lb. medium shrimp, peeled and deveined
3   Tbsp. soy sauce
2   Tbsp. canola oil
1   tsp. sriracha sauce
1   tsp. toasted sesame oil
1   tsp. packed brown sugar
1   cucumber, halved lengthwise and thinly sliced
12 leaves Bibb lettuce
3   cups cooked jasmine rice
½   cup chopped fresh basil, cilantro, and/or mint leaves
1   thai, fresno, or jalapeño pepper, stemmed and sliced (tip, page 28)

1. Zest one lime. Sprinkle zest, ¼ tsp. salt, and ¼ tsp. black pepper over shrimp. Steam in a steamer basket 4 to 5 minutes or until shrimp turn opaque.

2. Meanwhile, for dressing: Juice the 2 limes into a large bowl. Add soy sauce, canola oil, sriracha, sesame oil, and brown sugar. Whisk to combine. Add shrimp and cucumber slices to dressing; toss to coat.

3. Place lettuce leaves on plates. Top each leaf with rice, shrimp mixture, herbs, and pepper slices. Serves 4.

EACH SERVING *397 cal, 11 g fat (1 g sat fat), 201 mg chol, 629 mg sodium, 51 g carb, 4 g fiber, 4 g sugars, 26 g pro*

CURRY CHICKEN
SALAD WITH
COUSCOUS

CURRY CHICKEN SALAD WITH COUSCOUS

Of the two styles of curry powder, Madras is hotter than common.

TOTAL TIME 30 min.

- 1   cup Israeli couscous, uncooked
- 6   green onions, trimmed and chopped
- ¼   cup olive oil
- ¼   cup white wine vinegar
- 1   Tbsp. honey
- 2   cloves garlic, halved
- 2   skinless, boneless chicken breast halves, cooked and sliced
- 1   tsp. Madras curry powder
- 2   cups sliced kohlrabi, carrots, and/or celery

1. Cook couscous according to package instructions.
2. For dressing: In a blender combine green onions, olive oil, vinegar, honey, garlic, ¼ tsp. salt, and ¼ tsp. black pepper. Cover; blend until smooth.
3. In a medium bowl toss chicken with curry powder.
4. To serve, top couscous with vegetables and chicken. Drizzle with dressing. Season to taste. Serves 4.

EACH SERVING *442 cal, 18 g fat (3 g sat fat), 78 mg chol, 446 mg sodium, 43 g carb, 3 g fiber, 7 g sugars, 26 g pro*

ROASTED SALMON WITH RADISHES & FENNEL

ROASTED SALMON WITH RADISHES & FENNEL

There are many radish varieties, like Easter Egg, Black Spanish Round, and White Icicle, that pop up at farmers markets. This recipe opts for Watermelon, which are larger and milder than typical radishes.

HANDS-ON TIME 15 min.
TOTAL TIME 30 min.

- 1   lb. watermelon radishes or other radishes, cut into 1-inch pieces
- 1   fennel bulb, trimmed, quartered, and cored, fronds chopped
- 4   Tbsp. olive oil
- 4   6-oz. salmon fillets
- ½   tsp. orange zest
- 3   Tbsp. orange juice
- 3   Tbsp. white wine vinegar
- 1   Tbsp. honey
- 1   orange, peeled, quartered, and thinly sliced

1. Preheat oven to 400°F. Line a 15×10-inch pan with foil; lightly oil foil. Toss radishes and fennel with 2 tsp. olive oil, ¼ tsp. salt, and ¼ tsp. black pepper. Spread on one side of prepared pan. Roast 15 minutes.
2. Meanwhile, season salmon with ¼ tsp. salt and ¼ tsp. black pepper. Arrange skin side down on opposite side of pan. Drizzle 1 tsp. olive oil over salmon. Roast 10 to 15 minutes or until fish flakes easily when tested with a fork and radishes and fennel are fork-tender.
3. For vinaigrette: In a screw-top jar combine 3 Tbsp. olive oil, the orange zest and juice, vinegar, and honey. Cover; shake well to combine. Season to taste with salt and pepper. Drizzle vinaigrette over salmon and vegetables. Top with orange slices and fennel fronds. Serves 4.

EACH SERVING *543 cal, 36 g fat (7 g sat fat), 92 mg chol, 381 mg sodium, 17 g carb, 4 g fiber, 13 g sugars, 37 g pro*

THE POWER OF SOUR

Tart ingredients brighten and balance many dishes and beverages. This collection of recipes celebrates the sour sensation.

LEMON TIRAMISU

Skip what you know about traditional tiramisu. This recipe puts a tart spin on the layered espresso dessert: ladyfinger cookies dipped in lemon simple syrup, lemon curd, and zest-spiked whipped mascarpone.

HANDS-ON TIME 45 min.
TOTAL TIME 5 hr. 45 min., includes chilling

LEMON CURD
3 lemons (zest and ¾ cup juice)
1 cup sugar
2 eggs
2 egg yolks
½ cup unsalted butter, cut into cubes
¼ tsp. vanilla

LEMON SYRUP
2 lemons (zest and ½ cup juice)
¼ cup sugar

MASCARPONE CREAM
½ cup heavy cream

1 8-oz. container mascarpone cheese
⅓ cup sugar
½ lemon, zested
12 crisp Italian ladyfingers, halved crosswise
Sweetened whipped cream (optional)

1. For the lemon curd: In a medium saucepan combine zest and juice of three lemons, 1 cup sugar, eggs, egg yolks, butter, and pinch of salt. Cook, stirring constantly, over medium until mixture thickens and starts to bubble. Remove from heat. Stir in vanilla. Strain through a fine-mesh sieve. Transfer to a bowl. Cover surface with plastic wrap. Refrigerate 1 to 2 hours or until chilled. (Lemon curd can be made a week ahead.)

2. For syrup: In a small saucepan combine zest and juice of two lemons, ¼ cup sugar, and ¼ cup water. Heat over medium just until sugar is dissolved. Transfer to a small bowl; let cool.

3. For mascarpone cream: In a small bowl beat cream with a mixer on medium until stiff peaks form. In a medium bowl beat mascarpone, ⅓ cup sugar, and zest of half lemon with the mixer until smooth. Fold in whipped cream.

4. To assemble: Spoon one-third of the mascarpone cream into eight (4- to 6-oz.) glasses or ramekins. Dip ladyfinger halves into lemon syrup, coating both sides. Place about half the ladyfingers in glasses, breaking or cutting to fit. Top with half of the lemon curd and another third of mascarpone cream. Repeat cookie, curd, and cream layers. Cover each serving. Refrigerate at least 4 hours or overnight. If desired, top with sweetened whipped cream and additional zest. Serves 8.

EACH SERVING *533 cal, 34 g fat (19 g sat fat), 213 mg chol, 85 mg sodium, 54 g carb, 1 g fiber, 46 g sugars, 7 g pro*

DRIVEN BY GLOBAL FOOD TRENDS AND AN APPETITE FOR ASSERTIVE, COMPLEX FLAVORS, SOUR IS SHOWING UP EVERYWHERE. THE BITE OF ACID BALANCES SWEET AND SALTY, COUNTERS BITTER, AND AMPLIFIES THE FLAVORS OF INDIVIDUAL INGREDIENTS.

**CHICKEN
ADOBO WITH
COCONUT RICE**
Recipe on page 66

**MOZZARELLA-STUFFED
KIMCHI MEATBALLS**
Recipe on page 66

CITRUS AND VINEGARS ARE OBVIOUS
CHOICES FOR A SPIKE OF SOUR. THESE
RECIPES, HOWEVER, HIGHLIGHT OTHER
OPTIONS—LIKE FERMENTED INGREDIENTS
AND CULTURED DAIRY—FOR NUANCED TANG.

CHICKEN ADOBO WITH COCONUT RICE

Photo on page 64

Most adobo recipes call for marinating then braising meat or seafood for hours. This speedy rendition still relies on the tangy vinegar sauce but shortcuts the process. You can pull it off any weeknight.

HANDS-ON TIME 20 min.
TOTAL TIME 1 hr.

1   cup apple cider vinegar
⅓   cup reduced-sodium soy sauce
6   cloves garlic, minced
1   Tbsp. grated fresh ginger
1   Tbsp. packed brown sugar
1   serrano pepper, stemmed, seeded, and minced (tip, page 28)
2   bay leaves
1   Tbsp. freshly cracked black pepper
6   bone-in, skin-on chicken thighs (3 to 3½ lb.)
1   cup long grain white rice
1   14-oz. can unsweetened coconut milk
¼   cup toasted unsweetened coconut chips*
3   green onions, sliced

1. For chicken: In a 5- to 6-qt. Dutch oven combine vinegar, soy sauce, garlic, ginger, brown sugar, serrano, bay leaves, and black pepper. Add chicken, skin side down. Bring to boiling; reduce heat. Simmer, covered, 15 minutes. Turn chicken; simmer 15 minutes more. Place chicken skin side up on a foil-lined rimmed baking sheet.
2. For sauce: Bring cooking liquid to boiling over medium-high. Boil gently, uncovered, 10 to 12 minutes or until thickened and reduced to about 1 cup. Remove from heat. Discard bay leaves. Skim off fat.

3. Meanwhile, preheat broiler. Broil chicken 5 inches from heat 4 to 5 minutes or until skin is browned and crisp.
4. For coconut rice: Place rice in a fine-mesh sieve. Rinse with cold water. Place in a 2-qt. saucepan. Stir in coconut milk, ½ cup water, and ½ tsp. salt. Bring to boiling; reduce heat. Simmer, covered, 15 minutes. Remove from heat. Let stand 10 minutes.
5. Fluff rice with a fork. Stir in toasted coconut and half the green onions. Serve chicken with rice. Drizzle with sauce. Sprinkle with remaining green onions and, if desired, additional toasted coconut. Serves 6.
*Tip To toast coconut, preheat oven to 350°F. Spread coconut chips on a shallow baking pan. Bake 5 minutes or until golden brown, watching carefully to prevent burning.
EACH SERVING *758 cal, 49 g fat (21 g sat fat), 220 mg chol, 673 mg sodium, 34 g carb, 2 g fiber, 3 g sugars, 41 g pro*

MOZZARELLA-STUFFED KIMCHI MEATBALLS

Photo on page 54, 65

Chopped kimchi, a splash of its brine, and gochujang (a fermented chile paste) give spunk to the tomato sauce in this Korean-Italian crossover. The cheese-stuffed meatballs take their cue from South Korean cuisine, which is known for pairing sour fermented ingredients with mozzarella cheese.

HANDS-ON TIME 30 min.
TOTAL TIME 50 min.

3   Tbsp. olive oil
1   cup chopped onion
5   cloves garlic, minced
1   28-oz. can whole peeled Italian tomatoes in puree
1   cup chicken broth
⅓   cup brine from purchased kimchi

1¼   cups finely chopped kimchi
3   Tbsp. fish sauce
2   Tbsp. reduced-sodium soy sauce
1   Tbsp. gochujang sauce or paste
1   lb. ground beef (80% lean)
⅔   cup panko
¼   cup chopped green onions
4   oz. part-skim mozzarella, cut into ½-inch cubes (about 24)
    Cooked wide rice noodles and/or sautéed napa cabbage*

1. For sauce: In a 5- to 6-qt. Dutch oven heat 2 Tbsp. oil over medium. Add onion. Cook 5 minutes or until tender. Add three cloves garlic. Cook 1 minute more. Add tomatoes and their juices, crushing tomatoes with your hands as you add them to the pot. Add broth, brine, ¼ cup kimchi, 2 Tbsp. fish sauce, 1 Tbsp. soy sauce, and the gochujang. Bring to boiling; reduce heat to medium-low. Simmer, uncovered, 20 minutes or until sauce is thickened. Season to taste with salt and black pepper.
2. For meatballs: In a large bowl combine ground beef, remaining 1 cup kimchi, the panko, green onions, remaining two cloves garlic, remaining 1 Tbsp. fish sauce, remaining 1 Tbsp. soy sauce, and ¼ tsp. salt. Mix well with hands. With wet hands shape meat around a mozzarella cube to form 24 balls.
3. In an extra-large skillet heat remaining 1 Tbsp. oil over medium. Add half the meatballs. Cook 12 minutes or until browned and cooked through, turning occasionally. Remove; cook remaining meatballs. Transfer to the Dutch oven; heat through. Serve with noodles and/or cabbage. Serves 4.
*Tip To sauté cabbage, remove and discard ribs; cut leaves into wide ribbons. Cook cabbage in hot oil over medium-high 2 to 3 minutes or until softened.

Baking Option Place meatballs in a 15×10-inch baking pan lined with foil. Cover and chill 1 hour. Bake at 375°F for 18 minutes or until 160°F.

EACH SERVING *554 cal, 37 g fat (12 g sat fat), 98 mg chol, 2,456 mg sodium, 25 g carb, 6 g fiber, 11 g sugars, 32 g pro*

FERMENTED HOT SAUCE

If fermenting foods at home intimidates you, this subtly sweet hot sauce is an easy entry point.

TOTAL TIME 30 min., plus 1 to 2 weeks for fermenting

- 2   **cups chopped red bell peppers**
- 2   **to 3 habanero peppers, stemmed and seeds removed, if desired (tip, page 28**
- 1   **cup roughly chopped carrots**
- ½   **cup roughly chopped onion**
- 2   **cloves garlic**
- ⅓   **cup apple cider vinegar**
- ½   **tsp. smoked paprika**
- 1   **Tbsp. red miso paste**

1. In a food processor combine bell peppers, habaneros, carrots, onion, garlic, and 1½ tsp. salt. Pulse until finely chopped. Transfer to a wide-mouth quart jar, pressing to release some juices. Place a small plastic bag filled with water on vegetables to keep them submerged. Let stand 1 to 2 weeks in a cool, dark place.

2. In a food processor combine vegetables and their juices and apple cider vinegar. Puree until smooth. Strain through a fine-mesh sieve set over a bowl, pressing on solids. For a thicker sauce, add enough solids to reach desired consistency. Stir in paprika and miso. Season to taste with salt and black pepper. Makes 1½ cups.

EACH 1 TSP. *3 cal, 59 mg sodium, 1 g carb*

FERMENTED HOT SAUCE

THIS LASAGNA UPDATE HAS BIG PERKS: IT COMES TOGETHER IN A SKILLET, AND A FEW TART INGREDIENTS GIVE IT A MIDDLE EASTERN ACCENT.

VEGETABLE LASAGNA WITH LABNEH

Labneh, a Middle Eastern staple, is strained yogurt with a spreadable consistency akin to soft cream cheese. If you can't find it in large grocery stores or Middle Eastern markets, substitute 8 oz. whipped cream cheese, or it's fast and easy to make at home (see recipe, far right).

HANDS-ON TIME 45 min.
TOTAL TIME 1 hr. 30 min.

- 2 Tbsp. olive oil
- 1 large yellow straightneck summer squash (8 oz.), halved lengthwise and sliced into ¼-inch-thick half-moons
- 8 oz. cremini mushrooms, quartered
- 1 cup chopped yellow onion
- 1 bunch lacinato kale, stems removed and leaves coarsely chopped
- 3 large cloves garlic, minced
- 24 oz. cherry tomatoes, halved
- 9 dried lasagna noodles, broken
- 2 cups vegetable broth
- 1½ cups labneh*
  Zhoug
- 4 oz. fresh or part-skim mozzarella cheese, sliced
  Cherry tomatoes, flat-leaf parsley, and/or fresh cilantro (optional)

1. For vegetables: In an extra-large straight-sided skillet heat 1 Tbsp. oil over medium-high. Add squash in an even layer. Season to taste with salt and black pepper. Cook 2 minutes or until browned, without stirring. Turn; cook 2 minutes more or until browned. Transfer to a bowl. In same pan, brown mushrooms. Transfer to bowl with squash.

2. Add remaining 1 Tbsp. olive oil to skillet. Add onion; cook and stir until softened. Add kale; season with salt and pepper. Cook and stir 3 minutes or until kale is wilted and tender. Add garlic; cook and stir 1 minute more. Transfer to bowl with squash and mushrooms.

3. Add tomatoes to skillet. Season with salt and pepper. Cook 5 to 10 minutes or until tomatoes are softened and juices have thickened slightly. Transfer to bowl with vegetables and stir to combine. (Vegetable mixture can be kept refrigerated up to 3 days.)

4. Preheat oven to 400°F. Spoon about ⅓ cup vegetable mixture into a large oven-safe skillet. Cover with three noodles. Top with one-third vegetable mixture. Repeat layers twice. Gently pour broth over noodles. Bring to boiling over medium-high; reduce to medium. Cook, uncovered, 20 minutes or until noodles are tender and broth is mostly absorbed, keeping noodles submerged.

5. Spread labneh and zhoug over top of lasagna, making sure to cover all the noodles. Arrange mozzarella evenly over top. Bake, uncovered, 30 minutes or until juices are bubbling and top is golden. If desired, top with cherry tomatoes, parsley, and/or cilantro. Serves 6.

*Labneh To make labneh, spoon 2 cups plain whole milk Greek yogurt into a large piece of 100% cotton cheesecloth; tie into a bundle. Tie bundle to handle of a wooden spoon; suspend over a deep bowl or pitcher. Refrigerate at least 2 hours or until most of the liquid has drained and mixture is the consistency of softened cream cheese.

Zhoug In a food processor combine ½ cup each packed fresh flat-leaf parsley and cilantro, 2 cloves garlic, and 1 seeded serrano pepper. Pulse until finely chopped. Add ¼ cup olive oil, 2 Tbsp. lemon juice, ½ tsp. each ground coriander and ground cumin, and ¼ tsp. ground cardamom. Pulse just until combined. Season to taste. (Store in refrigerator up to 1 week.)

EACH SERVING 494 cal, 29 g fat (11 g sat fat), 38 mg chol, 928 mg sodium, 45 g carb, 7 g fiber, 8 g sugars, 15 g pro

VEGETABLE
LASAGNA
WITH LABNEH

CITRUS-CUCUMBER
SLAW WITH
PICKLED SHALLOTS
Recipe on page 72

TAMARIND-PEACH
LASSI
Recipe on page 72

THE TAMARIND-PEACH LASSI GETS A FLAVOR BOOST FROM SWIPING RIMS OF GLASSES WITH LIME THEN DIPPING IN CHILE-LIME SEASONING.

SOUR PANTRY

Add these acidic ingredients to the staples of lemon and vinegar.

VERJUS A punchy, vinegarlike juice from unripe fruit (usually grapes).

CHILE-LIME SEASONING Acid meets heat and salt. Sprinkle on fruit or stir into salsa.

TAMARIND The sticky, sweet-tart pulp from the seeds of tamarind trees.

POMEGRANATE MOLASSES A reduction of fruit juice, sugar, and citrus or citric acid.

GROUND SUMAC A vibrant spice with a tangy, almost lemony flavor.

CITRUS-CUCUMBER SLAW WITH PICKLED SHALLOTS

Photo on page 70

The flavor of sweet-tart verjus—the pressed juice of unripened grapes—hits somewhere between vinegar and wine. Like wine, verjus is available in both red and white varietals. In this recipe white verjus is the base of the slaw vinaigrette, which doubles as a brine for the quick-pickled shallots. Any combination of red, green, and/or napa cabbage works in the slaw.

TOTAL TIME 25 min.

½   cup white verjus
¼   cup vegetable oil
3   Tbsp. lime juice
1   large shallot, thinly sliced
5   cups shredded green, red, and/or napa cabbage
2   grapefruit and/or pomelos, peeled, seeded, and sectioned
1   English cucumber, sliced
½   cup thinly sliced red onion
1   cup seeded and chopped roma tomatoes
1   large jalapeño, seeded and finely chopped (tip, page 28)

In a small bowl stir together verjus, oil, lime juice, shallot, ½ tsp. salt, and ¼ tsp. black pepper. Let stand 20 minutes or up to 8 hours. To serve, in an extra-large bowl combine cabbage, grapefruit, cucumber, onion, tomatoes, and jalapeño. Pour vinaigrette and shallots over cabbage mixture. Serve with a slotted spoon. Serves 12.
EACH SERVING *38 cal, 1 g fat (0 g sat fat), 16 mg sodium, 8 g carb, 2 g fiber, 5 g sugars, 1 g pro*

TAMARIND-PEACH LASSI

Photo on page 71

Akin to a smoothie, the Indian drink lassi is made with yogurt or buttermilk, then incorporates any number of spices, juices, and/or fruits—mango is particularly popular. This rendition combines tangy Greek yogurt with fresh peach slices and tamarind, a tropical fruit that starts sweet, finishes tart, and has an earthy, acidic almost indescribable note. Jarred tamarind paste is a dark, sticky paste made by pureeing the fruit pulp with water and sugar. Find it in Asian or Mexican markets or large grocery stores.

TOTAL TIME 15 min.

2   cups Greek yogurt
3   Tbsp. tamarind paste
1½   cups fresh or frozen peeled peach slices
8   fresh mint leaves
2   tsp. honey
     Chile-lime seasoning (optional)
     Mint leaves (optional)

In a blender combine yogurt, ¼ cup water, the tamarind paste, peach slices, mint, and honey. Blend until smooth, adding water as needed to reach desired consistency. If desired, rim glasses with chile-lime seasoning and top each lassi with mint leaves. Serves 4.
EACH SERVING *210 cal, 2 g fat (2 g sat fat), 10 mg chol, 46 mg sodium, 37 g carb, 2 g fiber, 33 g sugars, 12 g pro*

FAUX MEAT

The biggest news in meat this year isn't meat at all. Now that Impossible Burgers are on drive-through menus, plant-based "ground beef" look-alikes are also in meat cases of large grocers.

WHAT'S THE BEEF?

Ingredients vary brand to brand, but producers of plant-based "ground beef" have figured out how to replicate the texture, aroma, and taste of meat using plant proteins derived from soy, peas, beans, rice, and wheat. Beet juice, pomegranate fruit powder, and other fruit and vegetable extracts imitate beef's pink color. Coconut oil and cocoa butter add pockets of white marbling.

HOW DO THE NUTRIENTS STACK UP?

Plant-based meat and 80-percent-lean beef each have about 20 g protein in a 4-oz. patty. The similarities end there. Most faux ground meats have fewer calories and fat, none have cholesterol, and, unlike beef, the faux meats provide some fiber. Note: Plant-based patties tend to have more sodium, ranging from 370 to 580 mg versus 80 mg for an unseasoned meat patty. Lightly salted beef, however, is comparable to the low end of the faux meat range.

WHERE'S THE BEEF?

Look for fresh faux beef alongside its counterpart in the refrigerated meat case. Major brands offer 12- to 16-oz. bulk packages and 3- to 4-oz. patties. In large stores you might find patties containing a blend of ground beef and pea protein.

DOES IT COOK LIKE BEEF?

The short answer is, yes, you can cook these plant-based products as you would ground beef. Look for specific tips on package labels, and follow guidelines for freezing and thawing.

"BEEF" PICADILLO-STYLE TACOS

TOTAL TIME 35 min.

- 2 to 3 Tbsp. vegetable oil
- 1 12- to 16-oz. pkg. plant-based ground meat
- 1 cup chopped onion
- 1 poblano pepper, stemmed, seeded, and chopped (tip, page 28)
- 2 cloves garlic, minced
- 1½ cups diced russet potato
- 1 tsp. ground coriander
- ½ tsp. ground cumin
- 2 cups chopped tomatoes
- ½ cup vegetable broth
- 12 corn tortillas, warmed
  Chopped slivered almonds, chopped fresh cilantro, and/or sliced green olives

1. In an extra-large skillet heat 1 Tbsp. oil over medium. Crumble in plant-based meat. Cook and stir until browned; transfer to a bowl. Heat 1 Tbsp. oil in the skillet over medium-high. Add onion, poblano, and garlic. Cook and stir 4 minutes or until poblano is charred. Add potato, ½ tsp. salt, and ¼ tsp. black pepper. Cook and stir 5 minutes or until potato is browned. Add coriander and cumin. Cook and stir 1 minute. Add tomatoes and broth.

2. Bring to boiling, scraping up browned bits; reduce heat. Simmer, uncovered, 5 minutes. Stir in plant-based meat to warm. Serve in corn tortillas; top with almonds, cilantro, and/or sliced green olives. Serves 6.

EACH SERVING *369 cal, 17 g fat (2 g sat fat), 543 mg sodium, 41 g carb, 6 g fiber, 4 g sugars, 16 g pro*

**CITRUS SUGAR
COOKIE EGGS AND
GOLDEN GLITZ**
Recipe on page 90
Technique on page 91

april

Master the art of cooking eggs—any style. Then roll out cookie dough, cut egg shapes, and decorate them glamorously to celebrate spring. For easy weeknight meals, prepare a savory soup, hearty sandwich, or one-pan roasted dinner.

78

84

90

Perfecting
THE EGG

Ask 100 people how to cook eggs and you'll likely gather a confusing number of responses. For reliable and definitive advice, the staff of the *Better Homes & Gardens* Test Kitchen stepped in to crack hundreds of shells—then stirred, fried, scrambled, boiled, and poached—to show how you can serve eggs confidently every time.

WHEN CRACKING EGGS, TAP THEM ON A FLAT SURFACE RATHER THAN THE SIDE OF A BOWL OR SKILLET, WHICH CAN DRIVE THOSE HARD-TO-FISH-OUT SHELL FRAGMENTS INTO THE EGG WHITE.

CHOOSING EGGS

Egg cartons boast many terms, and here's what they mean.

WHAT'S THE DIFFERENCE?

Free range, pasture raised, organic, omega-3? Although the terms can be confusing, they reveal how chickens are raised as well as their diets. Free range and organic indicate that chickens have varying degrees of outdoor access; organic also means that the food chickens eat is free of fungicides, herbicides, and pesticides. Pasture-raised chickens graze outdoors as well as being supplied supplements. Chickens that lay omega-3-enriched eggs are fed supplements with omega-3-rich sources, such as flaxseeds.

WHAT DOES COLOR TELL US?

The pigment in eggshells does not indicate or affect egg quality. Young or small chickens tend to lay eggs with white shells; older, larger chickens tend to lay eggs with brown shells. Brown eggs tend to be more expensive because the hens are larger and eat more. Exotic or heirloom breeds often lay eggs with soft tints of color.

WHY READ THE DATE?

Each egg carton is stamped with a 3-digit number that corresponds to the day of the year. Cartons packed on January 1 read 001; cartons packed on December 31 read 365. Consumers can use that number to determine freshness. When refrigerated, fresh, uncooked eggs will last up to 5 weeks beyond the pack date.

SCRAMBLED EGGS

If you prefer soft and creamy, try the stirred method. If fluffy is your pick, go with the folded method.

Stirred In a bowl whisk together 8 eggs and 3 Tbsp. milk. In a heavy 10-inch nonstick skillet heat 2 Tbsp. water over medium-low. Once the water starts to steam (about 2 minutes), add the egg mixture. Cook and stir constantly for 5 minutes or until the mixture is creamy and small curds form. Season with ½ tsp. salt and ¼ tsp. freshly ground black pepper. Serves 4.

Folded In a bowl whisk together 8 eggs and ½ cup milk. In a 10-inch nonstick skillet melt 2 Tbsp. butter over medium. Add egg mixture. Let stand 20 seconds or until mixture begins to set on bottom and around edges. Lift and fold toward center, allowing uncooked egg to flow underneath. Repeat just until eggs are set and slightly wet. Season with ½ tsp. salt and ¼ tsp. freshly ground black pepper. Serves 4.

STIR-INS

After scrambling, fold in cooked veggies, meat, cheese, and/or herbs. Try one of these combos:

1. Lox-style salmon, cream cheese, and fresh dill

2. Black beans, jalapeño, avocado, and fresh cilantro

3. Sweet potato, red onion, asparagus, and flat-leaf parsley

4. Bell pepper, green onion, and walnuts

POACHED EGGS

After experimenting and having minimal success, we turned to *Better Homes & Gardens New Cook Book* for the best results.

1. Boil water. In a large skillet bring 4 cups water and 1 Tbsp. vinegar to boiling. (The vinegar helps the protein in the whites firm quickly for a uniform shape.)

2. Add the egg. Break the egg into a cup. Hold cup lip close to the water and slip in the whole egg at once to keep the egg white intact.

3. Simmer away. Simmer, uncovered, 3 to 5 minutes or until whites are set and yolks begin to thicken but are not hard. Using a slotted spoon, remove eggs from the skillet.

A FRESH EGG POACHES BEST. TO TEST, PLACE A WHOLE EGG IN A GLASS OF WATER. IF IT SINKS TO THE BOTTOM, IT'S FRESH. IF THE WIDE END FLOATS UPWARD, THE EGG MAY BE OLD.

TOASTS WITH THE MOST

Toast is made to sop up runny yolks. Dress up the duo with these combos.

1 Sautéed mushrooms and fresh thyme

2 Ham, Swiss, and Dijon mustard

3 Fresh mozzarella, sautéed spinach, roasted cherry tomatoes, and fresh basil

4 Mashed avocado, seared corn, and pickled red onion

5 Romaine, bacon, and Caesar dressing

6 Smashed black beans, salsa, fresh cilantro, and green onion

FRIED EGGS

Timing and temp ensure cooked-through whites and fluid yolks for every style of fried egg. A well-seasoned cast-iron or nonstick skillet eliminates any sticking, and you can skip the basting some recipes suggest. For yolks that ooze at the pierce of a fork, remove them from the heat when the yolk edges are barely opaque.

Sunny-Side Up Cook over medium to set the whites without overcooking the yolks. Heat 2 Tbsp. butter over medium until melted and foamy. Add 2 eggs; cook 3 minutes.

Over Easy Flip the egg so both sides brown and the yolk stays runny. Heat 2 Tbsp. butter over medium until melted and foamy. Add 2 eggs; cook 2 minutes. Flip with a spatula. Cook 1 minute more.

Crispy Fry in olive oil over high heat to yield golden, lacy edges. Heat 2 Tbsp. olive oil over medium-high 2 minutes. Add 2 eggs; cook 2 minutes.

Extra Crispy Blend butter and oil to create brown edges and rich flavor. Heat 1 Tbsp. butter with 1 Tbsp. canola oil over medium-high 2 minutes. Add 2 eggs. Cook 2 minutes.

SUNNY-SIDE UP

CRISPY

OVER EASY

EXTRA CRISPY

SPRINKLE ONE ON
When eggs seem to call for a bit of seasoning, try one of these.

DUKKAH
Often the Egyptian mix includes toasted nuts, sesame, and cumin.

TOGARASHI
This Japanese chile blend provides heat.

ONION SALT
Plain onion salt or a blend with dried alliums adds flavor.

ITALIAN SEASONING
Especially good along with marinara.

EVERYTHING BAGEL
A savory blend to sprinkle lightly.

A CLASSIC. MASTERED. ONE, TWO, THREE ... THE PERFECT OMELET

OMELET

It's a simple dish that can make even the most practiced cooks break a sweat. But you can absolutely make a classic French omelet—no matter your skill level. Take a cue from culinary experts Jacques Pépin and Julia Child. The result is textbook: neat oval shape, pale yellow free of browning, a smooth and delicate sponge, and a custardy interior.

1. Beat Well. In a bowl beat 3 eggs, ¼ tsp. salt, and ⅛ tsp. black pepper with a fork until evenly mixed (no white strands) but not foamy.

2. Shake & Stir. In an 8½-inch nonstick skillet melt 2 Tbsp. butter over medium-high. When it starts to foam, pour in the eggs. Gently shake the skillet back and forth with one hand while stirring constantly with a fork in the other hand, to yield a small, silky curd. If you're concerned about scratching the skillet, use chopsticks or bamboo skewers.

3. All Set. Continue shaking and stirring, scraping around the edges occasionally, until the eggs are set but still slightly moist. At this point sprinkle on a little cheese. Then it's time to roll.

ROLL IT UP

The technique for a tidy omelet: Let gravity help.

TILT THE SKILLET Bring your hand palm side up under the handle and tilt the skillet to about a 45-degree angle.

GUIDE & ROLL Using a spatula, fold one-third of the omelet onto itself; repeat with opposite the third.

PLATE IT Angle the skillet over a plate and flip the omelet to land seam side down. Bon appétit!

HARD-COOKED EGGS

Turns out the best way to hard-boil eggs is to go easy. For soft to jammy to hard-cooked eggs, the gentle, consistent heat of steam works best. Plus, steamed eggs peel smoothly. Place up to six eggs in a steamer basket over a saucepan of boiling water. (More than six alters cook time.) Reduce heat, cover, and simmer according to the timings, right. Immediately transfer eggs to an ice bath to stop the cooking, then let cool slightly before peeling. For the easiest peeling, cook eggs that are at least two weeks old. As eggs age, the contents contract, enlarging the air cell. Steaming causes the whites to further pull away from the shell membranes.

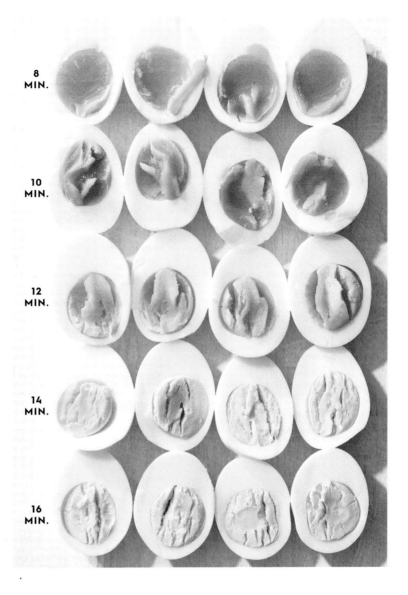

8 MIN.

10 MIN.

12 MIN.

14 MIN.

16 MIN.

Classic-ish Deviled Eggs Halve 6 hard-cooked eggs lengthwise. Mash yolks with ¼ cup mayonnaise, 1 tsp. Dijon mustard, 1 tsp. white wine vinegar, and a dash sriracha. Season with salt. Spoon or pipe into white halves. Sprinkle with chives and paprika. Serves 12.

Egg Salad Meets Avocado Toast Stir together 12 chopped hard-cooked eggs, ¼ cup finely chopped red onion, 2 Tbsp. mayonnaise, 1 Tbsp. lemon juice, 1 tsp. Dijon mustard, and ¼ tsp. salt. Gently fold in 1 chopped avocado. Serve on toasted bread. Serves 6.

FAST & FRESH

Easy, delicious recipes for a better dinner tonight.

BEANS & GREENS SOUPE AU PISTOU

Basil pesto is a yummy addition to almost any tomato-based vegetable soup. Consider making a double or triple batch to freeze and keep on hand.

HANDS-ON TIME 25 min.
TOTAL TIME 45 min.

- 1   lb. Swiss chard
- 2   cups vegetable broth
- 1   15-oz. can cannellini beans, rinsed and drained
- 2   medium tomatoes, cored and coarsely chopped
- 1   cup fresh basil
- 4   Tbsp. olive oil
- 6   Tbsp. finely shredded Parmesan cheese
- 2   cloves garlic
- 4   slices Italian bread

1. Remove stems from chard. Chop stems and greens separately.
2. In a 4-qt. pot combine broth, 2 cups water, the chard stems, beans, tomatoes, ½ tsp. salt, and ¼ tsp. black pepper. Bring to boiling; reduce heat. Simmer, covered, 15 minutes. Stir in chard greens. Cook, uncovered, 5 minutes more, stirring occasionally.
3. Meanwhile, for pesto: In a small food processor or blender combine basil, olive oil, 4 Tbsp. Parmesan, the garlic, and ¼ tsp. each salt and black pepper. Process until smooth.
4. Brush both sides of bread slices with olive oil. On a grill or grill pan toast bread on both sides; sprinkle with remaining cheese after turning once.
5. Ladle soup into bowls. Top each with pesto. Serve with bread. Serves 4.
EACH SERVING *409 cal, 25 g fat (4 g sat fat), 5 mg chol, 1,345 mg sodium, 36 g carb, 7 g fiber, 5 g sugars, 13 g pro*

GRILLED SAUSAGES WITH BALSAMIC ONIONS

Peppery arugula contrasts with the sweetness of grilled onions. Other tender greens, such as baby kale or spinach, work equally well.

TOTAL TIME 25 min.

- 1 red onion, halved and sliced ¾ inch thick
- 2 Tbsp. olive oil
- 4 chicken sausage links (12 oz.), cooked
- 4 cups arugula
- ¼ cup balsamic vinegar
- 1 to 2 Tbsp. fresh thyme leaves
- 4 oz. goat cheese, softened
- 4 hoagie rolls

1. Brush onion slices with 1 Tbsp. olive oil. Sprinkle with ¼ tsp. salt. Grill onion and sausage links on the rack of a covered grill directly over medium-high 8 to 10 minutes or until onion slices are tender and sausages are heated through, turning once.
2. In a large bowl combine arugula, onion slices, balsamic vinegar, thyme, 1 Tbsp. olive oil, and ¼ tsp. black pepper.
3. Spread goat cheese on hoagies. Top with sausages and arugula mixture. Serves 4.

EACH SERVING *612 cal, 25 g fat (9 g sat fat), 82 mg chol, 1,064 mg sodium, 67 g carb, 6 g fiber, 22 g sugars, 31 g pro*

ANCHO CHILE CHICKEN WITH POBLANOS AND TOMATILLOS

If fresh tomatillos aren't available, substitute six canned tomatillos. Omit the roasting, then chop the tomatillos and add them to the chicken mixture immediately before serving.

HANDS-ON TIME 20 min.
TOTAL TIME 40 min.

1	lb. skinless, boneless chicken thighs
2	Tbsp. olive oil
2	tsp. ground ancho chile pepper
2	poblano peppers, halved, stemmed, and seeded (tip, page 28)
1	onion, quartered
8	oz. fresh tomatillos, husked, rinsed, and halved
12	street-style taco flour tortillas
	Cotija or feta cheese (optional)

1. Preheat oven to 425°F. Line a 15×10-inch baking pan with foil. Coat chicken with 1 Tbsp. olive oil and the ground ancho pepper; arrange in a single layer on half the pan. Arrange poblanos, onion, and tomatillos on opposite half. Drizzle with 1 Tbsp. olive oil. Sprinkle chicken and vegetables with salt and black pepper. Bake, uncovered, 20 minutes or until chicken is done (170°F) and vegetables are charred.

2. Transfer pepper halves to a large bowl; cover with foil. Transfer chicken, onion, and tomatillos to a cutting board, reserving juices in pan. Chop onion and tomatillos. Slice chicken. Peel and chop peppers (discard skin). Return all to pan. Serve on tortillas. If desired, top with Cotija or feta cheese. Serves 6.

EACH SERVING *317 cal, 14 g fat (4 g sat fat), 81 mg chol, 26 g carb, 525 mg sodium, 4 g fiber, 3 g sugars, 21 g pro*

**BEJEWELED &
BEDAZZLED**
Recipe on page 90
Technique on page 91

**CITRUS SUGAR
COOKIE EGGS**
Recipe on page 90
Technique on page 91

MORE IS MORE

From a single cookie recipe, these eggs are dressed to impress in runway inspired sequins, glitter, and pearls.

LAYERED LOOK
Technique on page 91

TRIMS &
APPLIQUES
Technique on page 91

GOLDEN GLITZ
Technique on page 91

FIND BEAUTIFUL EMBELLISHMENTS IN THE CAKE DECORATING SECTION OF LARGE GROCERS AND CRAFTS STORES OR ONLINE.

CITRUS SUGAR COOKIE EGGS

Easily change the flavor of this cookie dough. Swap the orange zest and juice for lemon, lime, or any combination of the three.

HANDS-ON TIME 25 min.
TOTAL TIME 45 min.

1½	cups butter, softened
1	cup sugar
2	tsp. orange zest
¼	tsp. baking powder
1	egg
1	Tbsp. orange juice
1	tsp. vanilla
¾	tsp. salt
3½	cups all-purpose flour

1. Preheat oven to 375°F. In a large bowl beat butter with a mixer on medium to high 30 seconds. Add sugar, orange zest, and baking powder. Beat until combined, scraping sides of bowl occasionally. Beat in egg, orange juice, vanilla, and salt until combined. Beat in flour. Divide dough into two or three portions. On a lightly floured surface roll out dough one portion at a time to ⅛- to ¼-inch thickness.
2. Cut out egg shapes using 2- to 3-inch cookie cutters. (Dip cutters into additional flour to prevent sticking.) Place cutouts 1 inch apart on ungreased cookie sheets. Bake 6 to 8 minutes or until edges are firm but not brown. (Adjust timing for smaller and larger cookies.) Let cool on a wire rack. Makes 48 (2- to 3-inch) cookies.
EACH COOKIE *102 cal, 6 g fat (4 g sat fat), 19 mg chol, 86 mg sodium, 11 g carb, 4 g sugars, 1 g pro*

ROYAL ICING

Meringue powder is a mixture of pasteurized egg whites, sugar, and edible gums. Look for it in the baking aisle of large grocers or in the cake-decorating section of crafts stores.

TOTAL TIME 15 min.

4	cups powdered sugar
3	Tbsp. meringue powder
½	tsp. cream of tartar
½	cup warm water
1	tsp. vanilla
	Gel paste food coloring

In a large mixing bowl stir together powdered sugar, meringue powder, and cream of tartar. Add the warm water and vanilla. Beat with a mixer on low until combined. Beat on high 7 to 10 minutes or until stiff peaks form. Tint as desired with food coloring. Makes about 4 cups. Store unthinned icing, covered, in refrigerator up to 2 days.

ROYAL ICING HOW-TOS

Royal icing is a favorite of cookie decorators because icing consistency is easily tailored.

PIPING CONSISTENCY Transfer about 1 cup unthinned icing to a pastry bag fitted with a small round decorating tip (No. 2 or 3).

ICING CONSISTENCY Thin icing with warm water (4 to 5 tsp. per cup of icing). Icing should fall in ribbons from a spoon, and ribbons should disappear into icing surface in the bowl in 10 to 15 seconds. Dip cookie surface in icing; place on a wire rack to set (about 6 hours). One cup thinned icing covers about 36 (2- to 3-inch) cookies.

TRIMS & APPLIQUÉS

While icing is wet, attach edible wafer or rice paper flowers, painted gum paste blossoms, or small candies.

LAYERED

Ice cookies with white royal icing; let set. Mix ⅛ tsp. gel paste food coloring and 2 tsp. vodka. (Alcohol evaporates quickly without dissolving the icing.) "Paint" using clean artists brushes; add details with edible markers.

WAFER OR RICE PAPER FLOWERS
Pretty, pliable, and flavorless, these florals come in a variety of designs.

GUM PASTE BLOSSOMS
Gum paste looks like fondant but hardens to a porcelainlike finish. Brush with luster dust to color.

SUGAR FLOWERS
Made of sugar icing and widely available.

CANDY JEWELS
Gem-shape candies look like the real thing but melt in your mouth.

MORE TRIMS & APPLIQUÉS

If you like, cut out small flowers from the dough and bake. Use unthinned icing in a pastry bag to decorate and attach them to large egg cutouts. Pipe on additional accents as desired.

GOLDEN GLITZ

For edible gold leaf flake accents, let icing partially set (about 1 hour). Gold leaf is tricky to handle due to static; transfer flakes using a dry artists brush.

GOLD LEAF FLAKES
Yes, you can eat 24k gold flakes; look for food-grade leaf labeled as edible.

PEARLESCENT SHIMMER

While iced cookies are wet, attach small white or pearl nonpareils. When set, use a clean artists brush to apply pearlized white luster dust; tap off excess.

BEJEWELED & BEDAZZLED

While iced cookies are wet, sprinkle on edible metallic glitter. Using unthinned icing in a pastry bag, attach candy gems or pipe on geometric designs.

GLITTERS & DUSTS
Edible metallic glitter sparkles like crystals; sprinkle it on wet icing. Luster dust is a translucent powder. Use an artists brush to apply to dry surfaces, or mix with vodka (not water) and brush onto iced cookies.

**LAVENDER-HONEY
LEMON TART**
Recipe on page 96

may

Celebrate Mother's Day with luscious desserts. Lighten menus for spring with produce-forward recipes, then, guided by culinary experts, journey through a world of cuisines.

101

114

118

Spring Desserts
SWEET ON MOM

Berries. Lemon. Chocolate. Shower Mom with something sweet this Mother's Day: a special dessert in one of her favorite flavors. Vallery Lomas—food blogger and a winner on *The Great American Baking Show*—shares elegantly delicious recipes along with tips to guarantee success.

RASPBERRY AND RHUBARB SWISS ROLL

Valuable tips from Lomas ensure awesome presentation. First, beat whole eggs (rather than separate them, as some sponge cake recipes require). Second, begin rolling the spiral tightly, and complete rolling in one continuous movement. Third, use a serrated knife for clean slices without squishing the roll.

HANDS-ON TIME 25 min.
TOTAL TIME 2 hr. 25 min., includes chilling

	Nonstick cooking spray
4	large eggs
½	cup plus 2 Tbsp. granulated sugar
⅔	cup all-purpose flour
	Red food coloring
1	6-oz. pkg. fresh raspberries
½	cup sliced fresh or frozen rhubarb
3	oz. cream cheese, cut up and softened
⅔	cup whipping cream
2	Tbsp. powdered sugar, plus more for dusting
½	tsp. vanilla

1. Preheat oven to 400°F. Coat a 15×10-inch baking pan with nonstick cooking spray. Line pan with parchment paper; coat with cooking spray.

2. In a large bowl beat eggs, ½ cup granulated sugar, and a dash salt with a mixer on medium 2 minutes. Increase speed to medium-high; beat 8 to 10 minutes or until thick and light in color.

3. Sift flour over egg mixture; fold in until no streaks of flour remain. Place ⅓ cup batter in a small bowl. Add enough food coloring to tint pink. Place pink batter in a small resealable plastic bag. Snip off one corner. Randomly pipe small circles of batter in prepared pan. Bake 2 minutes. Spread remaining batter over circles. Bake 7 to 8 minutes or until cake is golden and springs back when lightly touched.

4. Line a baking sheet with parchment paper. Invert cake onto prepared sheet. Carefully remove parchment from cake. Dust a kitchen towel with powdered sugar. Use parchment to flip cake, pattern side down, onto towel. Roll up cake and towel, starting from a narrow side. Let cool completely on a wire rack.

5. For filling: In a medium saucepan combine raspberries, rhubarb, and remaining 2 Tbsp. granulated sugar. Bring to boiling, stirring to break up berries; reduce heat. Simmer, uncovered, about 10 minutes or until fruit is softened. Remove from heat; let cool slightly. Place in a blender or food processor. Cover; blend until smooth. Press mixture through a fine-mesh sieve to remove seeds. Let cool completely.

6. In a medium bowl beat cream cheese with a mixer on medium until smooth. Slowly beat in cream until smooth. Add 2 Tbsp. powdered sugar and the vanilla; beat until soft peaks form.

7. Unroll cake. Spread with half the fruit puree. Spread cream mixture over puree. Drizzle with remaining fruit puree. Using a knife, swirl mixtures together. Carefully reroll cake, using towel to help roll tightly. Place, seam side down, on a platter. Cover; chill at least 2 hours. Before serving, dust with additional powdered sugar. Serves 10.

EACH SERVING *212 cal, 11 g fat (6 g sat fat), 101 mg chol, 89 mg sodium, 25 g carb, 1 g fiber, 17 g sugars, 5 g pro*

A FLAWLESS SWISS ROLL IS COMPOSED OF A CAKE WITH SOME SPRING, DELICIOUS CREAMY FILLING, AND A DISTINCT SPIRAL. LOMAS EMBELLISHES THIS ONE WITH PINK POLKA DOTS IN THE CAKE. FOR THE FILLING, TANGY RHUBARB AND RASPBERRY PUREE IS SWIRLED INTO CREAM CHEESE.

TARTS TEND TO LOOK ELEGANT EVEN THOUGH PUTTING ONE TOGETHER IS FAIRLY SIMPLE. THIS TART CRUST, WHICH HAS ONLY FOUR INGREDIENTS, IS EASILY PRESSED INTO THE PAN—NO ROLLING REQUIRED.

LAVENDER-HONEY LEMON TART

Heighten the taste with a drizzle of lavender-infused honey and a few candied lemon slices. "Honey is just sweet enough to ensure lavender never tastes overpowering," Lomas says.

HANDS-ON TIME 10 min.
TOTAL TIME 6 hr., includes chilling

1	cup all-purpose flour
¼	cup powdered sugar
½	cup unsalted butter, melted
¾	cup honey
3	Tbsp. food-grade dried lavender buds
1	tsp. unflavored gelatin
4	large eggs
¾	cup granulated sugar
4	lemons (2 tsp. zest, ¾ cup juice)
2	Tbsp. unsalted butter, cut into pieces
	Whipped cream
	Candied Lemons

1. In a medium bowl whisk together flour, powdered sugar, and ¼ tsp. salt. Stir in melted butter until dough comes together. Press dough into bottom and up sides of a 14×4-inch rectangular or 9-inch round tart pan with removable bottom. Refrigerate crust at least 20 minutes or until firm.

2. Preheat oven to 350°F. Prick bottom of crust all over with a fork. Line crust with foil or parchment paper; fill with pie weights or dried beans. Bake 20 minutes. Remove foil and pie weights; bake 10 to 15 minutes more or until golden. Let cool on a wire rack.

3. For lavender honey: In a small saucepan combine honey and lavender buds. Heat over medium until honey simmers. Reduce heat to medium-low and simmer 15 minutes, stirring occasionally. Remove from heat; let stand 15 minutes. Pour honey through a fine-mesh sieve to remove lavender; discard lavender. Set honey aside.

4. In a small bowl sprinkle gelatin over 4 tsp. cold water; set aside.

5. In a medium saucepan whisk together eggs, granulated sugar, and lemon zest until combined. Whisk in lemon juice. Cook over medium, whisking constantly, 6 to 8 minutes or until thick and creamy. (Lemon curd will coat the back of a spoon, and a streak will remain visible if you run your finger across the spoon.)

6. Remove from heat; stir in cut-up butter until it melts into curd. Stir in gelatin until combined (the heat will melt gelatin). Pour curd into cooled crust. Refrigerate tart 4 hours or until completely set.

7. Top tart with whipped cream and Candied Lemons. Drizzle with remaining lavender honey. Serves 8.

Candied Lemons Preheat oven to 275°F. Thinly slice a small lemon, discarding ends. In a large straight-sided skillet heat ¼ cup lavender honey from Step 3 and ¼ cup water just to boiling, stirring to dissolve honey. Add lemon slices to skillet. Remove from heat and let stand 10 minutes. Line a baking sheet with parchment paper. Remove lemon slices from syrup; arrange in a single layer on prepared baking sheet. Bake 30 to 40 minutes or until lightly browned, turning once halfway through baking. Check slices every 10 minutes because some will brown more quickly than others. Remove as they brown.

EACH SERVING *386 cal, 18 g fat (10 g sat fat), 133 mg chol, 112 mg sodium, 55 g carb, 1 g fiber, 41 g sugars, 6 g pro*

WHAT'S BETTER THAN ONE TYPE OF CHOCOLATE? THREE—DARK AND WHITE CHOCOLATES, PLUS CRUNCHY CHOCOLATE CHIP COOKIE CRUMBLES.

TRIPLE-CHOCOLATE SHORTCUT MOUSSE

Lomas' whipped chocolate—simple ganache folded into whipped cream— tastes as decadent as mousse, minus the step of making a crème anglaise.

HANDS-ON TIME 25 min.
TOTAL TIME 2 hr. 25 min., includes chilling

4 oz. dark chocolate, finely chopped
2 oz. dark chocolate, finely chopped
4 oz. quality white chocolate, finely chopped
3 cups whipping cream
1 tsp. vanilla or vanilla bean paste
2 Tbsp. brewed espresso
6 crisp chocolate chip cookies
Unsweetened cocoa powder

1. In three separate medium bowls, place 4 oz. dark chocolate, 2 oz. dark chocolate, and the white chocolate.
2. In a small saucepan heat 1 cup cream over medium just until simmering.
3. Pour ½ cup warm cream over 4 oz. dark chocolate, ⅓ cup warm cream over 2 oz. dark chocolate, and remaining warm cream over white chocolate. Let stand 5 minutes without stirring. Stir each until smooth. If necessary to melt chocolate, place each bowl in a slightly larger bowl of hot water and stir until smooth. Stir vanilla into white chocolate mixture (it may be softer than dark chocolate mixtures.) Stir espresso into dark chocolate mixture made with 4 oz. dark chocolate.

4. In a large bowl beat the remaining 2 cups cream with a mixer on medium until soft peaks form. Divide whipped cream among the three bowls; fold into each until no streaks remain.
5. Spoon or pipe half the espresso chocolate mixture into the bottom of ten to twelve 3- to 4-oz. glasses. Tap glasses lightly to even layers. Crush two cookies; break remaining four cookies into pieces and set aside. Sprinkle crushed cookies over chocolate in glasses. Top with remaining espresso chocolate mixture, white chocolate mixture, then light chocolate mixture, lightly tapping glasses between layers. Chill at least 2 hours or until set. Sprinkle mousse with cocoa powder; top with broken cookie pieces. Serves 10 to 12.

Tip Choose good-quality white chocolate bars that contains at least 20% cocoa cutter, 14% milk solids, 3.5% milk fat, and a maximum of 55% sweeteners. Mousse is best served cold, straight from the refrigerator.

EACH SERVING *435 cal, 39 g fat (24 g sat fat), 84 mg chol, 70 mg sodium, 23 g carb, 2 g fiber, 17 g sugars, 5 g pro*

MEET VALLERY LOMAS

She began baking in earnest while in law school. And what started as a stress reliever for Lomas became a passion, then a blog. When asked what inspires her, she reminisces about her travels. She dreamed up the tart's lavender-honey syrup after a trip to Provence—and adds that a family love of baking is at the heart of her creations. "Baking is something you're mostly doing for other people," she says. "I always think about what's going to make them happy and what part of myself I can share."

ASPARAGUS SALAD WITH MARINATED PEAS & LITTLE GEM LETTUCE

A FRESH START

Say hello to light seasonal fare. It's time to brighten cooking and celebrate vibrant spring vegetables. Abra Berens, author of the produce-forward cookbook *Ruffage*, shows us how to make these refreshingly delicate ingredients sing.

ASPARAGUS SALAD WITH MARINATED PEAS & LITTLE GEM LETTUCE

When vegetables are as tender as in-season peas and asparagus, Berens often skips heat altogether. Instead, she "cooks" the peas in a quick marinade of citrus, oil, chives, and salt (à la ceviche), then tosses in bite-size bits of raw asparagus. She splashes in buttermilk and the dressing is complete.

HANDS-ON TIME 20 min.
TOTAL TIME 40 min.

1   cup shelled spring peas
¼   cup thinly sliced red onion or 2 thinly sliced green onions
1   lemon (2 tsp. zest, 3 Tbsp. juice)
¼   cup olive oil
1   Tbsp. chopped fresh chives, plus more for topping
1   lb. green or purple asparagus, trimmed and bias-sliced into ½-inch-long pieces
½   cup buttermilk
4   cups water
1   Tbsp. vinegar
4   eggs
2   heads Little Gem lettuce, cut into wedges, or 4 cups chopped romaine lettuce

1. In a medium bowl combine peas, onion, lemon zest and juice, olive oil, 1 Tbsp. chives, and ¼ tsp. salt. Cover; refrigerate 20 minutes or up to 3 days.
2. Add asparagus and buttermilk to bowl with peas; toss to coat. Season with salt and black pepper.
3. For poached eggs: In a large skillet bring 4 cups water and the vinegar to boiling; reduce heat to simmering. Break an egg into a cup; slip egg into simmering water. Repeat with remaining eggs, allowing each egg an equal amount of space. Simmer eggs, uncovered, 3 to 5 minutes or until whites are completely set and yolks begin to thicken but are not hard. Using a slotted spoon, remove eggs.
4. Serve asparagus mixture over lettuce with poached eggs. Top with additional fresh chives. Serves 4.

EACH SERVING *251 cal, 19 g fat (4 g sat fat), 187 mg chol, 279 mg sodium, 11 g carb, 4 g fiber, 6 g sugars, 11 g pro*

POACHED VEGGIES WITH WALNUT RELISH

Photo on page 102

"Poaching has gone a bit out of favor, but with vegetables it's so unobtrusive and subtle," Berens says. A few minutes in simmering water brings out each vegetable's flavor while retaining its color and crisp-tender texture.

HANDS-ON TIME 20 min.
TOTAL TIME 40 min.

4   cloves garlic, sliced
1   tsp. coriander seeds
1   tsp. fennel seeds
1   tsp. whole black peppercorns
5   sprigs fresh thyme
1   lb. asparagus, trimmed and halved lengthwise
8   spring onions or scallions, halved lengthwise but root intact
1   cup sugar snap peas and/or fresh spring peas
8   baby turnips, trimmed and halved
12   radishes, trimmed
10   to 12 shiitake mushrooms, stemmed and gills removed
10   to 12 baby carrots, halved if desired
8   baby artichokes, prepped* and halved
¼   cup lemon juice
     Walnut Relish

1. Tie garlic, coriander, fennel, peppercorns, and thyme into a 6-inch square of double-thick 100% cotton cheesecloth. Place in a large pot of 6 cups simmering water and 2 tsp. salt.
2. Add asparagus; cook 2 minutes. Add spring onions and peas; cook 2 minutes more. Using a slotted spoon, transfer vegetables to a shallow dish. Add turnips to pot; cook 3 minutes. Add radishes and mushrooms; cook 2 to 3 minutes more. Transfer to dish with asparagus. Add carrots to pot; cook 4 to 6 minutes or until crisp-tender. Transfer carrots to dish with asparagus. Add artichokes and lemon juice to pot; cook 7 to 8 minutes or until tender. Transfer artichokes to dish with vegetables. Serve with Walnut Relish. Serves 6.

Walnut Relish Preheat oven to 350°F. Spread 1 cup walnut halves in a shallow baking pan. Bake 7 to 10 minutes or until fragrant and lightly toasted. Cool slightly. Place toasted nuts in a resealable plastic bag; break into small pieces with the bottom of a skillet or mallet. In a medium bowl combine zest and juice of 1 lemon, ¼ cup sherry vinegar or red wine vinegar, ¼ cup olive oil, and 1 tsp. salt. Immediately stir walnuts into vinegar mixture. Just before serving, stir in 1 cup roughly chopped flat-leaf parsley. Season with salt and black pepper.

***Tip** To prep baby artichokes, stir 2 Tbsp. lemon juice into half a large bowl of water. Tear off tough outer leaves and peel off the tough outer layer of the stem, placing artichokes in the water mixture.

EACH SERVING *271 cal, 22 g fat (3 g sat fat), 449 mg sodium, 15 g carb, 6 g fiber, 5 g sugars, 6 g pro*

**POACHED VEGGIES
WITH WALNUT RELISH**
Recipe on page 101

WILTED LETTUCE
SOUP WITH SEARED
SALMON
Recipe on page 105

HERBED LINGUINE
WITH BURNT ORANGE

HERBED LINGUINE WITH BURNT ORANGE

Berens' favorite time to eat garlic is when it's still green, with immature heads and stalks that can be used like scallions. Like fresh fava beans, green garlic is an early-spring farmers market treasure, so snap them up while you can. Follow Berens' lead and pair these aromatic, almost grassy flavors with the bright spark of broiled oranges on a nest of fresh herbed pasta.

HANDS-ON TIME 1 hr.
TOTAL TIME 1 hr. 30 min.

2 cups all-purpose flour*
3 eggs*
2 Tbsp. chopped fresh herbs, such as basil, thyme, and/or sage
2 oranges, halved
2 Tbsp. olive oil
½ tsp. crushed red pepper
2 stalks green garlic or 6 cloves garlic, thinly sliced
1 to 2 cups fresh fava beans,** shelled, blanched, and peeled, or edamame
¼ cup butter
⅓ cup chopped flat-leaf parsley
2 Tbsp. chopped fresh tarragon
4 oz. ricotta cheese

1. In a food processor combine flour, eggs, the 2 Tbsp. herbs, and 1 tsp. salt; pulse until mixture resembles cornmeal. Transfer to a large bowl and knead into a cohesive ball. Cover with plastic wrap. Let rest at room temperature 30 minutes.
2. Cut dough ball into four pieces. With a pasta roller, roll dough until thin enough to see through the dough, lightly flouring dough as you roll, as necessary. (Or on a floured surface and using a rolling pin, roll dough pieces into a 12-inch circle, allowing to rest several times.) Roll sheet into a spiral. Cut into ¼-inch-wide strips.

Transfer to a baking sheet. Cover with a towel until ready to cook.
3. Preheat broiler. Slice 3 orange halves into ⅛-inch-thick half-moons, removing any seeds. Line a baking sheet with foil; arrange slices in a single layer on prepared baking sheet. Place remaining orange half, cut side up, on baking sheet. Broil 4 to 5 inches from heat 5 to 8 minutes or until edges start to brown. Let cool on baking sheet; coarsely chop slices and quarter the half.
4. In a large pot of heavily salted boiling water, cook pasta about 6 minutes or until al dente; drain, reserving ¼ cup cooking liquid.
5. Meanwhile, in an extra-large skillet heat olive oil over medium. Add crushed red pepper; cook 10 seconds. Add garlic and ¼ tsp. salt. Reduce heat to low; cook 1 minute or until soft but not browning. Add fava beans. Lightly toss to coat.
6. Add reserved cooking liquid to fava bean mixture and bring to boiling. Add butter; simmer gently, uncovered, 2 minutes to make a glossy sauce. Add pasta. Toss to coat. Add chopped orange slices, parsley, and tarragon. Spread ricotta over four plates, top with pasta mixture, and serve immediately with orange wedges. Serves 4.
*Tip To save time and skip making homemade noodles, use 12 oz. dried linguine. Add 2 Tbsp. chopped fresh herbs to the finished dish.
**Tip For 1 cup shelled, blanched, peeled fava beans, start with 2 lb. beans in shell. Remove beans from shell and cook in boiling water 1 minute. Drain and let cool. To peel, cut a small slit in outer coating and squeeze to remove bean.
EACH SERVING *545 cal, 25 g fat (11 g sat fat), 179 mg chol, 919 mg sodium, 63 g carb, 5 g fiber, 7 g sugars, 17 g pro*

WILTED LETTUCE SOUP WITH SEARED SALMON

Photo on page 103

"The idea of cooked lettuce makes everyone wrinkle their nose at first, myself included," Berens says. This soup, with its rich, wine-spiked broth and crispy salmon, will fetch smiles instead. Add chopped romaine right before serving: The hot broth softens lettuce to a silky texture.

TOTAL TIME 45 min.

¼ cup olive oil or grapeseed oil
4 4-oz. skin-on salmon fillets
1 yellow onion, thinly sliced
1 fennel bulb, halved, cored, and thinly sliced, plus 2 Tbsp. coarsely chopped fronds
⅔ cup dry white wine or hard cider
3 cups chicken stock
1 to 2 romaine hearts, trimmed and sliced crosswise into large pieces (6 cups)
1 cup fresh sugar snap peas, bias sliced or split horizontally
   Olive oil (optional)

1. In a large skillet heat 3 Tbsp. oil over medium-high until smoking. Pat skin side of fish dry with a paper towel. Season with salt. Sear fish skin side down until well-browned and moves freely in the pan, about 7 minutes.
2. Remove pan from heat and, with conviction, turn fish over and cook 1 minute. Transfer to a serving dish skin side up.
3. Wipe out skillet. Heat remaining 1 Tbsp. oil over medium until shimmering. Add onion, fennel, and a pinch of salt and black pepper. Cook 7 to 8 minutes or until vegetables are translucent and starting to brown. Add wine. Bring to boiling; reduce by half. Add chicken stock; return to boiling. Remove from heat. Add lettuce, allowing hot stock to wilt it.
4. Ladle into bowls. Top with salmon, fennel fronds, and snap peas. If desired, drizzle with additional olive oil. Serves 4.
EACH SERVING *371 cal, 21 g fat (3 g sat fat), 62 mg chol, 579 mg sodium, 12 g carb, 4 g fiber, 6 g sugars, 26 g pro*

"THE VIBRANCY OF SPRING VEGETABLES ALWAYS FEELS LIKE SUCH A REVELATION AFTER THE STEWS AND ROASTS OF WINTER." —ABRA BERENS

SPRING IS GRILLING SEASON, AND, ACCORDING TO BERENS, "IF YOU'RE GOING TO FIRE UP THE GRILL, YOU MIGHT AS WELL COOK EVERYTHING ON IT."

GRILLED CHICKEN THIGHS WITH SPRING ONIONS & BABY BOK CHOY

If you can find ramps—pungent wild spring alliums that taste like a cross between garlic and scallions—sub them in for the spring onions.

HANDS-ON TIME 20 min.
TOTAL TIME 50 min.

- 4 eggs, hard-boiled, peeled, and chopped
- ½ cup olive oil, plus more for drizzling
- 1 Tbsp. Dijon mustard
- 1 Tbsp. apple cider vinegar
- 2 Tbsp. capers, coarsely chopped
- 1 small shallot, minced or thinly sliced
- 2 Tbsp. chopped fresh dill
- 2 Tbsp. coarsely chopped flat-leaf parsley
- 8 bone-in, skin-on chicken thighs
- 4 heads baby bok choy, halved, or 2 heads bok choy, quartered lengthwise
- 24 spring onions,* green onions, or ramps

1. For relish: In a small bowl stir together eggs, ½ cup olive oil, the mustard, vinegar, capers, shallot, dill, and parsley. Season with salt and black pepper.
2. Season chicken thighs with salt and black pepper. Grill skin side down, covered, directly over medium 7 minutes or until golden brown. Move chicken off direct heat. Grill over indirect heat 20 to 25 minutes more or until cooked through (175°F).
3. Meanwhile, drizzle bok choy with a little olive oil and season with salt. Grill cut sides down directly over medium 3 minutes or until leaves are slightly charred. Move bok choy off direct heat.
4. Drizzle spring onions with olive oil. Season with salt. Grill onions with bulbs directly over medium and leaves over indirect heat so they don't singe.
5. Transfer chicken thighs, bok choy, and onions to serving platter. Serve with the relish. Serves 4.

*Tip Spring onions are bulb onions harvested before the bulb swells. Green onions are a good substitute. Or look for ramps, a wild spring allium also known as wild leeks.

EACH SERVING *701 cal, 57 g fat (11 g sat fat), 351 mg chol, 767 mg sodium, 10 g carb, 3 g fiber, 3 g sugars, 38 g pro*

"THE MISCONCEPTION ABOUT SPRING IS THAT IT ALL HAS TO BE LIGHT, BUT I REALLY LOVE USING EXTRA ACID OR EXTRA FAT TO GROUND SOME OF THOSE FLAVORS," BERENS SAYS. CASE IN POINT: BROWN BUTTER IS THE ACE INGREDIENT IN THIS VINAIGRETTE.

LAMB CHOPS WITH POTATOES & HERB-BROWN BUTTER VINAIGRETTE

Hot out of the pan and standing in for traditional oil, brown butter tames raw shallots and offsets the zing of fresh lemon and mint. Spoon some over baby potato slices and serve with a quick raw salad and pan-seared lamb chops.

HANDS-ON TIME 20 min.
TOTAL TIME 45 min.

⅓ cup salted butter
1 medium shallot, minced
1 large lemon (1½ tsp. zest, ¼ cup juice)
3 Tbsp. cider vinegar
¼ cup olive oil
2 Tbsp. fresh mint and/or dill, finely chopped
1 lb. baby potatoes and/or fingerling potatoes

8 1-inch-thick lamb rib or loin chops, fat trimmed if necessary
4 cups fresh spinach
½ cup quartered radishes and/or Persian cucumbers, sliced into strips
¼ cup fresh mint leaves

1. For dressing: In a small saucepan cook butter over medium 5 minutes or until toasty brown and fragrant. Place shallot in a medium bowl. Pour hot butter over shallot to soften; let cool completely.
2. Add lemon zest and juice, vinegar, 3 Tbsp. of the olive oil, 2 Tbsp. chopped mint, ½ tsp. salt, and ¼ tsp. black pepper to butter and shallot. Whisk to combine.
3. Bring a large pot of salted water to boiling. Using a mandoline or sharp knife, slice potatoes into ¼-inch-thick rounds. Add potatoes to boiling water. Cook 7 to 10 minutes or until tender but not falling apart. Immediately drain potatoes; toss with dressing. (Potatoes will absorb dressing as they cool.)

4. Season lamb chops liberally with salt and black pepper. In an extra-large skillet heat remaining 1 Tbsp. oil over medium-high. Add lamb chops. Cook 8 to 10 minutes or until 145°F, turning once. (Or grill, covered, 12 to 14 minutes over medium for medium rare [145°F], turning once.) Remove from skillet and let stand 5 minutes.
5. Toss spinach with radishes and mint leaves. Serve spinach mixture with potatoes and lamb chops; drizzle excess dressing over all. Serves 4.

EACH SERVING *544 cal, 38 g fat (16 g sat fat), 122 mg chol, 516 mg sodium, 23 g carb, 3 g fiber, 3 g sugars, 29 g pro*

SHRIMP & MANGO
RICE PAPER ROLLS
Recipe on page 118

NUOC CHAM
DIPPING SAUCE
Recipe on page 119

TASTE MAKERS

For curious cooks who are hungry for new flavor experiences, heed these four experts who make it easy to explore cuisines from around the world.

HUEVOS CON
MIGAS
Recipe on page 112

"MEXICAN COOKING IS ALL ABOUT BALANCING HOT AND MILD FLAVORS WITH ACIDITY, SPICE, AND FAT."

MEET GABRIELA CÁMARA

"I wrote a book that puts Mexican food on the level of everyday Italian food for an American public who's interested in Mexican cooking but who isn't going to make mole for dinner," says Gabriela Cámara, restaurant owner and author of *My Mexico City Kitchen*. It's not unusual for Cámara to compare the two cuisines: Her mother is Italian; her father is Mexican. Cámara credits both for an appreciation of fresh ingredients and her love of flavor. It's natural that Cámara's style—whether cooking at home or in her restaurants—focuses on seasonal ingredients combined with a minimum of fuss.

WHAT'S IN GABRIELA'S PANTRY

SEA SALT Cámara uses sea salt to temper the heat from fresh chiles. "You can't predict how spicy they will be while cooking," she says, "so add salt a little at a time."

LIMES "A squirt of lime juice is as essential as salt. It's the bright note that brings all the ingredients into harmony. To me, food tastes bland without it."

DRIED CHILES Dried chiles (guajillo, ancho, chile de arbol) give complexity to a dish. "A tiny bit will add spicy warmth." Toast dried chiles only until you can smell them.

FRESH CHILES Jalapeño, serrano, and habanero peppers have distinct flavor profiles and heat levels. "Heat may also vary from pepper to pepper."

HUEVOS CON MIGAS

Photo on page 111
TOTAL TIME 20 min.

8   **to 12 eggs**
2   **Tbsp. Crema Acida or crème fraîche**
½   **tsp. sea salt, plus more as needed**
⅓   **cup safflower oil**
4   **to 5 stale corn tortillas, cut into ⅜-inch squares**
     Salsa
1   **avocado, halved and cut into ½-inch-thick slices**

1. In a bowl whisk together eggs, Crema Acida, and ½ tsp. sea salt.
2. Heat the oil in a deep skillet or Dutch oven over high until it's hot but not smoking (it may seem like a lot, but the tortillas are very absorbent). Drop a piece of tortilla into the oil ; when it sizzles add remaining tortilla pieces. Cook, stirring with a wooden spoon. They will soften as they soak up the oil then turn crispy. Right after this happens, carefully pour off excess oil and turn the heat to low.
3. Add egg mixture to skillet and scramble together with the fried tortillas. Taste and add more salt if needed. Serve immediately topped with a spoonful of salsa and sliced avocado. Serves 4.
Crema Acida In a glass jar combine 2 cups heavy cream and ¼ cup buttermilk. Cover jar with several layers of cheesecloth or a dish towel. Let stand 24 hours at room temperature (between 70°F and 75°F). If your home is chilly, set the jar on top of refrigerator, which tends to be warmer, or in the oven with the oven light on. After 24 hours, replace cheesecloth with the jar lid. Refrigerate 24 hours before using. Store in the refrigerator up to 10 days.
EACH SERVING *415 cal, 35 g fat, 380 mg chol, 542 mg sodium, 11 g carb, 3 g fiber, 1 g sugars, 14 g pro*

SALSA WITH DRIED CHILES & TOMATILLOS

This is the salsa Cámara makes during the winter, subbing tomatillos for lackluster hothouse tomatoes. Toasting a combo of two varieties of dried chiles results in a fruity spice and deep red color.
TOTAL TIME 20 min.

10   **tomatillos, paper husks removed and discarded, rinsed**
10   **dried chiles de arbol, stemmed and seeded if desired**
2   **guajillo chiles, stemmed and seeded if desired (tip, page 28)**
4   **cloves garlic**
1   **tsp. sea salt, plus more as needed**

Heat an ungreased comal (griddle) or large skillet over medium. Add tomatillos; cook 10 minutes, turning halfway through so they cook evenly. Place tomatillos in a blender. Wipe comal clean; return to heat. Add all chiles; cook 2 minutes or until lightly toasted and begin to smell nutty, stirring constantly (don't let them brown or blister). Add chiles to blender. Add garlic to comal; cook until lightly browned on all sides. Add to blender with 1 tsp. sea salt. Cover and puree. Taste and add more salt if needed. Refrigerate in an airtight container up to 1 week. Makes 2 cups.
EACH ¼ CUP *11 cal, 71 mg sodium, 2 g carb, 1 g sugars*

SALSA
VERDE

SALSA WITH
DRIED CHILES
& TOMATILLOS

SALSA
MEXICANA

SALSA VERDE

Serve this salsa on everything from chilaquiles to tacos. It's a snap to make—just simmer and blend. Use the smallest tomatillos you can; they're fresher with only a mild bitterness.

TOTAL TIME 35 min.

- 1   small white onion
- 10   small tomatillos, papery husks removed, rinsed, and cut in half
- 2   to 4 serrano chiles, seeded if desired (tip, page 28)
- 11   large cloves garlic
- 1   Tbsp. sea salt, plus more as needed
- ½   cup finely chopped cilantro leaves

1. Cut onion in half; mince one half and set aside. In a medium saucepan combine tomatillos, chiles, onion half, garlic, sea salt. Add water to just cover; bring to boiling. Reduce heat; simmer until tomatillos are translucent and chiles are a faded khaki color.

2. Transfer to a blender; cover and puree. Return puree to saucepan; simmer over low until reduced by a third, about 10 minutes. Stir in minced onion and cilantro. Add more salt if needed. Refrigerate in an airtight container up to 1 week. Makes 2½ cups.

EACH ¼ CUP SERVING *4 cal, 168 mg sodium, 1 g carb*

SALSA MEXICANA

Onion, romas, and serranos blend into the little black dress of salsas.

TOTAL TIME 40 min.

- 2   Tbsp. olive oil
- 2   serrano chiles, seeded, if desired, and chopped (tip, page 28)
- 1   white onion, chopped
- 2   cloves garlic, chopped
- 5   roma tomatoes, cored, seeded, and chopped
- 1   tsp. sea salt, plus more as needed

In a small heavy-bottom saucepan heat olive oil over medium until hot but not smoking. Add chiles and onion; cook until onion is translucent but not browned. Add garlic and tomatoes; cook about 10 minutes or until vegetables look stewed. Transfer to a blender. Cover and puree. Return puree to pan; simmer over low 10 minutes or until reduced by a third. Add 1 tsp. sea salt. Add more salt if needed. This salsa is usually served hot. Refrigerate in an airtight container up to 5 days. Makes about 1½ cups.

EACH ¼ CUP *17 cal, 1 g fat (0 g sat fat), 108 mg sodium, 1 g carb, 1 g sugars*

IF YOU'RE NOT FAMILIAR WITH INDIAN CUISINE, DAL CAN BE CONFUSING BECAUSE IT IS BOTH AN INGREDIENT (DRIED LEGUMES, SUCH AS LENTILS) AND A RECIPE (A DISH OF SPICED LEGUMES).

MEET PRIYA KRISHNA

Priya Krishna wrote the cookbook *Indian(-ish)* to highlight 100 of her mother's recipes and to demystify Indian cooking. With the recipes and instructions, she hopes to bring Indian cooking firmly into American kitchens. "Ultimately, the food I grew up with is not that difficult to make," she says. When Ritu, Krishna's mother, immigrated to the U.S., she used American ingredients to re-create Indian recipes. "My mom wanted flavor in the quickest way possible, with minimal cleanup." Krishna follows her mom's lead, shopping locally for most of the foods in her recipes to show that ingredients can be easy to find.

WHAT'S IN PRIYA'S PANTRY

DAL (LENTILS) "Thin lentils cook fast; fat lentils cook slower." Krishna keeps quick-cooking varieties like split or whole red lentils, split green mung beans, and ivory-white lentils on hand.

ASAFETIDA "Asafetida, also known as hing, has a flavor similar to leeks and a strong funky scent that mellows after cooking." It is a coarse yellow powder made from a gum extracted from a ferula, an herb in the celery family. Buy it online or from Indian grocers.

GROUND TURMERIC Krishna notes that turmeric is better when cooked. "Sautéing the ground spice in oil brings out its earthy flavor."

BASMATI RICE "Long grain basmati rice is an auto-accompaniment to most Indian meals," Krishna says.

PRIYA'S DAL

HANDS-ON TIME 10 min.
TOTAL TIME 45 min., plus soaking

1   cup whole masoor dal (also known as whole red lentils or brown lentils)
1   bay leaf
1   tsp. ground turmeric
1   tsp. kosher salt
2   Tbsp. fresh lime juice
2   Tbsp. ghee* or olive oil
2   tsp. cumin seeds
2   dried red chiles (such as Thai)
    Pinch red chile powder (such as cayenne)
    Pinch asafetida (optional)

1. For lentils: Place lentils in a bowl; add water to cover. Soak at room temperature 1 hour; drain.
2. In a large pot combine lentils, bay leaf, turmeric, kosher salt, and 4 cups water. Bring to boiling over high; reduce heat to medium-high, stir lentils, and insert a large long-handled spoon into the pot (to break surface tension and prevent boiling over). Cook with spoon inserted until lentils are soft yet retain their shape and mixture resembles a thick soup, 20 to 30 minutes. Remove from heat; let stand 15 minutes. Add lime juice. Set aside.
3. For seasoning: In a small pan or butter warmer over medium-high warm ghee or oil. Once ghee melts or oil begins to shimmer, add cumin seeds and cook until they start to sputter and brown, which should take only seconds. Immediately remove pan from heat and stir in dried chiles, red chile powder, and asafetida (if using). Add to cooked dal and mix thoroughly. Serves 4.
*Tip Ghee is clarified butter. Find it at health food stores or large grocers, or make it by melting butter and skimming off the milky solids.
EACH SERVING *181 cal, 8 g fat (5 g sat fat), 18 mg chol, 282 mg sodium, 22 g carb, 3 g fiber, 1 g sugars, 8 g pro*

CHERRY TOMATO & CHILE PICKLE

The Indian table isn't complete without an assortment of condiments that function like ketchup, hot sauce, and salsa in other cuisines, and Krishna's shortcut pickle is one of those must-haves. Made with cherry tomatoes, serrano chiles, oil, lime, and a host of seeds, it comes together in less than 5 minutes. She serves it as a topping for many dishes, including her dal recipe.

TOTAL TIME 15 min.

2   Tbsp. olive oil
¼   tsp. fennel seeds
¼   tsp. nigella seeds
¼   tsp. cumin seeds
¼   tsp. black mustard seeds
¼   tsp. fenugreek seeds
¼   tsp. asafetida (optional)
4   long Indian green chiles or serrano chiles, halved lengthwise (tip, page 28)
1   cup cherry tomatoes, halved
¾   tsp. kosher salt
1   Tbsp. fresh lime juice

1. In a large nonstick skillet over medium-high warm oil. When oil begins to shimmer, add all of the seeds. Cook until seeds are slightly browned and start to sputter (cumin is the best indicator), about 1 minute. Stir in asafetida (if using) and chiles. Cook 2 minutes or until chiles brown and crisp on the sides.
2. Turn off heat; add tomatoes then immediately transfer to a serving bowl to stop cooking. Gently mix in salt and lime juice. Serve warm or at room temperature. Serves 4.
EACH SERVING *72 cal, 7 g fat (1 g sat fat), 0 mg chol, 213 mg sodium, 2 g carb, 1 g fiber, 1 g sugars, 1 g pro*

PRIYA'S DAL

SHRIMP & GRITS

RECIPES FOR THIS DISH VARY ACROSS THE SOUTH, ALTHOUGH THIS IS HOW CHEF SEAN BROCK PREPARES THE TRADITIONAL VERSION AT HOME.

SHRIMP & GRITS

TOTAL TIME 25 min.

- ½ cup all-purpose flour
- 1 Tbsp. kosher salt, plus more for seasoning
- ½ tsp. freshly ground black pepper, plus more for seasoning
- 1 tsp. canola oil
- 2 oz. country ham, cut into ¼-inch dice
- 1 lb. fresh or frozen (thawed) jumbo shrimp, peeled and deveined (21-25 count)
- 4 oz. small button mushrooms, quartered
- ¼ cup thinly sliced green onions
- ½ cup vegetable stock or broth
- 2 Tbsp. unsalted butter, diced
- 1 Tbsp. fresh lemon juice
  Stove Top Grits (right)

1. Combine flour, 1 Tbsp. kosher salt, and ½ tsp. freshly ground black pepper in a shallow bowl; mix well.
2. Heat canola oil in a large skillet over medium. Add ham and cook, stirring frequently, 3 minutes or until fat has rendered and ham is crisp.
3. Lightly dredge shrimp in seasoned flour, shaking off any excess, and carefully add them to hot skillet. Cook 1 to 2 minutes or until lightly browned on bottom. Turn shrimp; add mushrooms and green onions. Cook until shrimp are lightly browned on bottom and vegetables begin to soften, about 2 minutes. Add stock; bring to a simmer. Cook until reduced by half and shrimp are just cooked through, about 2 minutes. Stir in butter and lemon juice; season with salt and black pepper. Stir.
4. Divide Stovetop Grits among 4 warmed bowls. Spoon shrimp and mushrooms in broth over grits. Serves 4.
EACH SERVING *382 cal, 14 g fat (8 g sat fat), 195 mg chol, 1,646 mg sodium, 36 g carb, 3 g fiber, 1 g sugars, 27 g pro*

STOVE TOP GRITS

HANDS-ON TIME 10 min.
TOTAL TIME 1 hr. 25 min., plus 8 hr. soaking

- 1 1-liter bottle spring water* or regular water
- 1 cup coarse grits
- 1 fresh or dried bay leaf
- 1 Tbsp. kosher salt
- ½ tsp. freshly ground white pepper
- 2 Tbsp. unsalted butter
- 1 Tbsp. fresh lemon juice
- 1½ tsp. hot sauce

1. Combine the water and grits in a bowl, cover, and refrigerate 8 hours or overnight.
2. Use a fine-mesh sieve to gently skim any hulls or chaff from surface of water, being careful not to disturb water too much so none of the bits sink back into the grits. Transfer grits and their soaking water to a large saucepan. Bring to boiling over high, stirring constantly. Continue boiling, stirring, until grits thicken, 1 to 2 minutes. Remove from heat. Cover; let stand 10 minutes to allow the starch to hydrate slowly for creamier grits.
3. Uncover grits; add bay leaf and cook over low, stirring often, until very soft and tender, about 1 hour. Taste every 15 minutes or so to check texture.
4. Remove from heat. Remove and discard bay leaf; stir in kosher salt, white pepper, butter, lemon juice, and hot sauce. Serves 4.
Pressure Cooker Method Soak grits as directed in Step 1. Place grits, water, bay leaf, salt, and white pepper in a 6-qt. electric pressure cooker. Lock lid in place. Set cooker on high pressure for 15 minutes. Quick-release pressure. Carefully open lid. Stir in butter, lemon juice, and hot sauce. Discard bay leaf.
*Tip Brock uses spring water in his grits because it has a neutral flavor.
EACH SERVING *183 cal, 6 g fat (4 g sat fat), 15 mg chol, 890 mg sodium, 28 g carb, 2 g fiber, 3 g pro*

MEET SEAN BROCK

Chef Sean Brock is ready to dismantle any preconceived notion that Southern food is limited to fried chicken and biscuits. "Southern food is a very specific emotion," Brock says. "It's food designed to nurture." His cookbook *South* explores the regional cuisines of the South, which encompasses a landmass similar to Continental Europe and has, he argues, as many types of cooking styles. Corn bread served in South Carolina is slightly sweet to balance spicy BBQ; Nashville's hot-water corn bread is a salty deep-fried fritter. "The cuisine of the South is based on cultural influences and geography, but you can adapt it to any place in the world." In the Pacific Northwest, that might translate to Dungeness crab and grits; in Cleveland, it might be walleye and grits.

WHAT'S IN SEAN'S PANTRY

"When I cook, I start with what's fresh in market, plus these are staples."

APPLE CIDER VINEGAR "Every dish needs acid." Vinegar is how home cooks added acid before citrus was widely available.

HOT SAUCE For Brock, hot sauce is hardworking. "You get fermented, spicy, and acidic flavors from a splash." Red Clay is his go-to brand.

COUNTRY HAM Brock loves country ham so much that he mapped out his top nine makers. Try Bob Woods' hams from thehamery.com.

"VIETNAMESE FOOD IS HAVE-IT-YOUR-WAY FOOD," SAYS COOKBOOK AUTHOR ANDREA NGUYEN. "AT THE TABLE, DINERS GET TO DOCTOR THE DISH WITH DIFFERENT SAUCES, PICKLED VEGETABLES, AND FRESH HERBS TO MAKE IT THEIR OWN. THE CUISINE DOESN'T STAND STILL."

MEET ANDREA NGUYEN

In her most recent book, *Vietnamese Food Any Day*, Nguyen deliberately eschewed Asian cookware like woks and bamboo steamers in order to develop recipes that a home cook could make without special equipment. "It turned out to be surprisingly liberating," she says. "I don't have to cook exactly the way my mother cooked." She also stuck to readily available ingredients. "Mainstream supermarkets are so well stocked now with Asian ingredients," Nguyen says, "that anyone can find what they need without going to a specialty market."

WHAT'S IN ANDREA'S PANTRY

CHILE-GARLIC SAUCE "In Vietnamese food, chile peppers and garlic are balanced with sweet and sour." Chile-garlic sauce adds a tangy and moderate heat.

RICE NOODLES While working on her book, Nguyen had a revelation. Gluten-free rice-based spaghetti in the supermarket was a version of the rice noodles found at Asian markets. "I actually like them better."

FISH SAUCE She says, "A good fish sauce is umami-laden—savory with a hint of sweetness. An excellent fish sauce is fragrant like dried mushrooms." Store it in the refrigerator.

LEMONGRASS PASTE "I prefer fresh lemongrass, but it takes some prep. If you can't find it, no worries; a tube of lemongrass paste still brings the flavor."

SHRIMP & MANGO RICE PAPER ROLLS

Photo on page 110

Once you master how to make rice paper rolls, you're limited only by your creativity. "Almost anything can go into a roll as long as it's soft and thin," says Nguyen.

TOTAL TIME 45 min.

- 3 to 4 oz. dried small round rice noodles (maifun) or dried rice capellini
- 1 tsp. fine sea salt, plus more as needed
- 18 fresh or frozen (thawed) medium shrimp, peeled and deveined
- 1 16-oz. unripe mango, peeled, pitted, and cut into thin 4×½-inch strips
- 2 medium Persian cucumbers, halved lengthwise, seeded, and cut into thin 4-inch-long strips
- 1½ cups baby lettuce or thinly sliced napa cabbage
- 2 Tbsp. coarsely chopped fresh mint or basil
- 2 Tbsp. coarsely chopped fresh cilantro
- 12 8-inch rice paper rounds
- 1 cup Nuoc Cham Dipping Sauce (recipe, opposite)

1. Boil noodles in a pot of water 3 to 5 minutes or until chewy-soft. Drain; rinse under cold water. Set aside to drain; let cool to room temperature.

2. Fill a small saucepan half full with water, add 1 tsp. fine sea salt, and bring to boiling. Add shrimp; slide pan off heat and let stand 3 to 5 minutes or until shrimp are pinkish orange. Drain; let cool. Halve shrimp symmetrically. Season mango with salt.

3. Fill a shallow dish (something wider than rice paper) with about 1 inch of very warm water. Place noodles, shrimp, mango, cucumbers, lettuce, herbs, and rice paper nearby.

4. Slide a rice paper halfway into water then rotate the paper through your fingers until it is completely wet; transfer to a flat work surface. When paper is pliable and tacky, place a few leaves lettuce or 2 Tbsp. sliced napa on the lower third of paper in a 4×2-inch rectangle. Top with an egg-size mound of noodles, spreading into a rectangle. Arrange some cucumber and mango strips on top. Sprinkle with herbs.

5. Bring up the lower edge of rice paper to cover filling. Roll away from you, once, so lettuce faces you. Add three shrimp halves, cut sides up, to unrolled portion of rice paper, lining shrimp up snugly along partially finished roll. Fold in sides of rice paper to cover filling. Finish rolling to create a snug cylindrical package. The rice paper is self-sealing.

6. Repeat to make 12 rolls; cover to prevent drying. Serve with Nuoc Cham Dipping Sauce. Serves 4.

EACH SERVING *320 cal, 1 g fat (0 g sat fat), 94 mg chol, 1,741 mg sodium, 64 g carb, 3 g fiber, 15 g sugars, 16 g pro*

NUOC CHAM DIPPING SAUCE

Photo on page 110

This classic accompaniment to rice paper rolls and lettuce wraps is the Vietnamese version of a vinaigrette, with a refreshing mix of salty (fish sauce), sweet (sugar), spicy (chiles), and sour (lime juice and rice vinegar) ingredients.

TOTAL TIME 10 min.

- 2 to 2½ Tbsp. sugar, or 3 to 4 Tbsp. pure maple syrup
- 3 to 4 Tbsp. fresh lime juice
- ½ cup warm water, or as needed
- 2 tsp. unseasoned Japanese rice vinegar (optional)
- 3 to 4 Tbsp. fish sauce
- 1 large clove garlic, minced
- 1 to 2 Thai or serrano chiles, thinly sliced (tip, page 28), or 2 or 3 tsp. chile garlic sauce (optional)

1. In a small bowl combine 2 Tbsp. sugar, 3 Tbsp. lime juice, and the warm water. Taste; if needed, add the remaining 1½ tsp. sugar and/or 1 Tbsp. lime juice. If there's an unpleasant tart-bitter edge, add rice vinegar to correct the flavor.

2. Stir in fish sauce. Add garlic and, if desired, chiles. Keep sauce at room temperature up to 8 hours before serving. Makes 1 cup.

Tip Lime juice and vinegar can make the sauce bitter if held too long. Make up to 8 hours before serving.

EACH 1 TBSP. *8 cal, 265 mg sodium, 2 g carb, 2 g sugars*

1. THE DIP Slide half the rice paper into very warm water, then rotate it through your fingers until paper is completely wet.

2. BUILD IT Place wet rice paper on a flat surface. Wait about 1 minute before layering ingredients; the paper should be tacky like a sticky note. Start with a few leaves of baby lettuce and fresh mint; follow those with an egg-size mound of rice noodles, then cucumber and mango strips.

3. START TO ROLL Bring up the bottom edge of paper to cover filling. Then roll away from you once.

4. THE FINISH Place shrimp next to the rolled edge. Fold in both sides of paper. Roll to enclose filling.

"WHENEVER I SHOW PEOPLE HOW TO USE RICE PAPER, THERE'S ALWAYS THIS AHA MOMENT WHEN THEY REALIZE HOW EASY IT IS," NGUYEN SAYS. "DON'T SOAK THE RICE PAPER OR LEAVE IT IN THE WATER; IT MAY FALL APART."

SPANISH GIN TONIC
Recipe on page 137

june

Take advantage of summer weather and dine al fresco. Relax with friends while sipping cocktails on the patio, pack for a fun picnic, and savor the tastes of weeknight grilling.

PACK & GO
HOAGIES

everyone
LOVES A PICNIC

Treat the family to an idyllic afternoon of picnicking. Pick a sunny spot to spread a blanket, and then dig in to these easy summer sandwiches and sides.

PACK & GO HOAGIES

Get a head start on this recipe—the next time you grill, throw on extra pork tenderloin or steak for the sandwich fillings.

START TO FINISH 20 min.

4   8-inch-long soft baguettes (about 2 inches in diameter) or 1 long 14- to 16-oz. baguette cut crosswise into fourths
    Banh Mi or Caprese Steak filling

Using a serrated knife, slice bread lengthwise in half, cutting to but not through opposite side. Hollow out tops and bottoms; add desired filling. Place a filled sandwich in center of a wrap and fold burrito-style. Chill up to 4 hours. Makes 4 sandwiches.

Banh Mi Filling In a medium bowl combine 2 cups sliced vegetables, such as radishes, cucumber, carrot, and/or jalapeño peppers. Add 2 Tbsp. chopped fresh cilantro, 2 Tbsp. each vinegar and water, 2 tsp. sugar, and a pinch of salt. Stir to combine; let stand 10 minutes. Meanwhile, combine ¼ cup mayonnaise and 1 Tbsp. sriracha. Spread mayo mixture on cut sides of bread. Layer on sliced cooked pork tenderloin or deli ham (6 to 8 oz.) and pickled vegetables.
EACH SANDWICH *468 cal, 14 g fat (3 g sat fat), 42 mg chol, 874 mg sodium, 58 g carb, 1 g fiber, 3 g sugars, 19 g pro*
Caprese Steak Filling In a medium bowl combine 2 cups sliced tomatoes, 1 Tbsp. olive oil, 2 cloves minced garlic, and a pinch each of salt and black pepper. Toss to coat; let stand 10 minutes. Meanwhile, combine ¼ cup mayonnaise and 1 Tbsp. purchased pesto; spread mayonnaise mixture on cut sides of bread. Layer on sliced grilled steak or deli roast beef (6 to 8 oz.), sliced

THREE-BEAN SALAD WITH TAHINI-LIME DRESSING

tomatoes, ½ cup thinly sliced fresh mozzarella, and fresh basil leaves.
EACH SANDWICH *526 cal, 20 g fat (5 g sat fat), 50 mg chol, 822 mg sodium, 57 g carb, 1 g fiber, 2 g sugars, 23 g pro*

THREE-BEAN SALAD WITH TAHINI-LIME DRESSING

This summer-focused bean salad tastes best made well ahead of serving and packs well for a picnic.

START TO FINISH 25 min.

16 oz. fresh green beans and/or yellow wax beans, trimmed
1   cup frozen shelled edamame
1   cup fresh or frozen corn
1   15-oz. can garbanzo beans, rinsed and drained
¼   cup fresh cilantro, chopped
½   cup tahini (sesame seed paste)
⅓   cup fresh lime juice (3 medium)
1   Tbsp. olive oil
1   tsp. ground cumin

1. Cook beans, edamame, and corn in a large pot of boiling water 2 to 3 minutes or until beans are crisp-tender. Drain; transfer to a bowl of ice water. Let cool; drain and pat dry. Transfer to a serving bowl. Add garbanzo beans and cilantro; toss.
2. For dressing: In a small bowl whisk together tahini, lime juice, olive oil, 1 tsp. salt, and cumin. If needed, add water, 1 Tbsp. at a time, to reach desired consistency. Toss dressing with bean mixture. Season to taste with black pepper. Chill, covered, up to 24 hours. Serves 8.
EACH SERVING *198 cal, 12 g fat (2 g sat fat), 363 mg sodium, 20 g carb, 5 g fiber, 5 g sugars, 8 g pro*

FANCIER THAN PLAIN COOKIES AND
EASIER TO TOTE THAN CUPCAKES,
THESE CAKEY COOKIES SANDWICHED
WITH FLUFFY MARSHMALLOW FILLING
ARE CELEBRATION-WORTHY.

CREAM PIE
WHOOPIE PIES

*We pushed this handheld dessert a
step further with mix-and-match
flavors inspired by our favorite diner
cream pies. If you like, roll the filling
edges in sprinkles, nonpareils, or
toasted coconut.*

HANDS-ON TIME 20 min.
TOTAL TIME 1 hr. 20 min.

½   cup shortening
1   cup granulated sugar
1   tsp. baking soda
1   egg
1¼   cups buttermilk
3   tsp. vanilla
2½   cups all-purpose flour
½   cup butter, softened
1   7-oz. jar marshmallow creme
1½   cups powdered sugar

1. For cookies: Preheat oven to 350°F.
Line two cookie sheets with parchment
paper. In a large bowl beat shortening
on medium 30 seconds. Add granulated
sugar, baking soda, and ¼ tsp. salt; beat
until combined. Beat in egg, buttermilk,
and 1 tsp. of the vanilla. Beat in flour
until combined.
2. Using a large (3 Tbsp.) cookie scoop,
drop 20 mounds of dough 2 inches apart
on prepared sheets. Bake 10 minutes or
until edges are firm and bottoms start to
brown. Remove; let cool on wire racks.
3. For filling: In a medium bowl beat
butter on medium 30 seconds. Beat
in marshmallow creme and remaining
2 tsp. vanilla until fluffy. Beat in
powdered sugar.
4. Spread filling on bottoms (flat side)
of half the cookies. Top with remaining
cookies, flat side on filling. Wrap
individually and chill up to 3 days. Makes
10 whoopie pies.
EACH PLAIN WHOOPIE PIE *526 cal, 21 g fat
(9 g sat fat), 45 mg chol, 314 mg sodium,
79 g carb, 1 g fiber, 49 g sugars, 5 g pro*

Lemon Cream Prepare cookies and
filling as directed, except stir 2 tsp. lemon
zest into filling.
Double-Chocolate Cream Prepare
cookies as directed, except reduce flour
to 2¼ cups and combine with ¼ cup
unsweetened cocoa powder. Prepare
filling as directed, except add 1 Tbsp.
unsweetened cocoa powder with
powdered sugar.
Strawberry Cream Prepare cookies as
directed, except add ⅛ tsp. liquid red
food coloring to batter with buttermilk.
Prepare filling as directed, except fold
in 6 Tbsp. finely crushed freeze-dried
strawberries.
Banana Cream Mash 1 banana (½ cup)
with 1 Tbsp. lemon juice. Prepare cookies
as directed, except reduce buttermilk
to 1 cup; beat half the banana mixture
into cookie batter with buttermilk.
Prepare filling as directed, except beat
remaining banana mixture into filling
with marshmallow creme and increase
powdered sugar to 2½ cups.

LEMON
CREAM

DOUBLE-
CHOCOLATE
CREAM

STRAWBERRY
CREAM

BANANA
CREAM

GRILLED CHICKEN
WITH BLUEBERRY-
TARRAGON SAUCE

FAST & FRESH

Easy, delicious recipes for a better dinner tonight.

GRILLED CHICKEN WITH BLUEBERRY-TARRAGON SAUCE

If you don't want to use wine, ½ cup of pomegranate juice gives the sauce a similar tang.

HANDS-ON TIME 25 min.
TOTAL TIME 45 min.

- 2 cups blueberries
- 3 Tbsp. chopped fresh tarragon
- 3 cloves garlic, minced
- ½ cup dry red wine
- ½ cup chicken broth
- 2 Tbsp. honey
- 8 skin-on, bone-in chicken thighs
- 2 tsp. smoked paprika
- 2 lemons, halved
- 8 cups zucchini noodles
- 1 Tbsp. olive oil

1. For Blueberry-Tarragon Sauce: In a large saucepan combine blueberries, 2 Tbsp. tarragon, the garlic, wine, broth, and honey. Bring to boiling; reduce heat. Simmer, uncovered, 30 minutes or until sauce is reduced to about 1¼ cups. Season with salt and ground black pepper.
2. While the sauce simmers, season chicken thighs with paprika and ¼ tsp. each salt and black pepper. Grill chicken, covered, over indirect heat 30 minutes or until 175°F, turning once. Add lemon halves to grill rack directly over heat the last 5 minutes.
3. To serve, toss zucchini noodles with olive oil, remaining tarragon, ½ tsp. salt, and ¼ tsp. black pepper. Serve chicken with zucchini noodles, lemon halves, and sauce. Serves 4.
EACH SERVING *622 cal, 37 g fat (10 g sat fat), 148 mg chol, 323 mg sodium, 35 g carb, 7 g fiber, 23 g sugars, 36 g pro*

BEEF KABOBS WITH CORN & ORZO SALAD

Photo on page 129

This kabob-and-salad combo is a deconstructed steak taco, sans tortilla. If using wooden skewers, soak in water 30 minutes before building kabobs.

TOTAL TIME 25 min.

- ⅔ cup dried orzo
- 2 cups fresh corn planks or kernels
- 1 bell pepper, chopped
- ½ cup thinly sliced red onion
- ⅔ cup grape tomatoes, halved
- 2 limes (1 tsp. zest, ¼ cup juice)
- 2 Tbsp. olive oil
- 2 Tbsp. chopped fresh cilantro
- 4 tsp. chili powder
- 2 tsp. garlic salt
- 1 tsp. ground cumin
- 1 tsp. dried oregano
- 1½ lb. boneless beef sirloin steak, trimmed and cut into 1-inch pieces
  Lime wedges

1. For the corn and orzo salad: Cook orzo according to package directions, adding corn the last 1 minute of cooking. Drain in a colander. Rinse; drain again. In a large bowl combine orzo mixture, bell pepper, onion, and tomatoes.
2. For dressing: In a screw-top jar combine lime zest and juice, olive oil, cilantro, and ½ tsp. salt. Cover and shake well. Pour dressing over salad; toss to coat.
3. In a resealable plastic bag combine chili powder, garlic salt, cumin, and oregano. Add meat pieces, a few at a time; shake to coat. Thread meat onto skewers, leaving a ¼ inch between pieces.
4. Grill kabobs, covered, over medium 8 to 12 minutes or until meat is slightly pink in center, turning once or twice during grilling.

5. To serve, arrange salad on a large platter. Top with kabobs and, if desired, additional cilantro. Serve with lime wedges. Serves 6.
EACH SERVING *305 cal, 11 g fat (3 g sat fat), 61 mg chol, 431 mg sodium, 31 g carb, 4 g fiber, 6 g sugars, 25 g pro*

GRILLED EGGPLANT TARTINES

Photo on page 128

These open-face toasts are a beautiful blend of eggplant, Parmesan, bruschetta, and salad caprese.

TOTAL TIME 25 min.

- 1 1-lb. loaf Italian baguette
- 8 slices eggplant, ¾ inch thick
- ¼ cup olive oil
- 1 clove garlic, halved
- 1 8-oz. ball fresh mozzarella, sliced
- 4 roma tomatoes, thinly sliced
- ¼ cup shredded Parmesan cheese
- ¼ cup fresh basil leaves

1. Cut bread loaf in half lengthwise, then in half crosswise (for four pieces). Lightly sprinkle eggplant slices with salt and black pepper. Brush both sides of eggplant slices and cut sides of bread with olive oil.
2. Grill eggplant slices, covered, directly over medium 7 to 8 minutes or until browned and tender, turning once. Add bread, cut side down, to grill rack the last 1 to 2 minutes.
3. Rub toasted sides of bread with garlic. Arrange eggplant, mozzarella, and tomatoes on toasted sides of bread. Grill, covered, 1 to 2 minutes or until cheese softens. Top with Parmesan and basil. Drizzle with additional olive oil and sprinkle with cracked black pepper. Serves 4.
EACH SERVING *586 cal, 25 g fat (9 g sat fat), 44 mg chol, 1,007 mg sodium, 62 g carb, 4 g fiber, 6 g sugars, 20 g pro*

**GRILLED EGGPLANT
TARTINES**
Recipe on page 127

**BEEF KABOBS WITH CORN
& ORZO SALAD**
Recipe on page 127

GARDEN PARTY

When warm summer evenings inspire you to head outdoors for cocktails and appetizers, the season's riot of fresh herbs—picked from pots on the patio or from farmers markets will brighten happy hour.

WARM POTATO CHIPS WITH PARMESAN & HERBS

Season a bag of kettle-cooked potato chips with nutty Parmesan, sage, chives, and lemon zest. To prep these chips ahead of time, spread them in a baking pan and sprinkle with the cheese mixture up to 4 hours before baking.

TOTAL TIME 15 min.

1   8- to 9-oz. bag salted kettle-cooked potato chips
½   cup plus 2 Tbsp. finely grated Parmesan cheese
1½   Tbsp. chopped fresh sage or thyme
¼   cup chopped fresh chives
2   tsp. lemon zest
1   tsp. garlic powder

1. Preheat oven to 425°F. Arrange potato chips in a single layer in a 15×10-inch baking pan.
2. In a bowl combine ½ cup Parmesan, the sage, 1 Tbsp. chives, the lemon zest, and garlic powder. Sprinkle over chips.
3. Bake 5 minutes or until starting to brown. Sprinkle warm chips with remaining 3 Tbsp. chives and remaining 2 Tbsp. Parmesan. Serves 12.
EACH SERVING *109 cal, 6 g fat (1 g sat fat), 3 mg chol, 160 mg sodium, 12 g carb, 2 g pro*

STRAWBERRY-MINT LEMONADE

For a sweeter version of this summertime sipper, you'll want to use only 1½ cups lemon juice.

HANDS-ON TIME 15 min.
TOTAL TIME 1 hr. 20 min.

3   cups sliced fresh strawberries
1   cup sugar
1½   cups chopped fresh mint leaves
8   to 9 lemons (½ tsp. zest, 1½ to 1¾ cups juice)
    Lemon slices

1. For simple syrup: In a large saucepan combine 3 cups water, the strawberries, and sugar. Bring to boiling, stirring until sugar is dissolved. Reduce heat; simmer 5 minutes. Remove from heat. Add chopped mint; cover and let steep 30 minutes. Using a fine-mesh strainer, strain syrup to remove mint and berries. Let cool.
2. In a pitcher combine 3 cups cold water, the simple syrup, lemon zest, and lemon juice. Add lemon slices along with additional strawberry slices and mint leaves. Chill up to 4 hours before serving. Serves 8.
EACH SERVING *128 cal, 8 mg sodium, 33 g carb, 2 g fiber, 29 g sugars, 1 g pro*

THE G&T BAR

Take a tip from Spain and give the simple G&T a garden-inspired lift. Typically served in a balloon glass over lots of ice, Spanish-style gin tonics (hold the and) are typically finished with handfuls of fresh herbs, citrus or cucumber, and spices like peppercorns and juniper berries. They're completely customizable (including swapping in another spirit) and take advantage of overflowing herb pots. Recipe, page 137.

SPIRITS gin, vodka, silver tequila

HERBS & AROMATICS rosemary, basil, mint, tarragon, sage, lemon verbena, thyme, dill, fennel

FRUITS & VEGGIES lemon, lime, orange, grapefruit, English cucumber

SPICES peppercorns, star anise, juniper berries, fennel seeds

THE ALLURE OF THIS NONALCOHOLIC SANGRIA-INSPIRED SIPPER IS A MINT- AND BERRY-INFUSED SIMPLE SYRUP WITH LOTS OF FRESH FRUIT PLUS MINT TO FINISH. HAVE THIS ONE ON REPEAT ALL SUMMER.

**BAKED GOAT CHEESE
WITH HERB OIL**
Recipe on page 134

FOCACCIA WITH HERB OIL
Recipe on page 134

SHRIMP KABOBS WITH AJI VERDE
Recipe on page 137

CRISPY WHITE BEANS WITH GARLIC & HERBS
Recipe on page 137

FOR A SUMMERY TAKE ON BUBBLY BAKED CHEESE, DRIZZLE A SILKY CHÈVRE AND CREAM CHEESE MIX WITH VIBRANT HERB OIL

FOCACCIA WITH HERB OIL

Photo on page 133

This herb-studded focaccia is made with purchased pizza dough. Score the top, brush with herb oil, and scatter on chopped olives and fresh herbs before baking.

HANDS-ON TIME 20 min.

TOTAL TIME 2 hr. 20 min., includes standing

- ½ cup coarsely chopped fresh basil and/or flat-leaf parsley
- 1½ lb. purchased refrigerated pizza dough
- 3 Tbsp. olive oil
- 1 egg white, lightly beaten with 1 Tbsp. water
  Fresh basil and/or flat-leaf parsley leaves
  Herb Oil (far right)
- ¾ cup chopped pitted olives

1. Place chopped herbs on a work surface. Roll dough in herbs and knead lightly to work in. Shape into a ball. Use about 1 Tbsp. of the olive oil to lightly oil a bowl. Place dough ball in bowl and turn once to oil surface. Cover with plastic wrap. Let stand 45 to 60 minutes or until dough reaches room temperature.

2. Coat a 15×10-inch baking pan with remaining olive oil. On a lightly floured work surface, roll dough to a 15×10-inch rectangle, allowing dough to rest as needed during rolling to reach size. Press into prepared pan. Cover and allow dough to stand 1 hour or until slightly puffy and a few large bubbles of air form.

3. Preheat oven to 450°F. Using an extra-sharp knife, diagonally score squares across top of dough. Brush dough with egg white mixture. Arrange herb leaves on dough. Brush again with egg white mixture. Brush lightly with some of the Herb Oil. Sprinkle with olives.

4. Bake 15 minutes or until puffed and golden. Serve warm with Herb Oil for dipping. Serves 24.

EACH SERVING *96 cal, 3 g fat, 168 mg sodium, 13 g carb, 3 g pro*

BAKED GOAT CHEESE WITH HERB OIL

HANDS-ON TIME 10 min.

TOTAL TIME 25 min.

- 8 oz. goat cheese (chèvre), crumbled
- 1 8-oz. pkg. cream cheese, cut into pieces and softened
- 2 Tbsp. milk
- 2 tsp. lemon zest
- 1 tsp. chopped fresh lemon thyme or thyme
- ½ cup finely shredded Parmesan cheese
- ½ to ¾ cup cherry tomatoes (optional)
- 2 Tbsp. Herb Oil (right)

1. Preheat oven to 425°F. In a medium bowl combine goat cheese, cream cheese, milk, zest, lemon thyme, and ¼ tsp. each salt and pepper. Beat with a mixer on medium until smooth.

2. Spread cheese mixture in a 12- to 16-oz. gratin dish or two 8-oz. dishes. Sprinkle with Parmesan. If desired, top with cherry tomatoes. Bake 12 minutes or until lightly browned. Let cool slightly. Drizzle Herb Oil over cheese. Serve warm with crackers and vegetables. Serves 8.

EACH SERVING *270 cal, 23 g fat (13 g sat fat), 55 mg chol, 369 mg sodium, 5 g carb, 1 g sugars, 11 g pro*

HERB OIL

Use a single herb or your favorite combination to make this herb oil. We used tarragon and lemon thyme for the baked goat cheese, and paired basil and parsley in the oil for the focaccia.

TOTAL TIME 10 min.

- 4½ cups fresh herb leaves, such as tarragon, parsley, thyme or lemon thyme, and/or basil
- 1 cup avocado or canola oil

1. In a medium saucepan blanch herb leaves in boiling water 30 seconds. Remove with a slotted spoon and plunge into a bowl of ice water. (Blanching herbs keeps them bright green in the oil.) When completely cool, drain and squeeze herbs to remove water. Using a kitchen towel, pat herbs to dry thoroughly.

2. In a food processor combine blanched herbs and oil. Cover and process until well blended. Season with salt. Makes 1 cup. Refrigerate in an airtight container up to 4 days.

BAKED GOAT CHEESE
WITH HERB OIL

SHRIMP KABOBS WITH
AJI VERDE

AJI VERDE—A MILDLY SPICY PERUVIAN SAUCE MADE FROM CHILES, PARSLEY, AND CILANTRO—IS A TASTY ACCOMPANIMENT FOR GRILLED SHRIMP KABOBS.

SHRIMP KABOBS WITH AJI VERDE

HANDS-ON TIME 20 min.
TOTAL TIME 1 hr. 25 min., includes standing time

- 3   cloves garlic
- ¼   cup packed flat-leaf parsley (leaves and stems)
- ¼   cup packed fresh cilantro (leaves and stems)
- 2   Tbsp. extra virgin olive oil
- 1   large lime (1 tsp. zest, 2 Tbsp. juice)
- ½   tsp. freshly ground black pepper
- 1   lb. fresh extra jumbo shrimp in shells (16–20 per lb.), peeled and deveined
      Aji Verde (optional)

1. For marinade: In a small food processor combine garlic, parsley, cilantro, olive oil, lime zest and juice, 1 tsp. salt, and the pepper. Pulse until finely chopped.
2. In a medium bowl toss shrimp in marinade. Chill, covered, 1 hour. (Meanwhile, if using wooden skewers, soak them in enough water to cover for 30 minutes.)
3. Thread shrimp onto skewers. Grill, covered, over medium-high 4 to 5 minutes or until opaque, turning once. Top with additional chopped parsley and/or cilantro. Serve with lime wedges and, if desired, Aji Verde. Serves 8.
EACH SERVING (WITHOUT AJI VERDE) *77 cal, 4 g fat (1 g sat fat), 79 mg chol, 352 mg sodium, 1 g carb, 10 g pro*
Aji Verde In a food processor combine 1½ cups fresh cilantro leaves; 1 cup fresh flat-leaf parsley leaves; 3 jalapeños, stemmed and seeded; and 1 to 2 serrano peppers, stemmed and seeded. Process to a fine texture. Add 6 Tbsp. sour cream, ¼ cup olive oil, and ½ tsp. salt; process until smooth. Let stand 30 minutes before serving. Makes 1½ cups.
EACH 1 TBSP. *28 cal, 3 g fat (1 g sat fat), 51 mg sodium*

CRISPY WHITE BEANS WITH GARLIC & HERBS

Photo on page 133

When roasted with garlic oil and fresh rosemary, a can of white beans becomes a crunchy, poppable bar snack. Once roasted, these beans are crisp on the outside and smooth and buttery on the inside.

HANDS-ON TIME 10 min.
TOTAL TIME 1 hr., includes cooling

- 2   15-oz. cans cannellini or Great Northern beans, rinsed and drained
- ⅓   cup extra virgin olive oil
- 3   large cloves garlic, smashed
- 1   Tbsp. chopped fresh rosemary
- ½   tsp. freshly ground black pepper
- 2   Tbsp. fresh oregano leaves

1. Preheat oven to 425°F. Spread beans on a tray lined with paper towels; pat dry.
2. For garlic oil: In a small saucepan warm olive oil and garlic over medium-low 10 to 12 minutes or until simmering and aromatic and garlic starts to brown. Remove garlic with a slotted spoon; discard.
3. In a medium bowl combine beans, rosemary, 1 tsp. salt, and pepper. Toss with garlic oil. Arrange beans in a single layer in a 15×10-inch baking pan. Roast 35 minutes or until browned and crisp, stirring once.
4. Spread beans on a piece of foil; sprinkle with oregano. Let cool completely before serving. Serves 10.
EACH SERVING *155 cal, 8 g fat (1 g sat fat), 236 mg sodium, 17 g carb, 4 g fiber, 6 g pro*

SPANISH GIN TONIC

This cocktail is traditionally served in a balloon glass to ensure an herbal aroma with every sip.

TOTAL TIME 5 min.

- 2   oz. dry gin (or sub vodka or silver tequila)
- 4   oz. chilled tonic water
     Citrus (lemon, lime, orange, and/or grapefruit) slices, wedges, or twists
     Fresh herbs, such as mint, basil, sage, thyme, lemon thyme, fennel, tarragon, lemon verbena, dill, and/or lavender or edible flowers
     Spices, such as peppercorns, juniper berries, star anise, and/or fennel seeds
     English cucumber slices (optional)

For each cocktail, combine gin and tonic in a glass of ice. Garnish with citrus, herbs, spices, and, if desired, cucumber slices. Stir gently. Serves 1.
EACH COCKTAIL *196 cal, 30 mg sodium, 18 g carb, 17 g sugars*

SPANISH GIN TONIC

CHERRY CAPRESE SALAD
Recipe on page 152

july

Make room for seasonally abundant produce and flavorful dips and summer dishes to nosh. Take a road trip via foods along Route 66. Then discover a twist on a favorite breakfast choice.

FARMERS MARKET BOARD

When farmers markets and produce aisles overflow with the season's best, it's time to assemble this fresh and colorful grilled veggie spread.

GRILLED
LEMON
AÏOLI

CREAMY CASHEW
& ONION DIP

BUTTERMILK-MISO
RANCH

CREAMY CASHEW & ONION DIP

Cashew cream, shallots, and garlic are a vegan update to sour cream and onion dip.

HANDS-ON TIME 15 min.
TOTAL TIME 4 min.

10	oz. raw unsalted cashews
	Boiling water
3	Tbsp. neutral oil, such as avocado or grapeseed
1	cup thinly sliced shallots
3	cloves garlic, sliced
1	tsp. fine sea salt
¼	cup apple cider vinegar
1	tsp. smoked paprika

1. In a large bowl cover cashews in boiling water. Let stand 15 minutes.
2. In a large skillet heat oil over medium-low. Add shallots, garlic, and salt. Cook, covered, 12 minutes or until tender, stirring occasionally. Uncover; increase heat to high. Cook and stir 3 minutes or until golden brown. Drain cashews; transfer to a food processor bowl.
3. Add ½ cup water, the vinegar, and smoked paprika. Cover and process 5 minutes or until smooth. Fold in half the shallots mixture. Transfer to a serving bowl; top with remaining shallot mixture. Makes 2¼ cups.
EACH ¼ CUP *229 cal, 18 g fat (3 g sat fat), 255 mg sodium, 13 g carb, 2 g fiber, 3 g sugars, 6 g pro*

ADD A NOVEL VEGGIE OR TWO, HIT EVERYTHING WITH A LITTLE HEAT FROM THE GRILL, THEN ARRANGE IT ON A BOARD WITH SUPER-FLAVORFUL DIPS.

BUTTERMILK-MISO RANCH

Mild white miso mellows the tangy buttermilk in this ranch-style dip.

HANDS-ON TIME 15 min.
TOTAL TIME 35 min.

- ⅓ cup milk*
- ¼ cup buttermilk powder*
- ¼ cup white miso paste
- 1 tsp. white vinegar
- ½ tsp. onion powder
- ½ tsp. garlic powder
- ½ tsp. fine sea salt
- 1 tsp. cracked black pepper
- 1 cup sour cream
- 1 cup mayonnaise
- ¼ cup chopped flat-leaf parsley
- ¼ cup chopped fresh dill
- ¼ cup snipped fresh chives

In a large bowl whisk together milk, buttermilk powder, miso paste, vinegar, onion powder, garlic powder, salt, and pepper until smooth. Add sour cream and mayonnaise; stir to combine. Fold in parsley, dill, and chives. Makes 2½ cups.
*Tip Or use ⅓ cup buttermilk and omit milk and buttermilk powder.
EACH 2 TBSP. *109 cal, 10 g fat (2 g sat. fat), 12 mg chol, 248 mg sodium, 3 g carb, 2 g sugar, 1 g pro*

GRILLED LEMON AÏOLI

This aïoli shows a smoky side with grilled lemon.

HANDS-ON TIME 15 min.
TOTAL TIME 40 min.

- 1 large lemon, halved
- 3 large egg yolks*
- 2 tsp. Dijon mustard
- 1 clove garlic, minced
- ½ tsp. fine sea salt
- ½ cup avocado oil**
- ½ cup olive oil**

1. Grill lemon, cut sides down, 2 to 3 minutes or until lightly charred. Remove from heat; let cool. Juice lemon (about 2 Tbsp.).
2. Meanwhile, in a blender add egg yolks, mustard, garlic, salt, and lemon juice. In a 2-cup measure combine avocado oil and olive oil. Cover and turn blender to low. With the motor running, slowly drizzle in oil. Blend 2 to 3 minutes or until aïoli is thick and yellow. Makes 1¼ cups.
*Tip Use pasteurized egg yolks if serving to anyone with a compromised immune system.
**Tip Or use 1 cup olive oil total.
EACH 2 TBSP. *105 cal, 12 g fat (2 g sat fat), 28 mg chol, 64 mg sodium*

GET ON BOARD

These veggies contribute additional fresh flavor to the spread.

LETTUCE Sturdy enough to hold its own with a chunky dip, baby gem or the small inner leaves of romaine have a welcome crunch.

FLAKY SALT Set out a dish of flaky finishing salt and a small spoon for guests to sprinkle salt on veggies as they please.

NOT THE TYPICAL VEG Crisp raw kohlrabi tastes like a mild broccoli stem. Cut off greens, peel bulb, and slice into thin coins.

SWEET POTATO WEDGES

Cut sweet potatoes in half lengthwise, then slice each half lengthwise into wedges about 1 inch thick. Toss with a drizzle of oil and grill, covered, over medium-high 4 to 5 minutes or just until tender and charred, turning once.

ROAD TRIP EATS

A cross-country adventure inspires food writer and illustrator Casey Barber to re-create regional favorites at home.

U.S. Route 66 covers a lot of miles of experiences—more than 2,400 and plentiful food experiences. Casey Barber and her husband, Dan, have learned from decades of road-tripping that the foods they eat along while traveling reveals more about the people and places than any map or guide book ever could. So, last fall the couple set out in a rented camper to drive the length of Route 66, eating like locals along the way. "Every regional dish was an edible snapshot of our trip," Casey says. Back home again in New Jersey, Casey composed many of those memorable dishes, reliving the month-long adventure—and inviting friends to sample the tastes of local stops where the journey began.

ESTABLISHED IN 1926 AS AN EARLY SECTION OF THE U.S. HIGHWAY SYSTEM, ROUTE 66 EXTENDS THROUGH EIGHT STATES—FROM CHICAGO TO SANTA MONICA CALIFORNIA, IN THE WEST.

MINI CORN DOG BITES

You'll need 24 wooden crafts sticks for these corn dogs.

TOTAL TIME 40 min.

- 8 hot dogs
- 1¼ cups yellow cornmeal
- 1 cup all-purpose flour
- 2 Tbsp. sugar
- 1 tsp. kosher salt
- ½ tsp. baking powder
- ½ tsp. baking soda
  Vegetable oil
- 1 large egg, lightly beaten
- 1¼ cups buttermilk

1. Cut hot dogs crosswise into thirds then skewer each piece with a wooden crafts stick. In a large bowl stir together cornmeal, flour, sugar, salt, baking powder, and baking soda.
2. Preheat oven to 200°F. Line a rimmed baking pan with paper towels. Fill a 4- to 6-qt. Dutch oven with about 2 inches of oil (not more than halfway up the sides) or fill an electric deep-fat fryer with oil per manufacturer's instructions.
3. Heat oil to 350°F. Stir egg and buttermilk into dry ingredients.
4. Dip skewered hot dogs into batter to coat, spreading batter over ends of hot dogs. Fry battered dogs in hot oil 3 minutes or until golden brown, turning to cook evenly.
5. Transfer to prepared baking sheet; keep warm in oven. Repeat with remaining hot dogs and batter.* Makes 24 mini corn dogs.
*Tip Batter will thicken while standing. Add 1 to 2 Tbsp. buttermilk or water to thin batter if necessary.
EACH CORN DOG *119 cal, 7 g fat (2 g sat fat), 16 mg chol, 258 mg sodium, 11 g carb, 1 g fiber, 2 g sugars, 4 g pro*

VANILLA FROZEN CUSTARD

HANDS-ON TIME 25 min.
TOTAL TIME 8 hr. 45 min., includes freezing

4   **egg yolks**
½   **cup sugar**
2   **cups heavy cream**
1   **cup whole milk**
¼   **tsp. kosher salt**
1   **Tbsp. vanilla**

1. Place egg yolks in a medium-size heatproof bowl. Whisk in ¼ cup sugar. Continue to whisk about 1 minute or until mixture is slightly thickened (coats the back of a rubber spatula).

2. In a medium-size heavy saucepan combine cream, milk, remaining ¼ cup sugar, and salt. Cook over medium until liquid starts to steam and bubble at edges, stirring frequently with spatula. Reduce heat to medium-low.

3. Drizzle ½ cup hot mixture into egg yolks, whisking continuously to blend. Slowly whisk egg yolk mixture back into mixture in saucepan.

4. Cook and stir custard 5 to 10 minutes or until it thickens enough to coat the spatula in thick ribbons.

5. Strain custard through a fine-mesh sieve into a bowl. Stir in vanilla. Refrigerate, covered, at least 4 hours or overnight.

6. Pour cold custard into a 1½- to 2-qt. ice cream maker. Churn according to manufacturer's instructions. Freeze at least 4 hours before serving. Serves 8.

EACH SERVING *303 cal, 25 g fat (15 g sat fat), 163 mg chol, 69 mg sodium, 16 g carb, 16 g sugars, 4 g pro*

BATTERED & FRIED IN SPRINGFIELD, IL.

The Cozy Dog Drive In is the self-proclaimed home of the "original hot dog on a stick." For more than 70 years, the dogs have been dipped and fried to order. Casey Barber translated them into bite-size dogs.

SCOOPED UP IN ST LOUIS

Even in cold weather, fans queue up outside Ted Drewes Frozen Custard shops, including the stand that opened in 1941 along Route 66. The stands, ubiquitous in the St. Louis metro, also serve custard at the zoo and ballpark. Frozen custard is like a thick soft serve; extra egg yolks add body and rich, velvety texture. For the Ted Drewes version, top with any combo of sauces, nuts, cookies, fruit, or candy.

HOT OFF THE GRILL
IN EL RENO, OK.

There's certainly no shortage of burgers along Route 66—and Robert's Grill (est. 1926) is not only the oldest, but also a must-stop for a cheeseburger. Here, the grillmaster piles shaved raw onions onto quarter-pound patties, lets the burger sizzle a few minutes on the grill, flips it, applies firm pressure with a spatula, and lets the onions frizzle and caramelize under the meat. Tangy yellow mustard is served on the side. Casey's version follows a similar technique on the griddle, but piles the slaw on the burger.

SAUCED & SMOTHERED
IN ALBUQUERQUE

Casey and Dan had a rule rolling into New Mexico: Every meal they ate had to include green chiles, the culinary trademark of the state. At Frontier Restaurant, a 300-seat spot close to the University of New Mexico, a house-made green chile stew studded with pork and potatoes smothers the enchiladas.

TART & REFRESHING
IN ARIZONA

To Casey and Dan, it seemed like prickly pear was on every drink menu in the Southwest. The fruit of the opuntia (prickly pear cactus) tastes similar to kiwi or melon and is often made into an electric-pink syrup used in all sorts of drinks. Casey's Prickly Pear Limeade has lots of lime juice (naturally) and easily transitions into a shortcut margarita.

GRIDDLED ONION
CHEESEBURGER

HANDS-ON TIME 15 min.
TOTAL TIME 1 hr. 15 min.

1   14-oz. pkg. shredded cabbage with carrot (coleslaw mix)
½   cup yellow mustard
6   Tbsp. mayonnaise
2   Tbsp. sugar
½   tsp. celery seeds
1   lb. ground beef (80% lean)
    Kosher salt
    Black pepper
½   small white onion
4   slices American cheese
4   potato hamburger buns, split
    Ketchup, mustard, and/or dill pickle slices (optional)

1. For mustard slaw: In a large bowl combine coleslaw mix, mustard, mayonnaise, sugar, and celery seeds. Chill 1 hour or until ready to serve.
2. For burgers: Shape beef into four 4-oz. patties (3 to 4 inches in diameter). Season lightly with kosher salt and pepper.
3. Cut onion with a mandoline or sharp knife into paper-thin half-moons. Heat a griddle over medium-high at least 5 minutes.
4. Place patties on griddle; top each with a generous handful of onion slices.
5. Cook patties 6 minutes. Gently press down on each patty with a flat, heavy metal spatula occasionally during cooking to coat onions in beef juices.
6. Carefully flip the patties; smash by pressing down with a spatula to flatten and spread the onions on the griddle. Cook 2 minutes. Halve each cheese slice; place two halves on each patty.
7. Cook 1 to 2 minutes more or until onions are browned, an instant-read thermometer registers at least 160°F when inserted in burger, and cheese is just melted.
8. To assemble: Flip burger so onion is on top; place on bottom bun. Top with mustard slaw and, if desired, ketchup, mustard, and/or dill pickle slices. Makes 4 burgers.
EACH BURGER *731 cal, 49 g fat (16 g sat fat), 116 mg chol, 1,319 mg sodium, 40 g carb, 5 g fiber, 15 g sugars, 32 g pro*

GREEN CHILE ENCHILADAS

Casey's green chile stew recipe makes 8 cups. You'll need only 3 cups for each batch of enchiladas, but it's worth making a full batch to serve with nachos, tacos, or smothered burritos, or to eat it by the bowlful.

HANDS-ON TIME 30 min.
TOTAL TIME 1 hr. 20 min.

- 2 Tbsp. olive oil
- 2 cups finely chopped yellow onion
- 4 cloves garlic, minced
- 1 lb. ground pork
- 4 cups reduced-sodium chicken broth
- 1 lb. russet potatoes, peeled and cut into ½-inch dice
- 4 4-oz. cans diced Hatch green chiles (mild or hot), or four 4-oz. cans diced green chiles plus 1 fresh serrano chile, minced
  Kosher salt
- 2 Tbsp. yellow cornmeal
- ½ cup minced white onion
- 8 8-inch flour or corn tortillas
- 3 cups shredded sharp cheddar cheese (12 oz.)

1. For stew: Heat oil in a 5- to 6-qt. Dutch oven over medium. Add yellow onion and garlic; cook 5 minutes or until softened. Add pork. Cook 5 minutes, stirring to break pork into small pieces.
2. Stir in chicken broth, potatoes, chiles, and ½ tsp. each kosher salt and black pepper. Cover and bring to boiling; reduce heat. Simmer, uncovered, 40 minutes, stirring occasionally. In a small bowl combine cornmeal and 2 Tbsp. water; stir into pork mixture. Cook 2 to 3 minutes to thicken. Season to taste with kosher salt and black pepper.
3. Preheat oven to 375°F. Soak white onion in cold water 10 minutes (to mellow the flavor); drain. Spread about 1 cup stew in a 2- to 3-qt. rectangular baking dish to cover bottom. Line the center of each tortilla with about ⅓ cup cheese and 1 Tbsp. white onion. Roll up each tortilla and place seam-side down in prepared dish.
4. Ladle about 2 cups stew over the tortillas; sprinkle with remaining cheese. Bake 20 minutes or until cheese is melted and stew is bubbling. Makes 8 enchiladas.

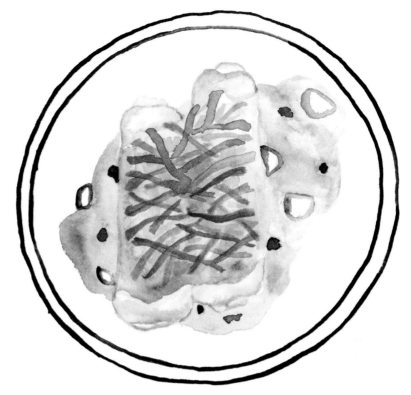

*Tip Store leftover green chile stew in an airtight container in the refrigerator up to 3 days or freeze up to 3 months. Thaw overnight in refrigerator and reheat in a saucepan over medium 8 minutes or until heated through.
EACH ENCHILADA *592 cal, 32 g fat (13 g sat fat), 82 mg chol, 1,249 mg sodium, 46 g carb, 2 g fiber, 5 g sugars, 28 g pro*

PRICKLY PEAR LIMEADE

Casey recommends Cheri's Desert Harvest for the prickly pear syrup.
HANDS-ON TIME 5 min.
TOTAL TIME 35 min.

- ½ cup fresh lime juice (3 to 4 limes)
- 3 Tbsp. Lime Simple Syrup
- 2 Tbsp. prickly pear syrup
- 1¼ cups water or plain seltzer

Stir all ingredients together in a small pitcher. Serve over ice. Serves 2.
EACH SERVING *126 cal, 6 mg sodium, 32 g carb, 28 g sugars*
Lime Simple Syrup Combine 1 cup sugar and 1 cup water in a small saucepan. Simmer over medium until sugar is dissolved, stirring occasionally. Remove from heat; stir in 1 Tbsp. lime zest. Cover; steep 30 minutes to 1 hour. Strain through a fine-mesh strainer into a jar; chill. Store, refrigerated, up to 1 month. Makes 1½ cups.

Prickly Pear Margaritas Pour 2 tsp. kosher salt onto a plate. Wet rims of two cocktail glasses with lime wedges; dip rims in salt. Fill glasses with ice. Fill a cocktail shaker halfway with ice. Add 3 oz. tequila, 1 oz. Cointreau or other orange liqueur, ⅓ cup fresh lime juice, ¼ cup Lime Simple Syrup, and 1 oz. prickly pear syrup. Shake until cold. Strain into glasses. Serves 2.
EACH SERVING *274 cal, 566 mg sodium, 39 g carb, 32 g sugars*

CHERRY-ORANGE
COBBLER

CHERRIES ON TOP

Pick the brightest of summer stone fruits—from tart to sweet—to star in desserts, main dishes, and salads.

CHERRY-ORANGE COBBLER

A bit of orange zest and orange juice balance the sweetness of this cobbler topped with browned butter biscuits— slightly reminiscent of graham crackers.

HANDS-ON TIME 15 min.
TOTAL TIME 2 hr., includes freezing

½   cup unsalted butter
2   cups all-purpose flour
½   cup plus 2 Tbsp. granulated sugar
2   tsp. baking powder
½   tsp. kosher salt
1   cup plus 1 Tbsp. half-and-half
1   Tbsp. turbinado (raw) sugar
2   Tbsp. cornstarch
2   oranges (1 tsp. zest, ½ cup juice)
½   tsp. ground cinnamon
2½   lb. fresh* dark sweet cherries, pitted (about 7 cups)
1   tsp. vanilla

1. In a small saucepan melt butter over medium. Cook 5 to 7 minutes more or until butter turns a deep golden brown. Pour into a small bowl. Let cool 5 minutes; freeze 1 hour or until solid.
2. Preheat oven to 375°F. For biscuit dough: In a medium bowl stir together flour, 2 Tbsp. granulated sugar, the baking powder, and ½ tsp. kosher salt. Using the large holes of a box grater, shred butter into flour mixture.** Combine with a fork. Make a well in center; add 1 cup half-and-half. Stir with a fork just until mixture comes together.
3. On a lightly floured surface gently knead dough into a ball; pat into a ½-inch-thick round. Using a floured 2½-inch round cutter, cut dough into eight circles, rerolling scraps as necessary. Brush tops with the remaining 1 Tbsp. half-and-half. Sprinkle with turbinado sugar.
4. In an extra-large bowl combine the remaining ½ cup granulated sugar, the cornstarch, orange zest, and cinnamon. Stir in cherries, reserved juice if using frozen, orange juice, and vanilla to combine. Spoon into a 2-qt. baking dish. Arrange biscuit cutouts on filling.
5. Bake 50 to 60 minutes or until biscuits are golden and filling is bubbly. Let cool slightly on a wire rack. Serve warm (with vanilla ice cream, if desired) or at room temperature. Serves 8.
*Frozen Cherries If using frozen, thaw two 1-lb. pkg. (32 oz. total) dark sweet cherries overnight in the refrigerator. Drain cherries, reserving ¼ cup juice. Follow recipe as directed.
**Tip If the last bit of butter is difficult to shred, finely chop it.
EACH SERVING *433 cal, 16 g fat (10 g sat fat), 42 mg chol, 214 mg sodium, 69 g carb, 4 g fiber, 38 g sugars, 5 g pro*

CHERRY MATH

FRESH

Cherries vary in size. Use these guidelines when buying and baking.

1 lb. (with pits) = about 3 cups

1 lb. (pitted) = 2½ to 2¾ cups

FROZEN

1-lb. pkg. (pitted) = 3 to 3½ cups

12-oz. pkg. (pitted) = 2 to 2½ cups

When using frozen cherries in our cobbler and slab pie recipes, measure cherries before thawing. Once thawed, reserve the amount of juice called for in each recipe.

ONE SIGN THAT SUMMER MARKETS ARE IN FULL SWING: BRIMMING BASKETS OF BRIGHT CHERRIES, DISPLAYED LIKE ARTWORK.

ELUSIVE TART VARIETIES, SUCH AS MONTMORENCY, MAKE A BRIEF APPEARANCE MID-JULY THROUGH EARLY AUGUST. TIME TO MAKE PIES, JAMS, SORBETS, AND SAUCES.

CHERRY PICKING

Cherries have a fleeting shelf life. Pay close attention to choosing and storing them.

BUY RIGHT Inspect cherries to avoid bruised or blemished fruit and look at the stems. Light green, firm stems indicate the fruit is fresh.

CHILL A bowl of cherries brightens a countertop, but they mold quickly at room temperature. Unwashed cherries last up to 1 week if you refrigerate them layered between paper towels to keep them dry.

CONSIDER BUYING EXTRA The real win is buying fresh cherries in bulk and freezing for when they're scarce. Line a baking sheet with parchment paper and spread pitted cherries in a single layer to make measuring easy once frozen. Transfer to a freezer container and freeze up to 6 months.

SWEET & SOUR CHERRY SLAB PIE

Cherry and almond are predictable flavor partners, so this recipe includes a hint of anise to break up the duo. No worries, it doesn't shout licorice. Baked in a 13×9-inch pan, this double-crust dessert makes enough to share and totes well.

HANDS-ON TIME 30 min.
TOTAL TIME 2 hr. 20 min.

- 3⅓ cups all-purpose flour
- 1½ cups unblanched almond meal
- 2 Tbsp. sugar
- 1 tsp. kosher salt
- 1 tsp. anise seeds
- 1½ cups cold unsalted butter, cut up
- ¼ cup ice water
- 1½ lb. fresh dark sweet cherries, pitted (about 4 cups)*
- 1½ lb. fresh tart red cherries, pitted (about 4 cups)*
- ¾ cup sugar, plus more for sprinkling
- ¼ cup cornstarch
- ¼ tsp. anise seeds, crushed
- 1 large egg

1. For dough: In a large bowl combine flour, almond meal, sugar, salt, and the anise seeds. Using a pastry blender, cut butter into flour until it resembles fine crumbs. Drizzle with the ice water and mix just until dough comes together, adding additional 1 Tbsp. ice water if needed.

2. Form one-fourth of the dough into a disk and wrap. Flatten and wrap remaining dough. Refrigerate both 1 hour.**

3. For filling: In a large bowl toss cherries, reserved juice if using frozen, sugar, cornstarch, and crushed anise.

4. Preheat oven to 375°F. On a 15×10-inch piece parchment paper roll a large portion of dough into a 14×10-inch rectangle. Transfer dough with parchment into a 13×9-inch baking pan. Press dough firmly against bottom and sides. Spread evenly with filling.

5. On a lightly floured surface roll small portion of dough to ⅛-inch thickness. Cut into strips. Place strips diagonally across filling, some filling exposed. As necessary, fold dough edges down and gently press into strips.

6. In a small bowl whisk together egg with 1 Tbsp. water. Brush pastry with egg wash and sprinkle with sugar. Bake 70 minutes or until crust is dark golden brown and filling is bubbling. Let cool in pan on a wire rack. Use parchment to lift uncut pie from pan. Serves 24.

***Frozen Cherries** Thaw two 12-oz. pkg. frozen tart cherries and two 12-oz. pkg. dark sweet cherries overnight in the refrigerator. Drain, reserving ½ cup juice. Prepare as directed.

****Tip** Dough can be made ahead and kept chilled up to 2 days or frozen up to 1 month. Thaw frozen dough in the refrigerator overnight.

EACH SERVING *291 cal, 15 g fat (8 g sat fat), 38 mg chol, 56 mg sodium, 35 g carb, 2 g fiber, 18 g sugars, 4 g pro*

PORK CARNITAS
TACOS WITH
CHERRY-CHIPOTLE
SALSA
Recipe on page 152

CHERRY CAPRESE SALAD
Recipe on page 152

CHOOSE SWEET VARIETIES LIKE THE PLENTIFUL BING OR THE MUCH-ANTICIPATED, BLUSH-TINGED YELLOW RAINIER FOR EATING OUT OF HAND, MUDDLING INTO COCKTAILS, AND FLAVORING SAVORY DISHES AND SALADS.

PORK CARNITAS TACOS WITH CHERRY-CHIPOTLE SALSA

Photo on page 150

Traditionally carnitas are cooked in manteca (fresh lard). Avoid the shelf-stable lard at grocery stores; instead look in the deli section of a Latin market. If you can't find fresh lard, use coconut oil.

HANDS-ON TIME 30 min.
TOTAL TIME 5 hr. 30 min.

2   tsp. kosher salt
1   tsp. ground cumin
1   tsp. dried oregano, crushed
1   tsp. ground chipotle chile powder
½   tsp. black pepper
½   tsp. ground cinnamon
2½   lb. boneless pork shoulder, trimmed and cut into 2- to 3-inch pieces
¼   cup manteca or coconut oil
1¼   lb. fresh sweet cherries, pitted (about 3½ cups)
12   cloves garlic
¼   cup finely chopped red onion
¼   cup chopped fresh cilantro
2   Tbsp. lime juice
12   to sixteen 5- to 6-inch corn tortillas, warmed

1. In a large bowl combine 1 tsp. kosher salt, cumin, oregano, ½ tsp. chile powder, the black pepper, and cinnamon. Add pork; toss to coat.
2. Spread manteca in the bottom of a 3½- or 4-qt. slow cooker. Place pork on manteca. Add 1½ cups cherries and the garlic. Cover and cook on high 4 to 5 hours or low 8 to 10 hours.
3. Meanwhile, for salsa, chop remaining 2 cups cherries. In a medium bowl combine chopped cherries, onion, cilantro, lime juice, remaining 1 tsp. kosher salt, and remaining ½ tsp. chile powder. Chill, covered, until serving.

4. Preheat broiler. Using a slotted spoon, remove pork to a shallow baking pan. Using two forks, shred pork. Spread evenly. Broil 4 inches from heat 4 minutes.
5. Remove cherries and garlic from slow cooker with a slotted spoon; stir into crisped pork. Serve carnitas in warm tortillas with cherry salsa, additional cilantro and red onion, sliced radishes, and lime wedges. Serves 6.
EACH SERVING *442 cal, 11 g fat (4 g sat fat), 125 mg chol, 492 mg sodium, 41 g carb, 6 g fiber, 13 g sugars, 45 g pro*

CHERRY CAPRESE SALAD

Photo on page 151

Heirloom cherry tomatoes provide an array of color in this salad. Serve any extra balsamic reduction on the side or refrigerate up to 1 week.

TOTAL TIME 30 min.

1   cup balsamic vinegar
8   oz. burrata cheese
1   lb. fresh dark sweet cherries (about 3 cups), pitted, or ½ lb. each tart red and dark sweet cherries, pitted
1   cup cherry tomatoes, halved
½   cup fresh basil leaves
2   Tbsp. extra virgin olive oil
     Flaky sea salt
     Black pepper

1. In a small saucepan bring balsamic vinegar to simmer over medium. Simmer, uncovered, 12 minutes or until reduced to ¼ cup; let cool.
2. Drain and pat dry burrata; cut in half. Spread burrata over bottom of platter. Arrange cherries, tomatoes, and basil on cheese. Drizzle with 1 Tbsp. balsamic reduction and the olive oil. Sprinkle with sea salt and pepper. Serves 6.
EACH SERVING *221 cal, 13 g fat (6 g sat fat), 27 mg chol, 168 mg sodium, 18 g carb, 1 g fiber, 15 g sugars, 8 g pro*

GRILLED CHICKEN & CHERRY SALAD

The epitome of summer: lots of crunchy vegetables, bursts of fresh cherries, and all the elements of an exceptional chicken salad (creamy lemon-tarragon dressing, herbs, and dried fruit).

TOTAL TIME 40 min.

4   cups baby kale and/or baby spinach
12   oz. fresh sweet or tart red cherries, pitted and halved (about 2 cups)
1   cup small broccoli florets
1   cup matchstick carrots
½   cup thinly sliced red onion
¼   cup dried tart red cherries
¼   cup roasted, salted sunflower kernels
¼   cup mayonnaise
2   to 3 Tbsp. chopped fresh tarragon
1   Tbsp. cider vinegar
1   Tbsp. lemon juice
2   tsp. sugar
½   tsp. kosher salt
¼   tsp. ground mustard
     Pinch black pepper
1   lb. skinless, boneless chicken breast halves, grilled and sliced

1. In a large bowl combine greens, fresh cherries, broccoli, carrots, onion, dried cherries, and sunflower kernels.
2. For dressing: In a small bowl whisk together mayonnaise, tarragon, vinegar, lemon juice, sugar, salt, mustard, and pepper.
3. Drizzle dressing over salad; toss to combine. Top with chicken. Serve immediately or chill, covered, up to 2 hours. Serves 6.
EACH SERVING *243 cal, 12 g fat (2 g sat fat), 63 mg chol, 258 mg sodium, 16 g carb, 3 g fiber, 10 g sugars, 20 g pro*

GRILLED CHICKEN
& CHERRY SALAD

SOUR CHERRY
SORBET

NO ICE CREAM MAKER REQUIRED. SCOOP INTO CONES, OR MAKE A FIZZY FLOAT WITH COLA OR SPARKLING ROSÉ.

SOUR CHERRY SORBET

If you've got 10 minutes, you've got time to make this tart sorbet. Blend frozen cherries and simple syrup in a food processor, then pour the sorbet into a freezer-safe container.

HANDS-ON TIME 10 min.
TOTAL TIME 10 hr. 10 min., includes freezing

1   lb. pitted fresh or frozen tart red cherries (about 3 cups)
¼   cup sugar

1. If using fresh cherries, spread onto a parchment paper-lined rimmed baking sheet. Freeze, uncovered, 6 hours or overnight.
2. For syrup: In a small saucepan combine sugar and ¼ cup water. Bring to a simmer, whisking to dissolve sugar. Remove from heat; let cool slightly. Chill 1 to 2 hours or until cooled completely.
3. Combine cold syrup and frozen cherries in a food processor fitted with chopping blade attachment. Process 3 to 5 minutes or until mixture is smooth, scraping down sides of bowl after each minute.
4. Transfer sorbet to a freezer-safe container. Freeze at least 4 hours. Serves 6.

EACH SERVING *70 cal, 3 mg sodium, 18 g carb, 1 g fiber, 15 g sugars, 1 g pro*

CHERRY-GINGER COOLERS

CHERRY-GINGER COOLERS

Muddling cherries, fresh mint, and ginger together releases and blends their juices into a refreshing mixer. For an afternoon sipper, top it off with iced green tea. When happy hour calls, pour in a splash of Aperol to make a spritz, or vodka for an updated Moscow mule.

TOTAL TIME 10 min.

6   fresh dark sweet cherries, pitted
4   slices fresh peeled ginger
1   sprig fresh mint

Cherry-Ginger Sweet Tea Muddle cherries, ginger, and mint in a pint glass. Fill glass with ice and 1½ cups sweetened iced green tea; stir. Garnish with a cherry. Serves 1.

EACH DRINK *150 cal, 87 mg sodium, 35 g carb, 1 g fiber, 28 g sugars, 1 g pro*

Cherry-Ginger Spritz Muddle cherries, ginger, and mint in a wineglass. Add 3 Tbsp. dry vermouth, 3 Tbsp. Aperol, and ice. Top with sparkling water; stir. Serves 1.

EACH DRINK *124 cal, 18 mg sodium, 12 g carb, 1 g fiber, 7 g sugars, 1 g pro*

Cherry-Ginger Mule Muddle cherries, ginger, and mint in a cocktail shaker. Add 3 Tbsp. vodka, 1½ Tbsp. lime juice, and 1 cup crushed ice. Shake vigorously. Pour into an ice-filled copper mug or glass. Top with ¼ cup sparkling water. Garnish with a mint sprig and/or a lime wedge. Serves 1.

EACH DRINK *143 cal, 10 mg sodium, 12 g carb, 1 g fiber, 7 g sugars, 1 g pro*

EGG-IN-A-BASKET

This dish has dozens of names, but every version is basically an egg fried in a piece of toast. This upgrade features everything bagels and a tumble of flavorful toppings.

SHEET-PAN EGGY BAGELS

You might know this breakfast classic as egg-in-a-hole, birdies-in-a-nest, or toad-in-the-hole.

TOTAL TIME 30 min.

- 8 everything bagel halves or ½-inch-thick slices country-style bread
- 8 eggs
- 1½ cups cherry tomatoes, halved
- ½ cup pitted, sliced Kalamata olives
- ½ to 1 cup chopped fresh herbs (oregano, parsley, and/or mint)
- ½ cup crumbled feta

1. Preheat oven to 400°F. Coat a 15×10-inch baking pan with nonstick cooking spray. (For bagels with small holes or for bread slices, use a 2-inch round cutter to enlarge or cut holes.) Arrange bagels, cut sides down, on prepared baking pan. Crack an egg into a glass measuring cup and pour into a bagel hole. Repeat with remaining eggs and bagel halves. Season eggs with ½ tsp. salt and ¼ tsp. pepper. Top with tomatoes, olives, half of the herbs, and the feta.

2. Bake 10 to 12 minutes or until bagels are toasted and eggs are desired doneness. Let stand 5 minutes before serving. Top with remaining herbs. Serves 8.

EACH SERVING *444 cal, 19 g fat (8 g sat fat), 210 mg chol, 912 mg sodium, 52 g carb, 3 g fiber, 7 g sugars, 18 g pro*

EGG TIMER

For runny yolks, bake about 10 minutes. If you prefer slightly thicker (jammy) yolks, bake 12 minutes.

FLAVOR CHANGE-UP

For an Italian spin, start with Asiago cheese bagels and use roasted red peppers instead of olives, basil and oregano for the herbs, and shredded Parmesan for the cheese.

MELON & SALT
Recipe on page 165

august

Pick a bounty—from gardens, farmers markets, or grocery aisles—to celebrate the best of summer fruits, vegetables, and herbs. And call on frozen puff pastry to bake a batch of Danish pastries.

TRIPLE-MELON
SALAD

in season
THE JUICY FRUIT

The darling of the melon patch, watermelon has a lot of fans this time of year, and for good reason. Yet its cantaloupe and honeydew cousins are just as deserving of attention. Here, the trio get equal billing in nine refreshing seasonal recipes.

TRIPLE-MELON SALAD

Customize this salad with your favorite melon combination cut any way you like, and paired with your choice of herbs.

TOTAL TIME 25 min.

3   cups baby arugula
6   cups cut-up melon, such as watermelon, cantaloupe, and/or honeydew
½   cup thin red onion wedges
½   cup crumbled feta cheese (2 oz.)
¼   cup orange juice
1   Tbsp. lime juice
1   Tbsp. honey
2   cloves garlic, minced
¼   cup olive oil
½   cup chopped fresh herbs, such as mint, basil, and/or parsley

1. Arrange arugula, melon, and onion on a platter. Sprinkle with cheese.
2. For dressing: In a small bowl whisk together orange and lime juices, honey, garlic, ¼ tsp. salt, and ¼ tsp. black pepper. Whisking constantly, add oil in a thin stream. Top salad with dressing and herbs. Serves 6.
EACH SERVING *193 cal, 12 g fat (3 g sat fat), 11 mg chol, 237 mg sodium, 20 g carb, 2 g fiber, 17 g sugars, 4 g pro*

MINT VINAIGRETTE DRIZZLE

Oil and vinegar might not be the first thing you think of serving over a simple melon slice, but this fresh mint vinaigrette goes with every type of melon and tastes slightly different on each.

TOTAL TIME 5 min.

½   cup white wine vinegar
6   Tbsp. olive oil
¼   cup finely chopped fresh mint
½   tsp. salt
½   tsp. black pepper

In a small bowl whisk together vinegar, oil, mint, salt, and pepper. Drizzle over fresh melon. Serves 8.
EACH 2 TBSP. *96 cal, 10 g fat (1 g sat. fat)*

HOW TO CHOOSE A GOOD MELON

Once a melon is harvested, its sweetness and flavor are set. To make sure you buy one picked at its prime, look for these clues: The ground spot on the underside of a watermelon should be more golden than white; if the stripes on the rind show signs of yellow, the melon is overripe. A cantaloupe or honeydew is ripe when you can gently depress the skin at the blossom end (opposite the stem); if you break the skin, the melon is overripe.

THE ASSERTIVE GARLIC-CITRUS DRESSING MAKES THIS VERSION OF THE POPULAR MELON AND FETA SALAD DISTINCTIVE.

MINT VINAIGRETTE DRIZZLE

CANTALOUPES LOVE PEACHES, WATERMELONS ARE SIMPATICO WITH BERRIES, AND HONEYDEWS HAVE A THING FOR LIMES. CALL IT SERENDIPITY IF YOU LIKE. WE CALL IT FORTUITOUS. THESE PARTNERS INTENSIFY THE FLAVOR AND COLOR OF SUMMER SIPPERS.

CANTALOUPE-PEACH AGUA FRESCA

Serve this drink over frozen cubed melon to avoid diluting the flavor with ice. Not a fan of coconut water? Substitute water and increase the lemon juice to 1/3 cup.

HANDS-ON TIME 30 min.
TOTAL TIME 2 hr. 30 min., includes chilling

6   cups cubed cantaloupe
2   fresh peaches, coarsely chopped
3   cups coconut water, chilled
¼   cup fresh lemon juice
    Frozen cubed cantaloupe
    Fresh peach slices
    Fresh lemon slices (optional)

1. In a blender combine 3 cups cantaloupe, 1 peach, and ¼ cup coconut water. Blend until smooth. Pour through a fine-mesh sieve, pressing on solids to release juice. Transfer juice to a 2-qt. pitcher. Repeat with remaining cantaloupe and peach and ¼ cup coconut water.
2. Stir remaining coconut water into mixture; chill 2 hours or until ready to serve. Stir and serve over frozen melon cubes with peach and lemon slices, if desired. Makes 7 cups.
EACH ¾ CUP *89 cal, 1 g fat (0 g sat fat), 146 mg sodium, 22 g carb, 4 g fiber, 17 g sugars, 3 g pro*

WATERMELON-BERRY-BASIL BLEND

HANDS-ON TIME 30 min.
TOTAL TIME 2 hr. 30 min., includes chilling

9   cups cubed watermelon
3   cups fresh raspberries
¾   cup fresh basil leaves

In a blender combine 3 cups watermelon, 1 cup raspberries, and ¼ cup basil. Blend until smooth. Pour through a fine-mesh sieve, pressing on solids to release juice. Transfer juice to a 2-qt. pitcher. Repeat twice with remaining watermelon, raspberries, and basil. Chill, covered, at least 2 hours and up to 24 hours. Serve over ice with additional raspberries and basil. Makes 6 cups.
EACH ¾ CUP *56 cal, 2 mg sodium, 13 g carb, 3 g fiber, 8 g sugars, 1 g pro*

HONEYDEW-GINGER LIME FIZZ

HANDS-ON TIME 20 min.
TOTAL TIME 2 hr. 50 min., includes chilling

¼   cup sugar
1   1-inch piece fresh ginger, thinly sliced
1   lime, zested and juiced
1   honeydew melon, seeded and halved
1   liter sparkling water, chilled

1. In a small saucepan stir together 1 cup water, the sugar, ginger, and lime zest over medium until sugar is dissolved. Let stand, covered, 30 minutes. Pour through a fine-mesh sieve into a bowl.
2. Use a melon baller to remove fruit from half the melon. Add to syrup; stir to coat. Chill, covered, 1 hour.
3. Meanwhile, remove rind from remaining melon half; cut melon into small chunks. Puree in a blender until smooth. Transfer to a 2-qt. pitcher. Cover; chill 2 hours or until ready to serve.
4. To serve, add melon balls with syrup and lime juice to puree in pitcher. Add sparkling water. Serve with lime slices. Makes 8 cups.
EACH 1 CUP *80 cal, 44 mg sodium, 21 g carb, 1 g fiber, 18 g sugars, 1 g pro*

CANTALOUPE-
PEACH AGUA
FRESCA

WATERMELON-
BERRY-BASIL
BLEND

HONEYDEW-GINGER
LIME FIZZ

MELON & SALT

SPRINKLING SALT
ONTO MELON
IS A SOUTHERN
TRADITION. TO
THE GENIUS
WHO STARTED IT,
WE'D LIKE TO SAY
THANK YOU.

MELON & SALT

In small doses salt magnifies melon's sweetness and heightens its flavor. Store in an airtight container up to 1 month.

TOTAL TIME 10 min.

¼ cup kosher salt
½ tsp. smoked paprika or ½ Tbsp. dry red wine (such as Cabernet Sauvignon) or sweet white wine (such as Riesling)
    Cubed watermelon

In a small bowl stir together the salt and paprika or wine. Sprinkle flavored salt over watermelon; serve with toothpicks. (Store any leftover flavored salt in an airtight container up to 6 months. If storing salt with wine, spread on a plate and dry for 24 hours before placing in storage container.) Makes 24 servings.
EACH SERVING *560 mg sodium*
Vanilla Salt In a small bowl stir together ¼ cup kosher salt, 1 Tbsp. sugar, and the seeds from 1 vanilla bean pod. Cover and let stand 1 to 2 weeks to develop flavor.
EACH SERVING *2 cal, 1 g carb, 1 g sugar*

LEMONDROP
MELON &
CHILE GRANITA

LEMONDROP MELON & CHILE GRANITA

This granita pairs a sweet-tart lemondrop melon with a serrano pepper syrup and herbal cilantro that will make you think of a spicy margarita with the refreshing icy texture of a snow cone.

HANDS-ON TIME 20 min.
TOTAL TIME 4 hr. 50 min., includes freezing

¾ cup sugar
1   serrano or jalapeño pepper, stemmed and sliced (leave seeds) (tip, page 28)
6   cups cubed lemondrop melon or honeydew melon
¼ cup packed fresh cilantro leaves
    Chile-lime seasoning, such as Tajín

1. In a small saucepan stir sugar and ¾ cup water over medium until sugar is dissolved. Stir in pepper. Let stand, covered, 30 minutes.
2. Meanwhile, puree melon and cilantro in a blender or food processor, in batches if necessary. Transfer to a 1½- to 2-qt. baking dish. Strain syrup into puree; stir to combine. Freeze, covered, 3 to 4 hours or until frozen. Use a fork to break mixture into slushy chunks, allowing coarse ice crystals to form. Freeze 1 to 2 hours more or until solid again. Use a fork to scrape the frozen surface into fine icy shards (it will look like shaved ice). For a smoother granita, process frozen mixture in a food processor 1 minute or until smooth. Freeze at least 1 hour more before serving.
3. Serve sprinkled with chile-lime seasoning. Makes 4 cups.
EACH ¼ CUP *110 cal, 111 mg sodium, 28 g carb, 1 g fiber, 27 g sugars, 1 g pro*

SHORTCUT PASTRIES

If the idea of baking cream cheese Danishes at home is intimidating, pick up a package of frozen puff pastry. This simple ingredient is the secret to these warm and fruity pastries.

CREAM CHEESE DANISHES

HANDS-ON TIME 30 min.
TOTAL TIME 45 min.

- 1½ cups fresh or frozen fruit
- 1 8-oz. pkg. cream cheese, softened
- ⅓ cup sugar
- 1 tsp. lemon or lime juice
- ½ to 1 tsp. vanilla, almond, or lemon extract
- ½ cup fruit preserves, jam, or marmalade
- 2 sheets frozen puff pastry, thawed in refrigerator
- 1 egg, lightly beaten

1. Thaw fruit if frozen. Preheat oven to 400°F. Line two baking sheets with parchment paper.

2. In a medium bowl beat cream cheese with a mixer on medium until smooth. Beat in sugar, lemon juice, and vanilla. In a small bowl stir together fruit and preserves.

3. On a lightly floured surface, roll one puff pastry sheet into a 10½-inch square. (Keep remaining sheet chilled.) Cut into nine 3½-inch squares; place on a baking sheet. Prick with a fork to within ½ inch of edges. Combine egg and 1 Tbsp. water; brush over squares. Spread each square with 1 Tbsp. cream cheese mixture; top with about 1½ Tbsp. fruit mixture.

4. Bake 15 to 18 minutes or until golden. transfer to wire racks to cool. Repeat with remaining puff pastry. Makes 18 Danishes.

EACH DANISH *200 cal, 11 g fat (6 g sat fat), 23 mg chol, 139 mg sodium, 23 g carb, 1 g fiber, 10 g sugars, 3 g pro*

FAST & FRESH

Easy, delicious recipes for a better dinner tonight.

CHICKEN COBB PITAS

All the best of a traditional Cobb salad fills pita pockets. For an even more flavorful aïoli, stir together the mayo mixture and refrigerate for an hour before assembling pitas.

TOTAL TIME 25 min.

½ cup mayonnaise
3 Tbsp. chopped green onion
2 tsp. lemon juice
1 clove garlic, minced
¼ tsp. cracked black pepper
2 6- to 7-inch pitta pockets, halved
1½ cups shredded deli-roasted chicken
4 strips bacon, crisp-cooked
1 hard-boiled egg, coarsely chopped
1 avocado, halved and sliced
1 roma tomato, sliced
¼ cup crumbled blue cheese

1. For aïoli: In a small bowl stir together mayonnaise, green onion, lemon juice, garlic, and pepper.

2. Open each pita half and spread with 1 Tbsp. aïoli. Gently stuff with chicken, bacon, egg, avocado, and tomato. Top with blue cheese. Serve with remaining aïoli for dipping. Serves 4.

EACH SERVING *500 cal, 36 g fat (8 g sat fat), 130 mg chol, 758 mg sodium, 23 g carb, 5 g fiber, 2 g sugars, 25 g pro*

CHICKPEA SALAD WITH TUNA

This main-dish salad can be prepared through Step 1, then chilled, covered, up to 4 hours.

HANDS-ON TIME 20 min.
TOTAL TIME 35 min.

- ¼ cup lemon juice
- 2 cloves garlic, minced
- ½ tsp. ground cumin
- ¼ cup olive oil
- ½ tsp. kosher salt
- 2 15- to 16-oz. cans chickpeas, rinsed and drained
- 4 green onions, bias-sliced into 1-inch pieces
- ½ cup chopped roasted red peppers
- ½ cup chopped flat-leaf parsley
- 1 12-oz. can oil-packed tuna, drained and broken into chunks
- ½ cup crumbled feta cheese

1. In a large bowl whisk together lemon juice, garlic, cumin, olive oil, kosher salt, and ¼ tsp. black pepper. Add chickpeas, green onions, roasted red peppers, and parsley; stir to combine. Let stand at room temperature 15 minutes.
2. Fold in tuna. Top with cheese, additional parsley, and black pepper. Serves 6.

EACH SERVING *316 cal, 17 g fat (4 g sat fat), 19 mg chol, 630 mg sodium, 21 g carb, 5 g fiber, 4 g sugars, 20 g pro*

THIS LEMONY BEAN SALAD IS LOOSELY BASED ON THE MIDDLE EASTERN DISH BALILAH. IT'S A GOOD BASE FOR RAW, ROASTED, OR GRILLED VEGETABLES IN THE FRIDGE.

CREAMY GAZPACHO

This cold soup takes advantage of summer produce, and blending in silken tofu increases the body and richness. Any combo of fresh herbs with delicate leaves (parsley, cilantro, basil, mint, and/or dill) works well.

TOTAL TIME 20 min.

1½ lb. roma tomatoes, coarsely
     chopped
1   cup roasted red peppers
4   cloves garlic
1   12-oz. pkg. silken tofu, cut into
     pieces
1   cup fresh herbs, chopped
¼   cup red wine vinegar
4   green onions, chopped
     Grilled baguette slices (optional)
     Shaved Parmesan cheese
     (optional)
     Olive oil (optional)

1. In a large food processor combine tomatoes, roasted red peppers, garlic, tofu, fresh herbs, vinegar, green onions, 1 tsp. salt, and ½ tsp. black pepper. Cover and process 1 minute or until nearly smooth.

2. Serve gazpacho (chilled if desired) with grilled baguette slices and finish with additional herbs, black pepper, shaved Parmesan, and/or a drizzle of olive oil. Serves 4.

EACH SERVING *102 cal, 2 g fat (0 g sat fat), 831 mg sodium, 13 g carb, 3 g fiber, 5 g sugars, 9 g pro*

ANTIPASTO SANDWICHES

A quick blitz in the food processor turns pesto and chopped veggies into a giardiniera-like relish. Serve any extra as a side salad or over eggs, grilled meat, or roasted veggies.

TOTAL TIME 20 min.

6	Tbsp. basil pesto
1	Tbsp. lemon juice
¾	cup chopped cauliflower
¾	cup cherry tomatoes
1	stalk celery, coarsely chopped
1	cup baby arugula
4	slices ½-inch-thick Italian bread
3	oz. salami, thinly sliced
2	oz. fresh mozzarella, thinly sliced

1. For relish: In a food processor combine ¼ cup pesto, the lemon juice, cauliflower, cherry tomatoes, and celery. Pulse a few times until mixture is coarsely chopped.

2. Divide arugula between two bread slices; add salami and cheese. Top cheese with relish. Spread remaining 2 Tbsp. pesto onto remaining bread slices; place on top. Cut sandwiches in half. Serves 4.
EACH SERVING *264 cal, 18 g fat (5 g sat fat), 34 mg chol, 826 mg sodium, 14 g carb, 2 g fiber, 3 g sugars, 12 g pro*

BIG-BATCH ROSEMARY LEMONADE
Recipe on page 179

HERB-ROASTED SHRIMP & SUCCOTASH RELISH

GRILLED ZUCCHINI & GOAT CHEESE TOASTS
Recipe on page 176

ROASTED CARAWAY CARROTS WITH FENNEL AÏOLI
Recipe on page 176

PRESERVING TRADITION

For a blogger and lifelong gardener, pickling veggies is a joyful family affair.

To Kaleb Wyse, nostalgia is the taste of a homemade pickle: sweet and salty with a bright, mouth-puckering kick. Some of his happiest memories of growing up on a fourth-generation family farm in southeast Iowa involve sitting at the kitchen table while his mother worked the stove-top canner and his grandmother mixed brine, offering him little samples as she added an extra pinch of this and a little sprinkle of that. *"During the process you wouldn't even think, Oh, we're making pickles,"* Kaleb says. "You would be hearing Grandma's stories about when she was little and about her mother. We had the best talks during those days in the kitchen."

At 32, Kaleb lives on the same property, down the road from the house where he was raised. And pickling remains a highly anticipated family tradition. These days, he plans around visits from his sister, Kelsey, who heads back to the farm every summer. Kaleb and his mother, both accomplished gardeners, harvest whichever vegetables are at their peak, and the Wyse clan gets to work putting up a mix of traditional recipes—dilly beans, Kirby cukes—and new experiments. "I'll pickle just about anything," Kaleb says, pointing to Curried Cauliflower with Turmeric and Smoky Paprika Carrots as two recent favorites. "And, of course, while we're cooking, we always get to reminiscing."

HERB-ROASTED SHRIMP

Top oven-roasted shrimp with a bright take on succotash, complete with barely cooked veggies and a vinegary punch.

TOTAL TIME 30 min.

1½ lb. fresh or frozen jumbo shrimp (14 to 16 per lb.), thawed if frozen, peeled, and deveined
2 Tbsp. olive oil
2 tsp. lemon juice
2 cloves garlic, minced
1 tsp. chopped fresh marjoram or oregano
1 tsp. chopped fresh thyme leaves

Preheat oven to 375°F. Pat shrimp dry. Arrange in a single layer in a 15×10-inch baking pan. Drizzle with the olive oil and lemon juice. Sprinkle with garlic, marjoram, thyme, and 1 tsp. salt. Roast, uncovered, 8 to 10 minutes or until shrimp are opaque. Serves 8 for appetizers.
EACH SERVING *94 cal, 4 g fat (1 g sat fat), 119 mg chol, 379 mg sodium, 15 g pro*

SUCCOTASH RELISH

HANDS-ON TIME 20 min.
TOTAL TIME 50 min., includes chilling

2 Tbsp. safflower or vegetable oil
¼ cup chopped yellow onion
½ cup chopped red bell pepper
¾ cup fresh or frozen (thawed) baby lima beans or edamame
1 cup fresh corn kernels (2 ears)
¼ cup apple cider vinegar
1 Tbsp. sugar
½ tsp. dry mustard
2 Tbsp. chopped fresh dill weed
1 Tbsp. chopped green onion

1. In a 12-inch skillet heat oil over medium-high. Add onion and bell pepper to skillet; cook 4 minutes or until softened and onion is translucent. Stir in lima beans; cook 1 minute. Add corn; cook 5 minutes or until heated through and bright yellow, stirring occasionally.
2. Add vinegar, sugar, mustard, ½ tsp. salt, and ½ tsp. black pepper. Cook, uncovered, 8 to 10 minutes or until the liquid has almost completely evaporated. Let cool to room temperature. Chill at least 30 minutes in an airtight container. Serve cold sprinkled with dill and green onion. Serves 6.
EACH SERVING *107 cal, 5 g fat (0 g sat fat), 210 mg sodium, 14 g carb, 2 g fiber, 5 g sugars, 3 g pro*

PRESERVED VEGETABLES ARE A WAY TO SHARE HIS FAMILY, FARM, AND HISTORY.

"I WANT TO SHARE THE SIMPLICITY OF PICKLING. MAYBE YOU DON'T KNOW HOW TO PICKLE, MAYBE YOU DIDN'T DO IT WITH YOUR GRANDMA, BUT IT'S NOT HARD. YOU CAN START DOING IT NOW AND MAKE MEMORIES TOO."

GRILLED ZUCCHINI & GOAT CHEESE TOASTS

Photo on page 172

"Like everyone who grows squash, I end up with too much of it. I'm always looking for new ways to use it." Here, za'atar, a Middle Eastern spice blend with a tinge of citrus, gives the veg some oomph.

TOTAL TIME 40 min.

2 medium zucchini (20 to 24 oz. total)
3 Tbsp. olive oil
1 to 2 Tbsp. za'atar seasoning
1 8-inch baguette, cut into twelve ½-inch-thick slices
4 oz. goat cheese, softened
   Snipped fresh chives (optional)

1. Preheat grill to medium. Cut zucchini in half lengthwise; brush cut sides with 1 Tbsp. olive oil. Sprinkle with za'atar and ½ tsp. salt. Brush remaining 2 Tbsp. olive oil on both sides of baguette slices; sprinkle with ground black pepper.
2. Grill zucchini halves, cut sides down, 10 to 12 minutes or until charred and beginning to soften. For the last 4 minutes, grill baguette slices until lightly charred and toasted, turning once. Let cool 5 minutes.
3. Slice zucchini into 2-inch-thick halfmoons. Spread baguette slices with goat cheese; top with zucchini. If desired, sprinkle with chives. Serves 6.
EACH SERVING *231 cal, 11 g fat (4 g sat fat), 9 mg chol, 576 mg sodium, 24 g carb, 1 g fiber, 2 g sugars, 7 g pro*

ROASTED CARAWAY CARROTS

Photo on page 172

Kaleb briefly roasts carrots before finishing them under the broiler. His two-step process ensures a crisp-tender texture and a bit of char. Serve them warm or at room temp with a fennel-packed dip.

HANDS-ON TIME 10 min.
TOTAL TIME 30 min.

1½ lb. carrots, peeled, halved, and cut into 4- to 5-inch sticks
1   medium fennel bulb, trimmed, cored, quartered, and thinly sliced
2   Tbsp. olive oil
1½ tsp. ground coriander
1   tsp. ground caraway
½   tsp. caraway seeds, toasted*
     Fennel Aïoli (right)

1. Preheat oven to 425°F. Place carrots and fennel in a 15×10-inch baking pan. Drizzle with oil and sprinkle with 1½ tsp. salt, the coriander, ground caraway, and caraway seeds. Toss to combine; spread evenly in pan.
2. Bake 20 minutes or until carrots are crisp-tender and starting to brown, stirring once. To brown the carrots a little more, preheat broiler and broil 4 inches from the heat for 2 minutes. Serve warm or at room temperature with Fennel Aïoli. Serves 6.
*Tip Toast small amounts of seeds in a dry skillet over medium heat 3 to 5 minutes, stirring frequently.
EACH SERVING *95 cal, 5 g fat (1 g sat fat), 672 mg sodium, 13 g carb, 4 g fiber, 6 g sugars, 2 g pro*

FENNEL AÏOLI

Photo on page 172
TOTAL TIME 15 min.

1   egg*
2   tsp. lemon juice
1   tsp. Dijon mustard
1   clove garlic
2   Tbsp. chopped fennel fronds, plus more for garnish
¾   cup safflower oil or olive oil

In a blender or small food processor combine egg, lemon juice, mustard, ¾ tsp. black pepper, ½ tsp. salt, the garlic, and 2 Tbsp. fennel fronds. Blend 20 to 30 seconds or until smooth. With blender running, add oil in a thin stream until the mixture is thick and white, about 1 minute. Season with salt and black pepper to taste. Chill in an airtight container up to 2 days. Makes 1 cup.
*Tip Raw eggs may carry harmful bacteria. If you are pregnant or immunocompromised, substitute eggs pasteurized in the shell.
EACH 1 TBSP. *95 cal, 11 g fat (1 g sat fat), 12 mg chol, 81 mg sodium*

BIG-BATCH ROSEMARY LEMONADE

Photo on page 172

For a boozy version, substitute an equal amount of Amaretto liqueur for the Almond Simple Syrup.

HANDS-ON TIME 15 min.
TOTAL TIME 2 hr. 15 min., includes chilling

In a 1½-qt. pitcher combine 2 cups fresh lemon juice (8 to 10 lemons), 1 cup Almond Simple Syrup or almond beverage syrup (such as Torani), and 4 fresh rosemary sprigs. Cover; chill 2 hours or until ready to serve. Stir in 1 cup club soda and serve in ice-filled glasses. Makes 4 cups.

Almond Simple Syrup In a saucepan heat ¾ cup water and ½ cup sugar over medium-high 5 minutes, stirring until sugar is dissolved. Stir in 1½ tsp. almond extract. Refrigerate in an airtight container up to 1 week.

EACH 1 CUP *134 cal, 15 mg sodium, 34 g carb, 28 g sugars*

PICKLED BEETS

Photo on page 180

HANDS-ON TIME 45 min.
TOTAL TIME 2 hr. 35 min.

- 2½ cups distilled white vinegar
- ½ cup sugar
- 2 Tbsp. kosher salt
- 3 4½-inch strips orange zest
- 2 Tbsp. Szechwan peppercorns
- 10 cups sliced cooked beets*

In a 3-qt. saucepan combine vinegar, 2 cups water, the sugar, salt, and orange zest. Bring to boiling. Boil, uncovered, 1 minute. Reduce heat to low; cover and let steep 10 minutes. Discard orange zest; keep brine hot. Place 1 tsp. Szechwan peppercorns in a hot, clean canning jar. Pack with beets, leaving ½-inch headspace. Pour hot brine over beet slices, maintaining ½-inch headspace. Add lid and screw band. Repeat for a total of six jars. Place jars in a water-bath canner. Process 30 minutes, beginning timing when water returns to a boil. Let jars cool on wire racks at least 4 hours. Makes 6 pints.

*Tip For 10 cups cooked beets, trim and peel 5 lb. beets; place in a 6-qt. pot with enough water to cover. Bring to boiling; reduce heat. Simmer, covered, 1 hour or until tender. Drain, cool, and slice ¼ inch thick.

EACH ¼ CUP *23 cal, 60 mg sodium, 5 g carb, 1 g fiber, 4 g sugars, 1 g pro*

HOW-TO: WATER-BATH CANNING

Preserve your favorite produce for year-round use when you master the basics of water-bath canning (aka boiling-water canning). Here's the process.

STEP ONE To prep jars and lids, wash both in hot, soapy water; rinse well. Fill canner with water; bring to a simmer. Place jars in canner until ready to fill; place lids in a heatproof bowl and cover with hot water to soften the sealant.

STEP TWO Use a jar funnel to fill jars. Run a wooden skewer or knife around the inside edge of jar to release any air bubbles. (Note: Fill only as many jars as will fit in your canner at one time.)

STEP THREE Measure headspace—the unfilled space between top of jar and top of food—according to recipe. Headspace allows food to expand a bit when heated and the vacuum seal to form. Adjust headspace by removing or adding food or brine.

STEP FOUR Wipe jar rims with a damp paper towel. Place lids on jars, then secure by screwing on bands no more than fingertip tight. Transfer to canner. If necessary, add boiling water so water covers jars by at least 1 inch. Start timer when water returns to a boil.

STEP FIVE Let jars cool at least 4 hours. Test seals by pressing on center of each lid. If lid moves or makes a clicking sound, it didn't properly seal. (Refrigerate any unsealed jars up to 1 week.) Store properly sealed canned food in a cool, dry place up to 1 year.

DILL BEANS

CURRIED
CAULIFLOWER

PICKLED
BEETS

HOT
PEPPERS

SMOKY
CARROT
STICKS

DILL BEANS

For the best fit, trim beans to a length even with the bottom of the neck of the jar.

TOTAL TIME 35 min.

2½ cups distilled white vinegar
3 Tbsp. kosher salt
3½ lb. fresh green beans, trimmed and cut into pieces
6 heads fresh dill weed or 6 Tbsp. dillseeds

In a 3-qt. saucepan combine vinegar, 2½ cups water, and salt. Bring to boiling. Boil, uncovered, 1 minute. Cover; keep hot on low. Pack a hot, clean pint canning jar with beans and a dill head, leaving ½-inch headspace (See how-to, page 179.) Pour hot brine over beans, maintaining ½-inch headspace. Add lid and screw band. Repeat for a total of six jars. Place jars in a water-bath canner. Process 5 minutes, beginning timing when water returns to a boil. Let cool on wire racks at least 4 hours. Makes 6 pints.
EACH ⅓ CUP *14 cal, 38 mg sodium, 3 g carb, 1 g fiber, 1 g sugar, 1 g pro*

HOT PEPPERS

HANDS-ON TIME 45 min.
TOTAL TIME 55 min.

6 cups apple cider vinegar
¼ cup sugar
1 Tbsp. kosher salt
1 Tbsp. celery seeds
12 cloves garlic
3 lb. mixed hot peppers, stemmed, seeded (if desired), and sliced

In a 3-qt. saucepan combine vinegar, 2 cups water, the sugar, and the salt. Bring to boiling. Boil, uncovered, 1 minute. Cover; keep hot on low. Place ½ tsp. celery seeds and 2 cloves garlic in a hot, clean pint canning jar. Pack with peppers, leaving ½-inch headspace. (See how-to, page 179) Pour hot brine over peppers, maintaining ½-inch headspace. Add lid and screw band. Repeat for a total of six jars. Place jars in a water-bath canner. Process 10 minutes, beginning timing when water returns to a boil. Let jars cool on wire racks at least 4 hours. Makes 6 pints.
EACH 2 TBSP. *13 cal, 11 mg sodium, 3 g carb, 2 g sugars, 1 g pro*

CURRIED CAULIFLOWER

HANDS-ON TIME 45 min.
TOTAL TIME 55 min.

5 cups distilled white vinegar
2 Tbsp. kosher salt
1 Tbsp. curry powder
½ tsp. ground turmeric
1 Tbsp. cumin seeds
10 cups cauliflower florets (two 2½-lb. heads)
6 serrano peppers, seeded (if desired) and sliced

In a 3-qt. saucepan combine vinegar, 2 cups water, the salt, curry powder, and turmeric. Bring to boiling. Boil, uncovered, 1 minute. Cover; keep hot on low. Add ½ tsp. cumin seeds to a hot, clean pint canning jar. Pack with cauliflower and a pepper, leaving ½-inch headspace. (See how-to, page 179.) Pour hot brine over cauliflower, maintaining ½-inch headspace. Add lid and screw band. Repeat for a total of six jars. Place jars in a water-bath canner. Process 10 minutes, beginning timing when water returns to a boil. Let jars cool on wire racks at least 4 hours. Makes 6 pints.
EACH ⅓ CUP *9 cal, 32 mg sodium, 1 g carb, 1 g fiber, 1 g sugars, 1 g pro*

SMOKY CARROT STICKS

HANDS-ON TIME 30 min.
TOTAL TIME 45 min.

4 cups distilled white vinegar
¼ cup sugar
2 Tbsp. kosher salt
1½ Tbsp. smoked paprika
6 4-inch sprigs fresh thyme
4 lb. carrots, cut into sticks

In a 3-qt. saucepan combine vinegar, 2 cups water, the sugar, salt, and paprika. Bring to boiling. Boil, uncovered, 1 minute. Cover; keep hot on low. Pack a hot, clean pint canning jar with 1 thyme sprig and carrots, leaving ½-inch headspace. (See how-to, page 179.) Pour hot brine over carrots, maintaining ½-inch headspace. Add lid and screw band. Repeat for a total of six jars. Place jars in a water-bath canner. Process 15 minutes, beginning timing when water returns to a boil. Let jars cool on wire racks at least 4 hours. Makes 6 pints.
EACH ⅓ CUP *23 cal, 58 mg sodium, 5 g carb, 1 g fiber, 3 g sugars*

TIME TO BRINE

Jars of preserved produce capture the essence of sun-soaked summer days. Kaleb's shares tips to turn the process into a family get-together.

THINK AHEAD "Gather your recipes, ingredients, and equipment in advance," Kaleb says. "Pickling is time-sensitive, so avoid hitting the pause button midpickling while you run to the store for a last-minute ingredient."

KEEP IT FRESH If you don't have a garden, shop your farmers market or farm stand for the freshest veggies you can find. "If you use produce that's been sitting around, your pickles won't have the same great crunch," Kaleb says.

RECRUIT THE KIDS "Small hands are an asset when you're putting food in jars," Kaleb says. If little ones aren't up for assembly-line work, get them involved decorating labels.

MAKE IT QUICK (PICKLE)

To skip the canning step and quick-pickle instead, halve the recipe, blanch the veggies (excluding cucumbers) 2 minutes, and store in brine-filled jars in the refrigerator at least 24 hours and up to 2 weeks.

**APPLE-CRANBERRY
BRAID**
Recipe on page 193

september

Zoë François shares bread-baking with a no-knead yeast dough.
Learn how to cook—and bake—with versatile cast iron.
Plus, fresh weeknight recipes your family will love.

187   188   205

MORNING GREENS

A salad for breakfast may seem like a stretch, but if you're the pizza-for-breakfast type (or someone who likes to get your greens in early), this bright, herbal salad deserves a spot on your morning menu.

BREAKFAST SALAD WITH AVOCADO & EGGS

For an extra boost of protein, top salad with crumbled bacon or crisped prosciutto.

TOTAL TIME 25 min.

- ½ cup packed flat-leaf parsley
- ½ cup packed fresh basil and/or dill
- 1 clove garlic, halved
- 1 lemon (½ tsp. zest, 2 Tbsp. juice)
- 1 small avocado, halved
- 2 Tbsp. olive oil
- 1 large carrot
- 2 heads butterhead lettuce, such as Bibb or Boston, torn into pieces (11 cups)
- 1¾ cups thinly sliced radishes
- 1½ tsp. white vinegar
- 6 eggs

1. For dressing: In a food processor pulse parsley, basil, and garlic until finely chopped. Add lemon zest and juice, half the avocado, the olive oil, 2 Tbsp. water, and ¼ tsp. each salt and black pepper. Cover; process until smooth.

2. Coarsely chop remaining avocado half. Using a peeler, shave carrot lengthwise into thin ribbons. In a large bowl toss lettuce, radishes, avocado, and carrot with dressing.

3. In a large skillet bring 6 cups water and the vinegar to boiling; reduce heat to simmering. One at a time, slip eggs into water. Simmer 3 to 5 minutes or until whites are set and yolks begin to thicken. Using a slotted spoon, remove eggs from water. Place eggs on salads. Serves 6.

EACH SERVING *176 cal, 13 g fat (3 g sat fat), 186 mg chol, 195 mg sodium, 8 g carb, 4 g fiber, 3 g sugars, 9 g pro*

BLITZED TOGETHER WITH HERBS, GARLIC, AND LEMON JUICE, AVOCADO GIVES BODY TO A GREEN GODDESS-INSPIRED DRESSING.

FAST & FRESH

Easy, delicious recipes for a better dinner tonight.

KALE-QUINOA BOWLS WITH MISO DRESSING & TUNA

TOTAL TIME 30 min.

⅔ cup quinoa, uncooked, rinsed, and drained
1 cup frozen edamame
¼ cup lemon juice
3 oranges (1 zested and juiced, 2 peeled and sliced)
3 Tbsp. vegetable oil
2 cloves garlic, minced
1 Tbsp. white miso paste
4 4-oz. tuna steaks
5 cups kale, stemmed and chopped
1 medium cucumber, sliced
Sesame seeds, toasted (tip, page 50) (optional)

1. In a small saucepan combine quinoa, 1⅓ cups water, and ½ tsp. salt. Bring to boiling; reduce heat. Simmer, covered, 15 minutes or until liquid is absorbed. Remove from heat. Stir in frozen edamame; let stand 10 minutes.

2. Meanwhile, for dressing: In a small bowl whisk together lemon juice, orange zest and juice, oil, the garlic, miso paste, ½ tsp. salt, and ¼ tsp. black pepper. Place tuna in a shallow dish. Drizzle with 2 Tbsp. dressing. Turn to coat.

3. Grill tuna on a grill or greased grill pan over medium 3 to 4 minutes per side (tuna will still be pink in center). Slice tuna.

4. Place kale in a large bowl; drizzle with 1 Tbsp. dressing. Massage kale 1 minute.

5. Divide quinoa mixture among bowls. Add kale, cucumber, orange slices, and tuna. Drizzle with dressing. If desired, sprinkle with sesame seeds. Serves 4.
EACH SERVING *456 cal, 15 g fat (1 g sat. fat), 44 mg chol, 216 mg sodium, 45 g carb, 10 g fiber, 13 g sugars, 39 g pro*

ROASTED CAULIFLOWER & CHICKPEAS WITH CHIMICHURRI

TOTAL TIME 30 min.

- 1 1½-lb. head cauliflower, trimmed and broken into bite-size florets
- 1 15-oz. can chickpeas, rinsed and drained
- ¼ cup plus 3 Tbsp. olive oil
- ½ tsp. crushed red pepper
- 1 cup packed flat-leaf parsley
- ½ cup packed fresh cilantro
- 1 shallot, coarsely chopped
- 1 lime, zested and juiced
- 4 pita bread, warmed
- 2 green onions, sliced

1. Preheat oven to 450°F. In a 15×10-inch baking pan combine cauliflower, chickpeas, 3 Tbsp. olive oil, ½ tsp. salt, and ¼ tsp. of the crushed red pepper; toss to coat. Spread in pan. Bake 25 minutes or until browned and tender, stirring once.

2. Meanwhile, for chimichurri, in a food processor or blender combine the parsley, cilantro, shallot, ¼ cup olive oil, the lime juice, remaining ¼ tsp. salt, and remaining ¼ tsp. crushed red pepper. Cover and process until finely chopped. Spread 1 Tbsp. on each pita.

3. Top pitas with cauliflower mixture and drizzle each with remaining chimichurri. Top with green onions and lime zest. Serves 4.

EACH SERVING *495 cal, 26 g fat (4 g sat. fat), 921 mg sodium, 55 g carb, 8 g fiber, 6 g sugars, 12 g pro*

VEGGIE FARFALLE WITH MEDITERRANEAN MEATBALLS

TOTAL TIME 30 min.

1 egg, lightly beaten
¼ cup panko
6 Tbsp. drained and chopped oil-packed dried tomatoes
5 Tbsp. grated Parmesan cheese
2 cloves garlic, minced
1 lb. ground chicken
8 oz. green beans, trimmed
8 oz. cremini mushrooms, quartered
4 Tbsp. olive oil
8 oz. dried farfalle pasta

1. Preheat oven to 400°F. Line one 15×10-inch baking pan with parchment paper. In a large bowl combine egg, panko, 4 Tbsp. tomatoes, 3 Tbsp. Parmesan, the garlic, ½ tsp. salt, and ¼ tsp. black pepper. Add chicken and mix well. Shape into 24 meatballs. Place in pan with green beans and mushrooms. Drizzle vegetables with 2 Tbsp. olive oil and season to taste. Bake 15 to 20 minutes or until meatballs are done (165°F) and vegetables are crisp-tender.

2. Meanwhile, cook pasta according to package directions. Drain, reserving ½ cup cooking liquid. Return pasta to pot. Add meatballs, vegetables, remaining Parmesan and tomatoes, 2 Tbsp. oil, and enough cooking liquid to moisten. If desired, lightly drizzle with additional olive oil, additional Parmesan, and/or fresh basil. Serves 4.

EACH SERVING *603 cal, 28 g fat (6 g sat. fat), 149 mg chol, 539 mg sodium, 55 g carb, 4 g fiber, 5 g sugars, 34 g pro*

PURCHASED PESTO WORKS WELL IN THIS RECIPE, BUT IF YOU WANT TO EXPERIMENT WITH MAKING YOUR OWN, TRY OUR SIMPLE RECIPE BELOW.

TOMATO & PROSCIUTTO TARTINES

TOTAL TIME 20 min.

- 1   Tbsp. olive oil
- 1   clove garlic, minced
- 4   ½-inch thick slices French bread
- ¾   cup purchased or homemade pesto
- 2   tomatoes, cored and thinly sliced
- 2   oz. thinly sliced prosciutto
- 4   to 6 oz. fresh mozzarella, thinly sliced
- ⅓   cup arugula

1. Preheat broiler. In a small bowl combine oil and garlic. Brush bread slices with oil mixture; arrange in a single layer on a baking sheet. Broil 4 inches from heat 2 minutes or until toasted, turning once.

2. Spread pesto on bread. Top with tomatoes, prosciutto, and mozzarella; broil 2 to 3 minutes more. If desired, drizzle with additional olive oil. Top with arugula. Serves 4.

EACH SERVING *443 cal, 34 g fat (9 g sat. fat), 38 mg chol, 766 mg sodium, 30 g carb, 3 g fiber, 3 g sugars, 17 g pro.*

Homemade Pesto Use any combination of fresh leafy herbs (such as parsley, cilantro, and basil) and hearty greens (such as kale and mustard greens). In a small food processor combine 3 Tbsp. olive oil, 2 cloves garlic, 1 cup herbs and/or greens, ½ cup toasted nuts (such as walnuts, pecans, pine nuts, and almonds), ⅓ cup grated Parmesan, 1 Tbsp. lemon juice, and ¼ tsp. salt. Process until nearly smooth.

APPLE-CRANBERRY BRAID
Recipe on page 193

1 dough,
4 ARTISANAL BREADS

Minneapolis-based cookbook author and baking instructor Zoë François shares these recipes that start with a simple no-knead yeast dough. The recipe makes enough for multiple loaves and holds up to two weeks, so you can bake when the mood strikes.

NO-KNEAD DOUGH

This dough keeps in the fridge up to 2 weeks. Remove portions to make a boule, a loaf, or rolls.

HANDS-ON TIME 15 min.
TOTAL TIME 2 hr. 15 min., includes rising

3   cups water (105°F to 115°F)
1   Tbsp. instant or active yeast
1   Tbsp. kosher salt
6½ cups unbleached all-purpose flour

1. In a 5-qt. nonreactive container, mix the water, yeast, and salt. Add flour; mix just until incorporated.
2. Cover dough loosely; allow to rise at room temperature about 2 hours.
3. Do not punch dough down. Shape and bake dough the day it's made or refrigerate in a lidded container (not airtight) up to 14 days. (The dough is easier to work with after several hours of refrigeration.) If dough is chilled, let it rest 30 minutes at room temperature before using. Makes 3½ lb.

Boule Remove a 1-lb. portion of dough. Dust dough with flour; shape a smooth ball by gently stretching and rotating dough from top to bottom. (Shaping should take no more than 40 seconds to avoid overworking.) Place dough on a large piece of parchment paper, sprinkle with flour, and cover. Let rest 1 to 1½ hours. Place a 6-qt. Dutch oven on rack in center of oven; preheat to 475°F. Dust dough with flour and use a sharp serrated knife to slash a ½-inch-deep cross in dough. Using parchment as a sling, carefully place dough (on parchment) into Dutch oven. Replace lid; bake 25 minutes or until loaf has risen and crust is golden. Remove lid; bake 10 to 15 minutes more or until crust is deep brown. Remove from Dutch oven; peel off parchment. Let cool. Makes 1 boule (12 slices).

EACH SLICE *78 cal, 83 mg sodium, 16 g carb, 1 g fiber, 2 g pro*
Loaf Remove a 2-lb. portion of dough. Generously grease a 9×5-inch loaf pan. Sprinkle dough with flour, and shape an oval by gently stretching and rotating surface of dough to bottom. (Shaping should take no more than 40 seconds to avoid overworking.) Place dough in pan; loosely cover. Let rest 1 hour 40 minutes. Combine 1 egg with 1 Tbsp. water. Just before baking, brush loaf with egg wash. Bake 50 to 60 minutes at 375°F or until top is a caramel brown. Spread with 2 Tbsp. softened butter as soon as it comes out of the oven. Let cool 5 minutes. Remove from pan; cool. Makes 1 loaf (12 slices).
EACH SLICE *172 cal, 3 g fat (1 g sat fat), 21 mg chol, 188 mg sodium, 31 g carb, 1 g fiber, 5 g pro*
Rolls Grease a 9-inch round cake pan. Remove a 1½-lb. portion of dough. On a floured surface, divide dough into eight pieces. With floured hands, shape into balls the size of small plums. Place in pan; cover loosely. Let rest 40 to 60 minutes. Combine 1 egg with 1 Tbsp. water. Just before baking, brush rolls with egg wash. Bake 25 to 30 minutes at 350°F or until lightly browned. Brush with ¼ cup melted butter. Let cool 10 minutes in pan; remove from pan. Makes 8 rolls.
EACH ROLL *225 cal, 7 g fat (4 g sat fat), 39 mg chol, 242 mg sodium, 35 g carb, 1 g fiber, 6 g pro*

ZOË FRANÇOIS

With eight baking cookbooks, almost 250,000 Instagram followers (@zoebakes), and a forthcoming show on *Magnolia Network*, it's safe to say Zoë knows baking.

"Growing up, I don't think my mom even knew which door was the oven," jokes Zoë. But even Zoë's mom has been able to successfully bake bread under Zoë's tutelage. "If my mom can bake bread, anyone can."

"CONSIDER THIS DOUGH A GATEWAY TO GEEKY, MORE COMPLEX BREAD-BAKING," ZOË SAYS. HER RECIPE CALLS FOR FOUR INGREDIENTS AND CAN BE SPUN INTO MULTIPLE CREATIONS.

NO-KNEAD BREAD DOUGH

More than a decade after the release of her original cookbook *Artisan Bread in Five Minutes a Day*, Zoë regularly returns to its no-knead bread recipe. "If only people knew how easy bread can be." Two inexpensive tools Zoë recommends:

DANISH WHISK "Someone gave me a Danish whisk on my first book tour, and I've never looked back." Its shape lessens resistance when stirring thick dough.

BENCH SCRAPER Zoë uses a bench scraper to cut and portion bread dough.

1 Stir together flour, salt, and yeast before adding water. Don't worry about combining salt and yeast (a common no-no when making a fermented bread like sourdough). "Salt can slow yeast activity," Zoë says. "But there's enough yeast here to prevent any hindrance."

2 Zoë suggests mixing dough in a 5- or 6-qt. container so the dough has plenty of room to rise. If your kitchen is cooler than 70°F, put the dough in the oven with the light on to create a warm environment for the 2-hour rise. Dough should double (or triple) in size.

3 Most bread doughs require some kneading to help develop the gluten structure. "Because this dough is so wet, the gluten proteins naturally align themselves during the rise, and you can get away without kneading." Don't punch down the dough; you want those big air pockets.

4 Shape and bake the day you mix the dough, or refrigerate the whole thing (approximately 3½ lb.) in a lidded container up to 14 days. "If your dough doesn't have a crazy amount of stretch, shape it and let it rest a bit before you bake."

APPLE-CRANBERRY BRAID

Photo on page 190

A braided loaf is all about striking presentation, even though the method is simple. Zoë breaks the process into steps that are doable by even the most novice baker.

HANDS-ON TIME 15 min.
TOTAL TIME 2 hr. 30 min., includes rise

- ⅓ cup almond paste
- 2 Tbsp. unsalted butter, softened
- 1 Tbsp. all-purpose flour
- 1 egg yolk
- ½ tsp. almond extract
- 1¼ cups fresh or frozen (thawed) cranberries
- ¼ medium orange, unpeeled
- ½ cup sugar
- 1 lb. No-Knead Dough (page 191)
- 1½ to 2 cups thinly sliced apple
- ¼ cup raw sliced almonds
- 1 egg, lightly beaten

1. In a small food processor, process almond paste, butter, flour, egg yolk, ¼ tsp. almond extract, and a pinch salt until smooth. Transfer to a bowl.

2. In the same food processor pulse to finely chop 1 cup cranberries, the orange, and 2 Tbsp. sugar.

3. To assemble braid, sprinkle 2 Tbsp. sugar over a 16×11-inch sheet of parchment paper. Place a 1-lb. portion of dough onto parchment; sprinkle top with 2 Tbsp. sugar and cover with plastic wrap. Roll out dough to a 10×12-inch rectangle.

4. Remove plastic wrap; spread almond paste mixture in a 2-inch-wide strip down center of dough. Top with cranberry mixture. Cover mixture with apple slices, then sprinkle with remaining ¼ cup cranberries.

5. Along each side cut eight evenly spaced horizontal slices toward filling. Starting from top, cross strips over filling. (Strips should cross each other about 1½ inches.) Do not stretch strips or they may break during baking. Folding last two strips under loaf.

6. Place braid on parchment onto a baking sheet; cover loosely. Let rest 45 minutes. (If any liquid leaks from braid, soak it up with a paper towel.) In a small bowl combine sliced almonds, 2 Tbsp. sugar, and ¼ tsp. almond extract.

Gently work mixture together until sugar resembles damp sand.

7. Preheat oven to 375°F. Combine egg with 1 Tbsp. water. Brush braid with egg wash and sprinkle with almond-sugar mixture. Bake 30 to 35 minutes or until golden brown. Makes 1 braid (8 slices).
EACH SLICE *288 cal, 8 g fat (3 g sat fat), 54 mg chol, 155 mg sodium, 47 g carb, 3 g fiber, 20 g sugars, 6 g pro*

Raspberry-Ricotta Prepare as directed, but omit almond paste mixture, cranberry filling, apple, and almond-sugar mixture. For ricotta filling: Mix ⅓ cup ricotta, 2 oz. cream cheese, ¼ tsp. orange zest, and 1 Tbsp. sugar. Spread on dough; spoon ⅓ cup raspberry jam over ricotta. Top with 1 cup fresh raspberries. Braid, brush with egg wash, and sprinkle with sugar; bake. Makes 1 braid.

1 To sweeten and tenderize dough, roll it over a dusting of sugar. If the dough doesn't roll easily, let it rest 20 minutes and try again. Top dough with almond crème and cranberry filling.

2 Place apple slices down the center and sprinkle with fresh or thawed frozen cranberries.

3 Cut strips in the dough on each side of the filling, then gently fold them over the filling as shown. Don't pull strips too thin or they may break as the braid bakes.

4 At the end of the braid, fold the last strips under the loaf and pinch to secure. If strips aren't secure, they may loosen during baking.

CHICKEN, SPINACH & FETA BRAID

Once you've baked a few successful loaves, have fun with different shapes and fillings. "Braids are simple yet look impressive—a good party trick."

HANDS-ON TIME 25 min.
TOTAL TIME 2 hr., includes rising

- 4 Tbsp. olive oil
- 2 garlic cloves, minced
- ¼ cup finely chopped flat-leaf parsley
- 2 Tbsp. thinly sliced green onion
- 8 cups chopped spinach
- 1 lb. No-Knead Dough (page 191)
- 4 oz. shredded chicken
- 3 oz. crumbed feta
- 3 oz. fresh mozzarella, thinly sliced
- 2 Tbsp. basil pesto
- 1 egg, lightly beaten
  Sesame seeds

1. In a large skillet heat 2 Tbsp. oil over medium. Add garlic, parsley, and green onion; sauté 1 minute or until wilted. Add spinach; cook 2 minutes or until wilted and liquid cooks off. Let cool.
2. Dust work surface with flour. Roll out dough to a 10×12-inch rectangle. Transfer to a lightly floured sheet of parchment paper; brush with 2 Tbsp. oil.
3. Place chicken down center of dough. Top with cheeses, pesto, and spinach mixture.
4. Braid following instructions in Step 5 of Apple-Cranberry Braid (page 193).
5. Place braid on parchment paper on a rimmed baking sheet. Let rest 45 minutes.
6. Preheat oven to 400°F. Combine egg with 1 Tbsp. water. Brush braid with egg wash and sprinkle with sesame seeds. Bake 30 to 35 minutes or until golden brown. Makes 1 braid (6 slices).
EACH SLICE *388 cal, 20 g fat (6 g sat fat), 71 mg chol, 483 mg sodium, 35 g carb, 3 g fiber, 17 g pro*

Sausage & Roasted Red Pepper Braid
Prepare as directed, but omit spinach mixture, chicken, feta, mozzarella, and pesto. Layer dough with 3½ oz. sliced fresh mozzarella, 5 oz. cooked Italian sausage, ½ cup roasted red pepper strips, 1 tsp. fresh thyme leaves, and an additional 3½ oz. fresh mozzarella. Drizzle with ¼ cup pasta sauce. Braid, brush with olive oil, sprinkle with sesame seeds, and bake. Makes 1 braid.

"MY GOAL IS TO STRIP AWAY ALL THE INTIMIDATION THAT GOES ALONG WITH BAKING YEAST BREADS," ZOË SAYS. FOR BEGINNER BAKERS, A NO-KNEAD BOULE IS AN EASY START.

BAKE IT OFF

Shape 1- to 2-lb. portions of Zoë's no-knead dough into dinner rolls, a loaf of sandwich bread, or an artisanal boule.

"Once you have this big batch of dough, it no longer feels like you have only one chance to nail it—like it's a precious loaf," Zoë says. "You can really play and experiment."

DINNER ROLLS After baking rolls in a cake pan, "immediately brush tops with a bit of butter to keep the crust soft."

LOAF Shape dough into an oval, and bake in a standard loaf pan. An egg wash results in a dark caramel top.

BOULE The straightforward shaping technique (a gentle stretch and tuck) for this rustic loaf is a good recipe for first-time bread-bakers. Scoring before baking gives dough more room for a final puff of yeast activity in the oven.

MAKE IT SWEET

Most sweet doughs, including brioche and laminated doughs, incorporate sugar and fat (usually egg or butter) for a tender finished product. By comparison, Zoë's dough is considered lean. It has a sturdy structure and the chewy texture you want in a dinner roll, but it's missing the delicate tenderness of pastry dough. Zoë's solution for tenderizing and sweetening her master dough for sweet braids is to roll it out on a surface dusted with sugar.

BREAD BASKET

After shaping the boule, use parchment paper as a sling to lower the dough into a preheated Dutch oven. After baking, use the paper to lift the boule out of the pot.

DINNER ROLLS

LOAF

BOULE

the original nonstick cookware
CAST IRON

Cast-iron cookware has made a resurgence. This versatile kitchen heavyweight can go straight from the stove-top to the oven, turns out beautiful cakes and breads, and performs like a champ on an outdoor campfire or grill, making it the perfect tool for culinary adventures.

EGGS & BACON BUCATINI

HAND-ON TIME 25 min.
TOTAL TIME 25 min.

8 oz. dried bucatini pasta
8 slices bacon, coarsely chopped
2 cloves garlic, minced
¼ tsp. crushed red pepper
7 eggs
½ cup grated or shredded Parmesan cheese
½ tsp. cracked black pepper
¼ cup chopped flat-leaf parsley

1. Preheat oven to 400°F. Cook pasta according to package directions; drain.
2. Meanwhile, in a 10-inch cast-iron skillet cook bacon over medium heat until lightly browned yet still pliable. Transfer to a paper towel-lined plate. Reserve drippings in skillet. Add garlic and crushed red pepper to reserved drippings. Cook, stirring, 1 to 2 minutes or just until garlic is fragrant. Transfer mixture to a large bowl; cool slightly.
3. Whisk one of the eggs, ¼ cup of the cheese, the black pepper, and ¼ tsp. salt into garlic mixture. Add cooked pasta and bacon; toss to coat.
4. Transfer pasta mixture to the cast-iron skillet. Twirl and pull with two forks to create six indentations. Bake 5 minutes. Sprinkle with remaining ¼ cup cheese. Break remaining eggs, one at a time, into a small dish; slide eggs into indentations. Sprinkle eggs with additional black pepper. Bake 10 to 15 minutes or until whites are completely set and yolks have thickened.* Cover; let stand 5 minutes. Sprinkle with parsley. Serves 6.
*Tip If you like soft egg yolks, bake only 10 minutes.
EACH SERVING *394 cal, 18 g fat (7 g sat fat), 248 mg chol, 603 mg sodium, 31 g carb, 1 g fiber, 2 g sugars, 20 g pro*

WHY CHOOSE CAST IRON

DURABILITY Unlike the average three- to five-year lifetime of a nonstick skillet, cast-iron pans are durable and can last indefinitely with proper care. With regular use, cast-iron pans become more seasoned and actually improve with age. Because these pans are cast from a single piece of metal, there are no joints or rivets to wear out.

VERSATILITY Use your cast-iron skillet on any cook surface—gas and electric stove tops, grills, and even open-flame fires. (For glass-top stoves, consult your owner's manual.) These pans can also be used in the oven for baking, as well as under the broiler. The only heat source where cast iron doesn't belong is the microwave.

NATURAL STICK PREVENTION With a good seasoning, cast-iron pans develop a naturally glossy surface that keeps food from sticking. Unlike traditional nonstick cookware coatings, such as Teflon, seasoned cast iron is able to withstand high temperatures and doesn't release harmful chemicals, such as perfluorinated compounds (PFCs).

HEAT RETENTION The density of cast iron is what helps it maintain heat so well. Once it's hot it holds the heat longer and more evenly than other metals, such as aluminum or stainless steel. (The handle gets hot, too, so use an oven mitt.) This quality makes cast iron ideal for searing meats and browning food.

CAST-IRON COOKWARE CAN DO IT ALL: FRY, SEAR, BRAISE, AND EVEN BAKE. LEARN TO TAKE GOOD CARE OF YOUR PAN SO IT WILL LAST FOR GENERATIONS TO COME.

**MUSHROOM & SPINACH
SKILLET PIZZA**
Recipe on page 200

CHILI-RUBBED BONE-IN STRIP STEAKS
Recipe on page 200

MUSHROOM & SPINACH SKILLET PIZZA

Photo on page 198
HANDS-ON TIME 30 min.
TOTAL TIME 55 min.

2   Tbsp. olive oil
6   cups sliced fresh cremini and/or button mushrooms (16 oz.)
¾   cup Alfredo pasta sauce
2   Tbsp. grated Parmesan cheese
¼   tsp. dried Italian seasoning, crushed
1   5- to 6-oz. pkg. fresh baby spinach
2   tsp. water
1   lb. purchased fresh pizza dough
1½   cups shredded mozzarella cheese (6 oz.)

1. Preheat oven to 450°F. In a 12-inch cast-iron skillet heat 1 Tbsp. of the oil over medium-high. Add mushrooms and ¼ tsp. salt; cook 8 to 10 minutes or until golden and most of the liquid is evaporated, stirring occasionally. Remove mushrooms from skillet. Cool skillet slightly; brush with 1 tsp. of the oil.
2. For sauce: In a small bowl combine Alfredo sauce, 1 Tbsp. of the Parmesan cheese, and the Italian seasoning.
3. In a large bowl sprinkle spinach with the water. Cover with a plate and microwave 45 seconds; toss. Microwave, covered, 15 seconds more or just until wilted. Let stand, covered, 2 minutes. Chop spinach and place in a sieve; press out excess liquid.
4. On a lightly floured surface, roll dough into a 14-inch circle. Transfer to prepared skillet; roll down excess dough to form edge of crust. Brush dough with remaining 2 tsp. oil; spread with sauce. Drain any liquid from mushrooms. Top dough with mushrooms and spinach. Sprinkle with mozzarella cheese and remaining 1 Tbsp. Parmesan cheese.
5. Cook pizza over medium-high 3 minutes. Transfer to the oven. Bake 18 to 20 minutes or until crust and cheeses are light brown. Let stand 5 minutes before serving. If desired, sprinkle with crushed red pepper. Makes 6 slices.
EACH SLICE *374 cal, 16 g fat (6 g sat fat), 40 mg chol, 871 mg sodium, 40 g carb, 2 g fiber, 3 g sugars, 15 g pro*

CHILI-RUBBED BONE-IN STRIP STEAKS

Photo on page 199
HANDS-ON TIME 30 min.
TOTAL TIME 55 min.

1   Tbsp. olive oil
1   cup chopped onion
1   lb. fresh tomatillos, husked and coarsely chopped
4   cloves garlic, minced
1   Tbsp. packed brown sugar
2   tsp. chili powder or ground chipotle chile pepper
1   tsp. kosher salt
2   bone-in beef top loin (strip) steaks, cut 1½ inches thick and trimmed
     Nonstick cooking spray
2   medium avocados, halved, seeded, peeled, and chopped
¼   cup chopped fresh cilantro
1   Tbsp. red wine vinegar
1   fresh red jalapeño, sliced (tip, page 28)

1. Preheat oven to 350° F. In a 10-inch cast-iron skillet heat oil over medium. Add onion; cook 5 minutes or until tender, stirring occasionally. Add tomatillos and garlic; cook, covered, 10 minutes, stirring occasionally. Cook, uncovered, 5 minutes more or until slightly thickened. Transfer to a bowl; cool.
2. Meanwhile, in a small bowl combine brown sugar, chili powder, and ½ tsp. of the salt. Rub mixture over steaks.
3. Wipe out skillet and coat with cooking spray; heat over medium-high. Add steaks; cook 10 minutes or until browned on both sides. Bake 20 minutes for medium rare (140°F). Cover; let stand 5 minutes.
4. Stir avocados, cilantro, vinegar, jalapeño pepper, and remaining ½ tsp. salt into tomatillo mixture. Serve with steaks. Serves 6.
EACH SERVING *646 cal, 47 g fat (16 g sat fat), 138 mg chol, 393 mg sodium, 14 g carb, 5 g fiber, 7 g sugars, 41 g pro*

TUNA-TOT CASSEROLE

HANDS-ON TIME 30 min.
TOTAL TIME 1 hr.

2   Tbsp. olive oil
3   cups sliced fresh cremini mushrooms (8 oz.)
3   cups 1-inch pieces fresh green beans
¾   cup finely chopped onion
3   cloves garlic, minced
2   cups half-and-half
2   Tbsp. Worcestershire sauce
1½   tsp. dried thyme, crushed
2   12-oz. cans solid albacore tuna (water pack), well drained
1   cup shredded white cheddar cheese (4 oz.)
½   of a 30-oz. pkg. frozen fried disc-shape potato nuggets
6   Tbsp. sliced green onions

1. Preheat oven to 425°F. In a 12-inch cast-iron skillet heat oil over medium. Add mushrooms, green beans, and onion; cook 7 to 8 minutes or until beans are nearly tender and liquid is evaporated, stirring occasionally. Add garlic; cook and stir 1 minute more.
2. Stir in half-and-half. Boil gently, uncovered, 5 to 10 minutes or until liquid lightly coats vegetables. Stir in Worcestershire sauce and thyme.
3. Stir in tuna; sprinkle with cheese. Top with potato nuggets. Bake 20 to 25 minutes or until potatoes are brown and center is bubbly. Let stand 10 minutes before serving. Sprinkle with green onions. Serves 8.
EACH SERVING *383 cal, 23 g fat (9 g sat fat), 62 mg chol, 698 mg sodium, 22 g carb, 3 g fiber, 6 g sugars, 24 g pro*

TUNA-TOT
CASSEROLE

CINNAMON
STREUSEL
COFFEE CAKE

CINNAMON STREUSEL COFFEE CAKE

HANDS-ON TIME 30 min.
TOTAL TIME 1 hr 30 min., including cooling

- 1¾ cups all-purpose flour
- ¾ cup granulated sugar
- ¾ tsp. baking powder
- ¼ tsp. baking soda
- 5 Tbsp. butter, cut up
- 1 egg, lightly beaten
- ¾ cup buttermilk or sour milk*
- 1 tsp. vanilla
  Streusel
  Powdered Sugar Icing (optional)
  Fresh raspberries (optional)

1. Preheat oven to 350°F. Lightly grease a 9- or 10-inch cast-iron skillet. In a large bowl stir together flour, granulated sugar, baking powder, and baking soda. Using a pastry blender, cut in butter until mixture resembles coarse crumbs. Make a well in center of flour mixture.
2. In a small bowl combine egg, buttermilk, and vanilla. Add egg mixture all at once to flour mixture. Stir just until moistened (batter should be slightly lumpy). Spread half of the batter into prepared skillet. Sprinkle with ¾ cup of the Streusel. Drop remaining batter in small mounds onto layers in skillet; sprinkle with the remaining Streusel.
3. Bake 30 to 40 minutes or until golden and a toothpick comes out clean. Cool in skillet on a wire rack 30 minutes. If desired, drizzle with Powdered Sugar Icing and sprinkle with raspberries. Serve warm. Serves 9.
*Tip For sour milk, combine 1 Tbsp. lemon juice or vinegar and enough milk to equal 1 cup; let stand 10 minutes.
Streusel In a medium bowl stir together ½ cup each packed brown sugar and all-purpose flour and 1 tsp. ground cinnamon. Cut in ¼ cup butter until mixture resembles coarse crumbs.
EACH SERVING *345 cal, 13 g fat (8 g sat fat), 52 mg chol, 218 mg sodium, 54 g carb, 1 g fiber, 30 g sugars, 5 g pro*
Powdered Sugar Icing In a small bowl stir together 1¼ cups powdered sugar, 1 Tbsp. milk, and ½ tsp. vanilla. Stir in additional milk, 1 tsp. at a time, to reach drizzling consistency.

BAKLAVA MONKEY BREAD

BAKLAVA MONKEY BREAD

HANDS-ON TIME 15 min.
TOTAL TIME 1 hr.

- ⅔ cup packed brown sugar
- ⅓ cup honey
- ⅓ cup heavy cream
- 3 Tbsp. butter
- 1 tsp. lemon zest
- ½ cup walnuts, finely chopped
- ½ cup pistachio nuts, finely chopped
- ⅓ cup granulated sugar
- 1 tsp. ground cinnamon
- 3 7.5-oz. cans refrigerated biscuits (30 total), halved crosswise

1. Preheat oven to 350°F. For syrup, in a medium saucepan combine brown sugar, honey, cream, butter, and lemon zest.
Bring to boiling; reduce heat. Simmer, uncovered, 5 minutes or until reduced to 1 cup. Cool slightly.
2. Meanwhile, in a small bowl combine walnuts, pistachios, granulated sugar, and cinnamon.
3. Generously grease a 10-inch cast-iron skillet. Spoon half of the nut mixture into prepared skillet. Top with half of the dough pieces and drizzle with half of the syrup. Repeat layers.
4. Bake 40 minutes or until golden. Let cool on a wire rack 5 minutes; invert onto a platter. Spoon any topping and nuts remaining in pan over bread. Serve warm. Serves 12.
EACH SERVING *424 cal, 18 g fat (8 g sat fat), 15 mg chol, 705 mg sodium, 61 g carb, 3 g fiber, 31 g sugars, 7 g pro*

EVERYDAY USE AND CARE

BARE CAST IRON As soon as your pan is cool enough to handle (but still warm), scrub it with a nylon scrub brush and hot water. If necessary, a plastic pan scraper may also be used. For tough jobs, add water and simmer for about 1 minute, cooling before scraping clean. Dry the pan immediately and thoroughly to keep from rusting, then rub a few drops of vegetable oil on the inside of the skillet. Hang or store in a dry place.

ENAMELED CAST IRON Wash using hot, soapy water and a plastic scrub brush. If light stains or metal scrape marks are present, remove them using cleaning products specially designed for enameled pots and pans. For burnt-on, crusty stains, fill the pan with 2 cups water and add ¼ cup baking soda. Bring to a simmer; use a plastic or wooden cooking utensil to loosen the blackened areas. Rinse with hot water and dry.

BEYOND THE SKILLET

Cast iron is used in the kitchen for more than just skillets. Two favorite options—a loaf pan and a fluted tube pan.

CAST-IRON LOAF PAN
Size: 8×4 inches

CAST-IRON FLUTED TUBE PAN
Size: 13-cup capacity

CARROT CAKE BREAD

HAND-ON TIME 25 min.
TOTAL TIME 2 hr. 20 min., plus standing overnight

- 1½ cups all-purpose flour
- 1 tsp. baking powder
- ½ tsp. ground cinnamon or ¼ tsp. ground ginger
- ¼ tsp. baking soda
- 2 eggs, lightly beaten
- 1½ cups lightly packed finely shredded carrots
- ¾ cup vegetable oil
- ½ cup granulated sugar
- ½ cup packed brown sugar
- 1 tsp. vanilla
- ½ cup chopped candied pecans or toasted pecans
  Cream Cheese Drizzle

1. Preheat oven to 350°F. Grease bottom and ½ inch up sides of an 8×4-inch cast-iron loaf pan. In a large bowl stir together flour, baking powder, ½ tsp. salt, the cinnamon, and baking soda. Make a well in center of flour mixture.

2. In a medium bowl combine eggs, carrots, oil, sugars, and vanilla. Add carrot mixture all at once to flour mixture. Stir just until moistened (batter should be lumpy). Fold in pecans. Spread batter into prepared pan.

3. Bake 55 to 60 minutes or until a toothpick inserted in center comes out clean. Cool in pan on a wire rack 10 minutes. Remove from pan; cool completely on wire rack. Wrap and store overnight before slicing. Before serving, top with Cream Cheese Drizzle and, if desired, additional candied pecans. Makes 12 slices.

Cream Cheese Drizzle In a small bowl combine 1 oz. cream cheese and 1 Tbsp. butter until smooth. Stir in ½ cup powdered sugar and enough milk (about 1 Tbsp.) to reach drizzling consistency.

EACH SLICE *322 cal, 18 g fat (3 g sat fat), 36 mg chol, 207 mg sodium, 38 g carb, 1 g fiber, 24 g sugars, 3 g pro*

MEYER LEMON-POPPY SEED CAKE

A cross between a mandarin orange and a regular lemon, Meyer Lemons are smaller, sweeter, and less acidic than regular lemons. They have smooth skin and dark yellow pulp.

HANDS-ON TIME 20 min.
TOTAL TIME 3 hr. 10 min., including cooling

2   to 3 Meyer lemons or lemons
    (1 Tbsp. zest; 3 Tbsp. juice)
3   eggs
1½ cups milk
1   cup butter, melted and cooled
1   Tbsp. poppy seeds
3   cups all-purpose flour
2   cups granulated sugar
1½ tsp. baking powder
1   tsp. salt
¼   tsp. baking soda
    Meyer Lemon Glaze

1. Preheat oven to 350°F. Grease and flour a 10-inch cast-iron fluted tube pan. In a large bowl whisk together eggs, milk, melted butter, poppy seeds, and lemon zest and juice. Whisk in flour, sugar, baking powder, 1 tsp. salt, and the ¼ tsp. baking soda until smooth. Spread batter into prepared pan.

2. Bake 50 minutes or until golden and a toothpick comes out clean. Cool cake in pan on a wire rack 10 minutes. Remove from pan; cool completely on wire rack. Drizzle with Meyer Lemon Glaze. Makes 16 slices.

Meyer Lemon Glaze In a small bowl stir together 1 cup powdered sugar and enough Meyer lemon or lemon juice (1½ to 2 Tbsp.) to reach drizzling consistency.

EACH SLICE *343 cal., 13 g fat (8 g sat. fat), 67 mg chol., 327 mg sodium, 52 g carb., 1 g fiber, 34 g sugars, 5 g pro*

BEET & ONION JAM
GALETTE
Recipe on page 220

october

Cool weather brings warming stews and seasonal recipes for earthy beets, winter squash, and sweet apples. A velvety fondue and festive cheese ball suggest entertaining.

209   214   224

CIDER-CHEESE
FONDUE

gatherings
BOARD GAME

Give the cheese board routine a fall spin with luscious three-cheese fondue, served with a spread of hearty dippers. Plus, stir up pumpkin, sage, and cheddar cheese to shape into a pumpkin.

CIDER-CHEESE FONDUE

Choose creative dippers for this fondue: sturdy fruits, such as apple and pear wedges or whole grapes pierced on forks. The cheese drapes deliciously over cubes of firm, full-flavor breads, such as pumpernickel, rustic sourdough, or whole grain. Also consider bite-size sausage chunks, chewy soft pretzels, and crisp-tender cooked broccoli, cauliflower florets, or small carrots.

TOTAL TIME 30 min.

1   clove garlic, halved
1½ cups apple cider or 12 oz. dry hard cider
2   tsp. hot pepper sauce
8   oz. Swiss cheese, shredded (2 cups)
8   oz. Gruyère cheese, shredded (2 cups)
8   oz. sharp cheddar cheese, shredded (2 cups)
2   Tbsp. cornstarch
     Assorted dippers

1. Rub garlic on bottom and sides of a heavy 4- to 5-qt. pot; discard garlic.
2. Add cider and hot pepper sauce to pot; bring to a simmer over medium. In a large bowl toss cheeses with cornstarch. Add a small handful at a time to cider, whisking constantly until melted before adding more.
3. Transfer to a fondue pot and serve with dippers. Serves 8.
EACH SERVING FONDUE *371 cal, 27 g fat (16 g sat fat), 86 mg chol, 458 mg sodium, 6 g carb, 1 g sugars, 23 g pro*

PUMPKIN CHEESE BALL

HANDS-ON TIME 15 min.
TOTAL TIME 4 hr. 15 min., includes chilling

2   8-oz. pkg. cream cheese, softened
2   cups finely shredded extra-sharp cheddar cheese
¾   cup canned pumpkin
¼   cup butter, softened
2   Tbsp. minced fresh sage
½   tsp. smoked paprika
¼   tsp. garlic powder
     Assorted crackers

1. In a large bowl combine cream cheese, 1¼ cups cheddar cheese, the pumpkin, butter, sage, paprika, garlic powder, and ¼ tsp. each salt and black pepper. Beat with a mixer on medium until fluffy. Chill, covered, 4 to 24 hours.
2. Wrap in plastic wrap and shape into a ball. Unwrap; roll ball in remaining ¾ cup cheddar cheese. Serve with crackers. (To shape a pumpkin, after rolling in remaining cheese, wrap in plastic wrap. Place a few rubber bands vertically around cheese ball to form ridges. Chill 30 minutes. Add a diagonally cut green bean and sage leaves to top.) Serves 24.
EACH SERVING *123 cal, 11 g fat (7 g sat fat), 34 mg chol, 159 mg sodium, 2 g carb, 1 g sugars, 4 g pro*

PUMPKIN CHEESE BALL

SHAPE A CHEESE BALL AS AN EDIBLE CENTERPIECE—THIS ONE IS A CHUBBY, FLAVORFUL PUMPKIN.

FAST & FRESH

Easy, delicious recipes for a better dinner tonight.

BUTTERNUT SQUASH & FETTUCCINE ALFREDO

Spiralize a 1- to 1½-lb. butternut squash for 5 cups of fresh noodles.

HANDS-ON TIME 10 min.
TOTAL TIME 25 min.

1   9-oz. pkg. refrigerated fettuccine
5   cups butternut squash spirals or two 12-oz. pkg. frozen butternut squash spirals
1   Tbsp. olive oil
1   cup chopped onion
1   13.5-oz. link smoked sausage, sliced
1   cup whipping cream
2   Tbsp. chopped fresh sage
¼   cup finely shredded Parmesan cheese
½   tsp. kosher salt

1. In a large pot cook pasta and squash in lightly salted boiling water 3 to 5 minutes or until tender. Drain; return to pot.

2. In a large skillet heat oil over medium-high. Add onion; cook and stir 3 minutes. Add sausage; cook and stir 2 to 3 minutes or until browned. Stir in cream; bring to boiling. Boil gently, uncovered, 1 minute. Add sage, cheese, salt, and ½ tsp. black pepper; stir to combine. Add to pasta and squash in pot; toss to coat. Serves 6.

EACH SERVING *529 cal, 37 g fat (17 g sat fat), 120 mg chol, 735 mg sodium, 33 g carb, 3 g fiber, 5 g sugars, 17 g pro*

CHICKEN-LENTIL TACOS

Adobo, the smoky, slightly sweet sauce chipotles are canned in, adds oomph to a finishing drizzle of sour cream.

TOTAL TIME 30 min.

- 1   cup sliced red onion
- 3   Tbsp. lime juice
- 1   tsp. kosher salt
- 1   8-oz. skinless, boneless chicken breast
- 1   tsp. chili powder
- ½   tsp. cumin
- 1   Tbsp. vegetable oil
- ½   cup reduced-sodium chicken broth
- 2   cups cooked brown lentils*
- 1   chipotle pepper in adobo, finely chopped, plus 1½ Tbsp. sauce
- ¼   cup sour cream
- 8   6-inch corn tortillas
- ¼   cup chopped flat-leaf parsley

1. For pickled onions: In a small bowl stir together onion, 2 Tbsp. lime juice, and ½ tsp. salt. Let stand 15 minutes.
2. Meanwhile, season chicken with remaining ½ tsp. salt, the chili powder, and cumin. In a 10-inch skillet heat oil over medium-high. Add chicken to skillet; cook 12 minutes or until done (165°F), turning occasionally. Remove and slice chicken. Add broth to skillet, stirring to scrape up browned bits. Stir in lentils, chipotle, and 1 Tbsp. adobo sauce. Bring to boiling; reduce heat. Simmer, uncovered, 3 to 5 minutes or until thickened. Carefully stir in chicken; heat through.
3. In a small bowl stir together sour cream, remaining 1 Tbsp. lime juice, and remaining ½ Tbsp. adobo sauce. Warm the tortillas and top with chicken mixture, pickled onions, and parsley. Drizzle with spiced sour cream. Serves 4.
*Tip For 2 cups cooked lentils: In a saucepan combine 2 cups water, ⅔ cup dried brown lentils, and ¼ tsp. salt. Bring to boiling. Reduce heat; simmer, covered, 20 to 25 minutes. Or use one 9-oz. pkg. steamed lentils.

EACH SERVING *325 cal, 9 g fat (2 g sat fat), 48 mg chol, 463 mg sodium, 40 g carb, 9 g fiber, 4 g sugars, 23 g pro*

SHORTCUT PHO

Fish sauce has a distinctive umami-rich profile with a hint of sweetness. It's an integral ingredient in pho, but feel free to adjust the amount to your liking.

TOTAL TIME 30 min.

1   lime, halved
4   cups 50%-less-sodium beef broth
1   Tbsp. fish sauce
⅛   tsp. ground cinnamon
⅛   tsp. ground coriander
1   dash ground cloves
12 oz. beef sirloin steak, very thinly sliced
8   oz. rice noodles, cooked
¼   cup fresh cilantro
¼   cup fresh mint leaves
1   bunch green onions, bias-sliced into 1-inch pieces
    Lime wedges

1. Juice half the lime; cut remaining half into wedges. In a 4-qt. pot combine lime juice, broth, fish sauce, cinnamon, coriander, and cloves. Bring to boiling; reduce heat. Simmer, uncovered, 15 minutes.
2. Drop beef into simmering broth. Cook 20 to 30 seconds or until cooked through.
3. Divide noodles among bowls. Spoon broth and beef over noodles. Top bowls with cilantro, mint, and green onions. Serve with lime wedges. Serves 4.
EACH SERVING *322 cal, 4 g fat (1 g sat fat), 46 mg chol, 991 mg sodium, 49 g carb, 2 g fiber, 1 g sugars, 21 g pro*

FOR A KICK, FINISH WITH SRIRACHA, CHILE SLICES, AND/OR CHILI OIL.

APPLE DUTCH BABY

Also known as a puffed or German pancake, a Dutch baby puffs in the oven then sinks as it cools, creating a crater for beautiful caramelized fruit.

DUTCH BABY WITH CARAMELIZED APPLES

This skillet pancake has a lightly crisped exterior and a custardlike texture.

HANDS-ON TIME 20 min.
TOTAL TIME 35 min.

3	eggs, lightly beaten
½	cup milk
½	cup all-purpose flour
1	Tbsp. granulated sugar
½	tsp. vanilla
¼	tsp. cinnamon
3	Tbsp. butter
1⅓	cups thinly sliced apple (any type)
2	Tbsp. brown sugar
2	Tbsp. maple syrup
	Powdered sugar (optional)

1. Preheat oven to 425°F. For batter: In a medium bowl combine eggs and milk. Whisk in flour, granulated sugar, vanilla, cinnamon, and ¼ tsp. salt.
2. In a 9- or 10-inch oven-going skillet melt 1½ Tbsp. butter over medium. Pour batter into skillet. Bake 15 minutes or until light brown and puffed.
3. Meanwhile, in a medium saucepan melt remaining 1½ Tbsp. butter over medium-high. Add apple slices; cook, stirring, 5 minutes or until crisp-tender and browning on edges. Stir in brown sugar and syrup; cook 2 to 3 minutes more or until tender. Serve Dutch baby with caramelized apples and, if desired, dust with powdered sugar. Serves 4.
EACH SERVING *287 cal, 13 g fat (7 g sat fat), 165 mg chol, 285 mg sodium, 35 g carb, 1 g fiber, 21 g sugars, 8 g pro*

WE DIG BEETS

Fans of the humble root consider beets "dirt candy." If you're on the fence, our recipes will leave you totally in love with this vibrant vegetable.

BEET SAMPLER PLATTER

Mighty when it comes to nutrients, beets are a good source of vitamin C, magnesium, and folate. They're also rich in nitrates that may help reduce blood pressure and improve exercise endurance.

TOUCHSTONE GOLD Extra sweet and less earthy than reds. It retains bright color after cooking.

RED ACE The diva of the red varieties, it has the deepest-color flesh and grows quicker than others.

AVALANCHE The creamy white beet is an award winner for its aromatic flavor, free of earthy notes.

BADGER FLAME The color of a dancing flame, this stunner has the best raw flavor. Shave it into ribbons for a salad.

CHIOGGIA Also known as candy cane beet, it is less likely to stain hands and surfaces than full red beets.

MARINATED BEET NOODLE SALAD

Marinate raw beet noodles in lemon juice and olive oil, then pile onto a swoosh of whipped yogurt and tahini. If you don't have a spiralizer, cut beets into matchsticks or thin strips.

TOTAL TIME 30 min.

2   small or 1 large Fresno pepper, finely chopped (tip, page 28)
1   medium shallot, finely chopped
2   Tbsp. olive oil
2   Tbsp. fresh lemon juice
4   medium or 2 large red and/or golden beets, spiralized and cut into 2- to 3-inch lengths (3 cups)
⅓   cup plain yogurt
¼   cup tahini
1   Tbsp. lemon juice
⅓   cup goat cheese or feta cheese, crumbled (optional)
½   cup pomegranate arils
⅓   cup chopped pistachios
⅓   cup chopped fresh mint
¼   cup chopped flat-leaf parsley

1. For marinade: In a large bowl combine pepper, shallot, oil, lemon juice, and ½ tsp. salt. (If using different color beets, divide marinade among bowls for one each color.) Add beets to marinade; stir to coat. Let stand at least 10 minutes, stirring occasionally.
2. Meanwhile, in a blender or mini food processor combine yogurt, tahini, and lemon juice. Cover; blend until fluffy.
3. To serve, spread yogurt mixture on a large platter using the back of a spoon to create a swoosh. Lift beets out of marinade, allowing excess to drip back into bowl. Place beets on yogurt swooshes. Sprinkle with cheese (if using),

pomegranate arils, pistachios, mint, and parsley. Drizzle with any beet marinade in the bowl. Serves 4.
EACH SERVING *335 cal, 23 g fat (5 g sat fat), 10 mg chol, 439 mg sodium, 25 g carb, 7 g fiber, 13 g sugars, 11 g pro*

"HEARTBEET" COOLER

Photo on page 217

If you're down to one red beet in your crisper drawer, here's a refreshing way to use it. Blend it with fresh ginger and lime juice into a batch of vibrant, antioxidant-rich drinks. You can freeze the beet-lime-ginger puree in ice cube trays up to 3 months.

TOTAL TIME 15 min.

1   medium red beet, scrubbed and cubed (1 cup)
1   1-inch piece fresh ginger, peeled and cut up
¾   cup fresh lime juice (about 6 limes)
1   32-oz. bottle Fuji apple juice or other unfiltered, unsweetened apple juice
    Lime slices
    Thinly sliced Chioggia beet (optional)

1. In a blender combine red beet, ginger, and lime juice. Cover and blend until smooth, adding a little water, if necessary. Pour through a fine-mesh sieve (you should have about 1 cup juice). Discard pulp.
2. In a large pitcher stir together beet mixture and apple juice. Serve over ice with lime slices and, if desired, beet slices. Serves 6.
EACH SERVING *85 cal, 14 mg sodium, 22 g carb, 1 g fiber, 16 g sugars, 1 g pro*

MARINATED BEET
NOODLE SALAD

**ROASTED BEET-CITRUS
SORGHUM BOWLS**
Recipe on page 219

"HEARTBEET" COOLER
Recipe on page 214

ROASTED BEET
CHIPS

TOASTING PAPER-THIN SLICES OF BEETS CONCENTRATES THE FLAVOR. WE CUSTOMIZED THIS SNACK BY COMBINING RED AND GOLD VARIETIES WITH SPICES THAT ENHANCE THEIR NATURAL FLAVOR.

ROASTED BEET-CITRUS SORGHUM BOWLS

Photo on page 216

Gluten-free sorghum anchors this dish. Cooked farro, quinoa, wheat berries, or brown rice would also be delicious.

HANDS-ON TIME 25 min.
TOTAL TIME 1 hr. 25 min.

5   to 6 small beets, any variety (1 lb. total)
3   Tbsp. olive oil
2   cloves garlic, smashed
1   fresh thyme sprig
1   cup uncooked whole grain sorghum
1   15-oz. can chickpeas, rinsed and drained
1   lemon, zest and juice removed
1   orange
¼   cup mayonnaise
¼   cup sour cream
3   oz. feta cheese, crumbled
2   cups baby arugula
1¼ cups halved and sliced English cucumber
1   avocado, halved, pitted, peeled, and quartered

1. Preheat oven to 375°F. Place beets in a 3-qt. rectangular baking dish. Drizzle with 1 Tbsp. oil and sprinkle with salt. Add 2 Tbsp. water, the garlic, and thyme sprig. Bake, covered, 45 to 50 minutes or until beets can be pierced easily with a paring knife; let cool. Using a paper towel, rub skins off beets. Cut beets into wedges. Toss with 1 Tbsp. oil, ¼ tsp. salt, and ⅛ tsp. ground black pepper.
2. Meanwhile, in a large saucepan with a tight-fitting lid combine 2 qt. water, the sorghum, and ½ tsp. salt. Bring to boiling; reduce heat. Simmer, covered, 50 to 60 minutes or until tender. Drain off any remaining liquid; let cool slightly.
3. While beets and sorghum cook, in a medium bowl combine chickpeas with remaining 1 Tbsp. olive oil and a pinch of salt. Add the lemon zest and juice. Zest the orange, then add zest to chickpeas. Peel then section orange over the bowl to catch any juice.
4. For dressing: In a blender or small food processor combine mayonnaise, sour cream, and feta; blend until smooth.
5. Divide sorghum among four bowls; top with roasted beets, orange sections, chickpeas, arugula, cucumber, and avocado. Drizzle any remaining citrus juices over each bowl. Top with dressing. Serves 4.
EACH SERVING *616 cal, 36 g fat (8 g sat fat), 32 mg chol, 1,102 mg sodium, 66 g carb, 13 g fiber, 13 g sugars, 15 g pro*

ROASTED BEET CHIPS

Red beets like five-spice powder, steak seasoning, or caraway. Golden beets love curry powder, sesame seeds, or chipotle pepper.

HANDS-ON TIME 15 min.
TOTAL TIME 1 hr. 5 min.

3   medium red, golden, and/or white beets (1 lb. total), trimmed and, if desired, peeled
1   Tbsp. vegetable oil
1   tsp. desired seasoning*

1. Preheat oven to 300°F. Line two large baking sheets with parchment paper. Use a mandoline to slice beets ¹⁄₁₆ inch thick. Layer slices between paper towels; press firmly to remove excess liquid. Toss beets with oil, desired seasoning, and ½ tsp. salt. (Separate different color beets in bowls.)
2. Arrange beet slices in a single layer on prepared baking sheets. Bake about 50 minutes, removing chips as they crisp. Let cool on paper towels. Serves 8.
Air Fryer Halve the recipe or fry half at a time. Preheat air fryer to 325°F. Coat air fryer basket with nonstick cooking spray. For each batch, arrange a layer of beets in basket, slightly overlapping. Cook 20 minutes or until crisp. Transfer chips to paper towels to cool.
*Tip Beet flavor varies by variety. Dark beets have the strong flavor. For red beets, use steak seasoning, five-spice powder, or caraway seeds. For golden beets, use curry powder, sesame seeds, or ½ tsp. ground chipotle chile pepper. For white beets, use za'atar, herbes de Provence, or Italian seasoning.
EACH SERVING *31 cal, 2 g fat (0 g sat fat), 175 mg sodium, 4 g carb, 1 g fiber, 3 g sugars, 1 g pro*

YOU CAN'T BEAT A GALETTE FOR EASY ELEGANCE. THIS ONE FEATURES A WALNUT PASTRY CRUST AND STEP-SAVING INGREDIENTS—PURCHASED ONION JAM AND GARLICKY CHEESE SPREAD.

BEET & ONION JAM GALETTE

The French term galette refers to a rustic free-form tart from a single crust of pastry or dough. Italian cooks use the term crostada. Whatever you call it, a galette doesn't require a special pan, and it is filled with a simple sweet or savory filling.

HANDS-ON TIME 25 min.
TOTAL TIME 1 hr. 40 min.

- ½ cup walnut pieces
- 1½ cups all-purpose flour
- ½ cup cold unsalted butter, cut into pieces (1 stick)
- 2 Tbsp. sour cream
- 1 to 2 Tbsp. ice water
- ½ cup plus 1 Tbsp. onion jam or fig jam
- 1 5.3-oz. pkg. semisoft cheese with garlic and fine herbs (such as Boursin)
- 1 Tbsp. chopped fresh thyme
- 1 lb. red beets, trimmed, halved if large, peeled, and sliced ⅛ inch thick
- 1 Tbsp. olive oil
  Chopped walnuts, toasted (tip, page 50)

1. In a food processor pulse walnut pieces until very finely chopped. Add flour and ½ tsp. salt; pulse to combine. Add butter; pulse until mixture resembles coarse bread crumbs. Add sour cream and 1 Tbsp. ice water; pulse until the mixture begins to come together, adding an additional 1 Tbsp. ice water if needed. Remove to a bowl. Knead dough gently until it comes together. Wrap pastry in plastic wrap, flattening into a disk. Chill 30 minutes.

2. Preheat oven to 375°F. Line a baking sheet with parchment paper.

3. On a lightly floured surface, roll out pastry to a 12-inch round. Transfer to prepared baking sheet. Spread ½ cup onion jam over pastry, leaving a 2-inch-wide border. Spoon small mounds of cheese over jam. Sprinkle with thyme. Layer the beets on top, overlapping as necessary. Fold pastry edge over beets, pleating as necessary. Drizzle beets and pastry with oil and sprinkle with salt and black pepper.

4. Place a foil-lined shallow baking sheet on oven rack below galette. Bake 45 to 50 minutes or until pastry is golden brown, juices are bubbling, and beets are tender. Brush with remaining 1 Tbsp. jam while warm. Let cool on baking sheet on a wire rack 30 minutes. Top with toasted walnuts and additional fresh thyme. Serves 8.

EACH SERVING *423 cal, 28 g fat (14 g sat fat), 52 mg chol, 300 mg sodium, 38 g carb, 3 g fiber, 13 g sugars, 6 g pro*

STEW SEASON

Cool weather invites warm-up recipes, like these hearty stews of seasonal vegetables, toothsome grains, and comforting flavor combinations. All are easy to tailor to your family's liking.

OVEN BEEF & BARLEY STEW

This only looks like a traditional beef stew recipe. While the beef braises in the oven, carrots, mushrooms, and onions roast on a sheet pan alongside for caramelized flavor.

HANDS-ON TIME 20 min.
TOTAL TIME 2 hr.

- 3 Tbsp. olive oil
- 2 to 2½ lb. beef or lamb stew meat
- 2 strips bacon, coarsely chopped
- 3 cloves garlic, thinly sliced
- 3 Tbsp. tomato paste
- 1 cup dry red wine or 50%-less-sodium beef broth
- 1 32-oz. box 50%-less-sodium beef broth
- 1 to 2 Tbsp. fresh thyme or rosemary, chopped
- ¾ tsp. kosher salt
- ¼ cup all-purpose flour
- ½ cup regular barley, farro, or brown rice*
- 4 carrots or parsnips, peeled and cut into 1- to 2-inch pieces, or 2 cups baby carrots
- 2 cups sliced cremini or button mushrooms
- 1 medium onion, cut into thin wedges
- 1 cup frozen peas
- 2 croissants, cut into 1½-inch chunks
- 2 Tbsp. butter, melted
- 2 cloves garlic, minced
- 1 Tbsp. finely chopped flat-leaf parsley

1. Arrange oven racks with one at the lowest level. Preheat oven to 325°F.
2. In a 5- to 6-qt. Dutch oven heat 1 Tbsp. olive oil over medium-high. Add half the beef and bacon; cook until browned, stirring occasionally. Using a slotted spoon, transfer meat to a bowl. Add an additional 1 Tbsp. olive oil, remaining beef and bacon, and the sliced garlic to Dutch oven. Cook 3 minutes, stirring occasionally. Return all meat to Dutch oven. Stir in tomato paste; cook and stir 2 minutes.
3. Carefully add wine, stirring to scrape up any browned bits from bottom of pot. Reserve ½ cup of the broth. Add remaining broth to meat mixture. Stir in thyme, and ½ tsp. each salt and pepper. Bring to boiling. Cover and place pot on the lower oven rack; braise 1 hour.
4. In a small bowl whisk together reserved ½ cup broth and the flour; stir into beef mixture. Stir in barley. Bake, covered, 35 minutes or until barley is tender and stew is thickened.
5. Meanwhile, in a shallow baking pan combine carrots, mushrooms, onion, remaining 1 Tbsp. olive oil, and ¼ tsp. each salt and black pepper; toss to coat. Place on a separate oven rack; roast, uncovered, 45 minutes, stirring once.
6. Stir vegetables and peas into stew; let stand, covered, 5 minutes. Increase oven temperature to 425°F.
7. For croutons: Line a shallow baking pan with foil. In a large bowl combine croissant chunks, melted butter, minced garlic, and parsley; toss to combine. Spread croissants in a single layer in the prepared pan. Bake 5 minutes or until toasted; let cool. Serve croutons on stew. Serves 6.

*Tip If you use brown rice, increase baking time in Step 4 to 45 minutes.
EACH SERVING *598 cal, 31 g fat (13 g sat fat), 119 mg chol, 971 mg sodium, 39 g carb, 7 g fiber, 8 g sugars, 36 g pro*

THIS ONE-POT WONDER TAKES ITS CUE FROM A NORTH AFRICAN TAGINE, A SPICED STEW COOKED IN A POT OF THE SAME NAME, WHICH SEALS IN STEAM AS THE MIXTURE SIMMERS.

STEW SWAPS: MEAT

Easily adapt these stew recipes to satisfy your family's preferences or to use what you have on hand. A few tips:

PORK SHOULDER Sub beef or lamb stew meat or cut-up beef chuck roast

CHICKEN Thighs and whole meaty chicken pieces result in the best flavor. To substitute breasts for thighs, use the following timings:

- bone-in breast half—35 minutes
- boneless half—15 minutes;
- cut-up breast pieces—8 to 10 minutes.

STEW SWAPS: VEGETABLES

Substitute veggies of similar textures so cooking time stays the same.

RUSSET POTATOES Sub any variety of potato or winter squash, peeled and cut up

CARROTS Sub parsnips, turnips, celery, green beans, or cored and chopped fennel

PEAS Sub corn, any type cooked dried beans (black-eyed, pinto, black), chickpeas

BELL PEPPERS Sub poblano

CAULIFLOWER Sub broccoli, summer squash, zucchini

ONIONS Sub leeks

MOROCCAN CHICKEN & CAULIFLOWER STEW

Cooked in a Dutch oven, the warming mix of spices (cumin, ginger, and cinnamon) is faithful to tagine steaming.

HANDS-ON TIME 20 min.
TOTAL TIME 1 hr. 40 min.

1	tsp. ground cumin
1	tsp. ground ginger
½	tsp. ground cinnamon
¼	tsp. cayenne or ½ tsp. crushed red pepper
½	tsp. kosher salt
2	lb. chicken thighs and/or drumsticks, skinned, if desired
1	Tbsp. coconut oil or olive oil
3	cloves garlic, minced
1	28-oz. can crushed tomatoes
1½	cups reduced-sodium chicken broth
2	cups small cauliflower florets and/or halved green beans
1	15-oz. can chickpeas, rinsed and drained
¼	cup coarsely chopped dried apricots
¼	cup coarsely chopped pitted green olives
3	cups hot cooked couscous or rice (optional)
	Chopped flat-leaf parsley and/or toasted slivered almonds (tip, page 50) (optional)

1. In a small bowl combine cumin, ginger, cinnamon, cayenne, and ½ tsp. salt. Rub chicken with half the spice mixture.
2. In a 4- to 6-qt. Dutch oven heat coconut oil over medium. Cook chicken 6 to 8 minutes or until browned, turning once. (Cook in batches if necessary to prevent crowding.) Add garlic around chicken; cook 1 minute more. Add remaining spice mixture, the crushed tomatoes, and broth. Bring to boiling; reduce heat. Simmer, covered, 45 minutes. Add cauliflower, chickpeas, apricots, and olives. Return to boiling; reduce heat. Simmer, covered, 25 minutes. Uncover; cook 10 minutes more or until chicken is tender, stirring occasionally. Remove and shred chicken, discarding skin and bones. Stir shredded chicken into stew. If desired, serve over couscous and top with parsley and/or almonds. Serves 4.

EACH SERVING *418 cal, 11 g fat (4 g sat fat), 90 mg chol, 1,317 mg sodium, 48 g carb, 11 g fiber, 19 g sugars, 34 g pro*

MOROCCAN CHICKEN
& CAULIFLOWER STEW

CORN & POTATO STEW
WITH CORNMEAL
DUMPLINGS

CORN & POTATO STEW WITH CORNMEAL DUMPLINGS

Coconut milk and pureed corn give this vegetarian stew serious body—and subtle sweetness—but it's the cornmeal dumplings that really steal the show.

HANDS-ON TIME 15 min.
TOTAL TIME 40 min.

- 2   12-oz. pkg. frozen whole kernel corn or 8 ears fresh corn, kernels removed
- 2   cups vegetable or chicken broth
- 1   lb. Yukon Gold potatoes and/or red potatoes, peeled and cut into ½-inch pieces
- 1   13.5-oz. can unsweetened coconut milk or 1¼ cups whole milk
- ½   cup chopped roasted red bell pepper
- 1   to 2 jalapeños, seeded and finely chopped (tip, page 28), or one 4-oz. can diced green chiles
- ¾   tsp. kosher salt
- ½   cup all-purpose flour
- ⅓   cup cornmeal
- ¼   cup crumbled Cotija or feta cheese
- 1   tsp. baking powder
- ½   tsp. ground cumin
- 1   egg, lightly beaten
- 2   Tbsp. olive oil
- ¼   cup chopped fresh cilantro or basil
       Sliced radishes (optional)
       Lime wedges

1. In a blender or food processor blend half the corn and half the broth until nearly smooth (mixture will be thick). Transfer to a 4- to 5-qt. Dutch oven; add remaining broth and the potatoes. Bring to boiling; reduce heat. Simmer, covered, 15 minutes, stirring occasionally. Reserve 2 Tbsp. coconut milk. Stir remaining corn, remaining coconut milk, bell pepper, jalapeño, ½ tsp. salt, and ¼ tsp. black pepper into broth mixture. Return to boiling; reduce heat to a simmer.
2. Meanwhile, for dumplings: In a medium bowl stir together flour, cornmeal, Cotija, baking powder, cumin, ¼ tsp. salt, and ⅛ tsp. black pepper. Combine egg, reserved 2 Tbsp. coconut milk, the olive oil, and 2 Tbsp. cilantro. Add to flour mixture; stir with a fork just until combined. Drop dumpling mixture in eight mounds on simmering stew. Cook, covered, 10 to 12 minutes or until a

toothpick inserted into a dumpling comes out clean. (Do not lift lid while cooking.)
3. Top stew with remaining cilantro, radishes (if using), and serve with lime wedges. Serves 4.
EACH SERVING *602 cal, 28 g fat (17 g sat fat), 54 mg chol, 713 mg sodium, 78 g carb, 7 g fiber, 8 g sugars, 13 g pro*

PORK & SQUASH STEW WITH GINGER-RED CABBAGE SLAW

HANDS-ON TIME 40 min.
TOTAL TIME 2 hr. 10 min.

- 1   tsp. kosher salt
- ½   to 1 tsp. curry powder or ¼ tsp. ground turmeric
- ¼   to ½ tsp. ground coriander
- ¼   tsp. ground allspice or five-spice powder
- 2   to 2½ lb. boneless pork shoulder, trimmed and cut into 1-inch pieces
- 2   Tbsp. olive oil
- 2   leeks, trimmed, halved lengthwise, rinsed, and sliced ¼ inch thick
- 2   stalks celery, chopped, or 1 bulb fennel, cored and chopped
- 1   32-oz. container reduced-sodium chicken broth
- 1½   to 2 lb. butternut squash, peeled, seeded, and cut into 1-inch pieces
- 2   cooking apples (such as Granny Smith or Jonathan), peeled, cored, and cut into 1-inch pieces
       Ginger-Red Cabbage Slaw

1. In a large bowl combine salt, curry powder, coriander, and allspice. Add pork to bowl; toss to coat. In a 4- to 6-qt. Dutch oven heat 1 Tbsp. oil over medium-high. Add half the pork; cook and stir until browned. Using a slotted spoon, transfer pork to a bowl. Repeat with remaining 1 Tbsp. oil and pork; transfer to the bowl. Add leeks and celery to Dutch oven; reduce heat to medium. Cook and stir 5 minutes, scraping up browned bits from bottom.
2. Add pork and broth to Dutch oven. Bring to boiling; reduce heat. Simmer, covered, 1 hour, stirring occasionally. Stir in squash and apples. Simmer, covered, 25 minutes. Uncover; cook 5 minutes more or until squash and pork are tender. Season to taste.
3. Just before serving, prepare Ginger-Red Cabbage Slaw; ladle stew into bowls and top with slaw. Serves 6.
Ginger-Red Cabbage Slaw In a large skillet heat 1 Tbsp. olive oil over medium-high. Add 3 cloves minced garlic and pinch salt. Cook and stir 15 seconds. Add 2½ cups shredded red cabbage. Cook and stir 3 minutes or until crisp-tender. Stir in 2 tsp. grated fresh ginger or ½ tsp. ground ginger. Remove from heat. Stir in 3 Tbsp. chopped fresh flat-leaf parsley and zest and juice from 1 small lemon.
EACH SERVING *372 cal, 12 g fat (3 g sat fat), 91 mg chol, 874 mg sodium, 27 g carb, 5 g fiber, 10 g sugars, 38 g pro*

PORK & SQUASH STEW WITH GINGER-RED CABBAGE SLAW

SWEET POTATO
MARSHMALLOW
MERINGUE PIE
Recipe on page 243

november

Plan Thanksgiving dinner from this array of creative recipes for sides, delectable desserts, and moist glazed turkey.

233   239   254

holidays
SPINS ON SIDES

Complete the Thanksgiving feast with outstanding sides that hint of traditional favorites—with just enough updates for today's tastes and convenience.

CUSTOMIZE IT

Dressing, a carbohydrate cornerstone of Thanksgiving, is called stuffing when it's cooked inside the bird. This recipe calls for ingredients from the pantry and fridge, allowing for substitutions that suit your family's tastes.

GRAINS farro, brown rice, wheat berries

BREAD sourdough, Italian, whole wheat, brioche, corn bread, rye

MEAT bacon, crumbled sausage, pancetta, sliced chicken sausage

VEGGIES mushrooms, leeks, celery, onions, carrots, kale

HERBS sage, thyme, parsley, oregano, basil

MAKE-AHEAD

Prep the bread, farro, and vegetables up to three days before assembling. Or make the entire dish and refrigerate 24 hours.

TWICE-TOASTED FARRO & MUSHROOM DRESSING

Streamline dinner prep by assembling this dish through Step 5 in the morning, then chill up to 6 hours. Increase covered baking time to 30 minutes.

HANDS-ON TIME 25 min.
TOTAL TIME 2 hr.

1¼ cups farro
1   lb. bread, cut or torn into ¾-inch pieces (8 to 10 cups)
8   slices thick-cut bacon
½   cup butter
16   oz. cremini mushrooms, quartered
1   large leek, sliced and rinsed
2   stalks celery, sliced
3   cloves garlic, thinly sliced
⅓   cup coarsely chopped celery leaves (optional)
¼   cup chopped fresh sage
2   Tbsp. fresh thyme leaves
½   tsp. kosher salt
¼   tsp. crushed red pepper
2   eggs
3   to 4 cups reduced-sodium chicken stock or broth

1. Preheat oven to 375°F. In a 3- to 4-qt. saucepan bring 3 cups lightly salted water to boiling. Meanwhile, in a large skillet toast farro over medium-high 5 minutes or until toasted and fragrant, stirring frequently. Carefully add farro to boiling water (mixture will bubble). Reduce heat to medium. Cover and simmer 18 to 20 minutes or just until tender but retains a little bite. Drain well; spread on a sheet pan to cool.*
2. Meanwhile, spread bread in a shallow baking pan. Bake 12 to 15 minutes or until golden brown, stirring once. Let cool. Transfer to an extra-large bowl.*

3. In a large skillet cook bacon over medium until crisp. Transfer bacon to paper towels to drain, reserving ¼ cup drippings in skillet. Let cool; crumble bacon. Add butter to skillet with drippings; stir until melted. Remove from heat. Add mushrooms, leek, celery, and garlic to baking pan used to toast bread. Drizzle with 3 Tbsp. butter mixture; toss to coat. Roast 20 minutes or until lightly browned, stirring once.
4. Return skillet to medium-high and add cooked farro. Cook and stir 5 to 6 minutes or until farro browns a bit more. Remove from heat. Stir in celery leaves (if using), sage, thyme, salt, and crushed red pepper.
5. Grease a 3-qt. baking dish. Add farro, mushroom mixture, bacon, and the remaining butter mixture to bread in bowl; toss to combine. In a medium bowl lightly beat eggs; stir in 2 cups of the stock. Pour over bread mixture; stir gently. Add enough remaining stock just until dressing is moistened. Spread in prepared baking dish. Cover with foil.
6. Bake 20 minutes. Remove foil and bake 20 minutes more or until top is golden brown and internal temperature is 165°F. (To bake alongside the turkey at 325°F, increase covered and uncovered bake times to 30 minutes each. If dressing was prepped and chilled, bake covered 40 minutes; bake uncovered 30 minutes.) If desired, top with additional sage and/or celery leaves. Serves 10.
*Tip Farro and bread cubes can be prepped 1 day ahead. Cover and chill farro. Cover bread and store at room temperature.
EACH SERVING *413 cal, 19 g fat (9 g sat fat), 71 mg chol, 705 mg sodium, 47 g carb, 5 g fiber, 4 g sugars, 13 g pro*

SPICED APPLE
RINGS WITH
BEETS

RED CABBAGE &
RADICCHIO SLAW

GINGER-CRANBERRY
RELISH

VIBRANT, ASTRINGENT TASTES DESERVE A SPOT ON YOUR THANKSGIVING BUFFET. THEY CUT THROUGH CARBS AND FATS (SUCH AS MASHED POTATOES AND GRAVY) AND HELP BALANCE SALTY AND SWEET.

SPICED APPLE RINGS WITH BEETS

Cinnamon sticks, star anise, and mustard seeds flavor the pickling liquid; beet slices add earthy flavor.

HANDS-ON TIME 15 min.
TOTAL TIME 6 hr. 45 min., includes chilling

- 1½ cups plus 1 Tbsp. cider vinegar
- ⅔ cup packed brown sugar
- 5 whole star anise
- 2 2- to 3-inch cinnamon sticks
- 2 tsp. yellow mustard seeds
- 2 bay leaves
- ½ tsp. whole allspice
- 1½ tsp. kosher salt
- 3 cooking apples, such as Granny Smith
- 1 medium beet
- ½ medium sweet onion, cut into thin wedges

1. For pickling liquid: In a 4- to 6-qt. pot combine 1½ cups water, 1½ cups vinegar, the brown sugar, star anise, cinnamon sticks, mustard seeds, bay leaves, allspice, and salt. Cook and stir over medium until sugar is dissolved. Reduce heat to medium-low; simmer, covered, 15 minutes.
2. Meanwhile, in a large bowl combine 3 cups water and remaining 1 Tbsp. vinegar. Peel apples. Trim ¼ inch from ends. Cut apples crosswise into ¼-inch slices. Remove seeds. Add slices to vinegar mixture to prevent browning. Peel beet; cut into ¼-inch slices. Add beet to pickling mixture in pot; return to simmer. Cook, covered, 5 minutes.

3. Drain apples; add to pot. Return to simmer; cook 8 minutes or just until apples and beets are tender. Gently stir in onion. Let cool to room temperature. Transfer to a glass container. Chill, covered, at least 6 hours or up to 1 week. Serves 6.

EACH SERVING *38 cal, 95 mg sodium, 9 g carb, 2 g fiber, 6 g sugars, 1 g pro*

RED CABBAGE & RADICCHIO SLAW

Fennel-spiced vinaigrette elevates this simple slaw, while the mild sweetness of red cabbage tempers radicchio's characteristic bite. Top with pomegranate arils for juicy pops of sweet-tart flavor in each crunchy bite.

HANDS-ON TIME 20 min.
TOTAL TIME 1 hr. 20 min.

- ⅓ cup olive oil
- 3 Tbsp. red wine vinegar
- 2 Tbsp. finely chopped red onion
- 1 Tbsp. sugar
- 2 tsp. fennel seeds, lightly crushed
- 1 tsp. sea salt
- ½ tsp. cracked black pepper
- 3 cups shredded red cabbage
- 2 cups shredded radicchio
- ¼ cup pomegranate seeds

1. In a medium bowl whisk together olive oil, vinegar, red onion, sugar, fennel seeds, salt, and pepper. Add cabbage and radicchio; toss to coat. Cover and chill at least 1 hour or up to 4 hours.
2. To serve, top slaw with pomegranate seeds. Serves 6.

EACH SERVING *140 cal, 12 g fat (2 g sat fat), 387 mg sodium, 7 g carb, 2 g fiber, 5 g sugars, 1 g pro*

GINGER-CRANBERRY RELISH

Crystallized ginger, walnuts, and sweet honey create a fresh interpretation of a traditional holiday favorite.

HANDS-ON TIME 20 min.
TOTAL TIME 1 hr. 20 min., includes chilling

- 1 large orange
- 1 12-oz. pkg. fresh or frozen cranberries, thawed if frozen (3 cups)
- 1 small red apple, cored and coarsely chopped
- ⅛ tsp. ground cloves
- ½ tsp. kosher salt
- ⅓ cup chopped walnuts, toasted (tip, page 50)
- ¼ to ½ cup honey
- 3 Tbsp. finely chopped crystallized ginger

1. Using a vegetable peeler, remove three wide strips of zest from orange. If necessary, use a spoon to scrape any white pith off strips. Coarsely chop 1 Tbsp. zest. Squeeze juice from orange (you should have ⅓ cup).
2. In a food processor combine zest, cranberries, apple, cloves, and salt; pulse until chopped. Add orange juice. Pulse three times or just until combined.
3. Transfer relish to a medium bowl. Stir in walnuts, honey, and ginger. Chill, covered, at least 1 hour or up to 1 day. If desired, garnish with additional toasted walnuts. Serves 6.

EACH SERVING *84 cal, 4 g fat (0 g sat fat), 95 mg sodium, 11 g carb, 2 g fiber, 5 g sugars, 1 g pro*

AT THANKSGIVING, THE HUMBLE POTATO SHEDS ITS UNASSUMING REPUTATION. BUT UNDERDRAINED OR OVERMIXED POTATOES CAN QUICKLY TURN INTO A STODGY, GLUEY MASS. WE'VE GOT THE SECRETS TO LIGHT AND FLUFFY POTATOES, EVERY TIME.

MASTER THE MASH

Here are a few Test Kitchen tips from years of practice:

START POTATOES IN COLD WATER so they cook evenly. After draining, return potatoes to the hot pan and let them stand a few minutes so the residual heat dries them out.

HEATING THE MILK before adding it to the potatoes helps keep them warm until they hit the table. Start by using the least amount of milk, then gradually add more until the potatoes reach your desired consistency.

MIX POTATOES JUST UNTIL FLUFFY Overworking breaks the starch cells and results in a glue-like texture.

MASHED POTATOES

HANDS-ON TIME 20 min.
TOTAL TIME 40 min.

3   lb. russet, Yukon Gold, or red potatoes, peeled* and cut into 2-inch pieces
¼   cup butter
½   to ¾ cup milk, whipping cream, or half-and-half

1. In a 4- to 5-qt. Dutch oven cook potatoes, covered, in enough lightly salted boiling water to cover 20 to 25 minutes or until tender; drain. Return the hot, drained potatoes to the hot Dutch oven. Add butter. Let stand, uncovered, 2 to 3 minutes. Meanwhile, in a small saucepan heat milk over low heat until very warm.
2. Mash potatoes with a potato masher or beat with an electric mixer on low speed just until light and fluffy. Stir in ½ cup warm milk, 1 tsp. salt, and ½ tsp. black pepper. Gradually stir in additional milk until potatoes reach desired consistency. Serves 10.
EACH SERVING *126 cal, 5 g fat (3 g sat fat), 13 mg chol, 281 mg sodium, 19 g carb, 2 g fiber, 1 g sugars, 3 g pro*
Garlic Mashed Potatoes Preheat oven to 400°F. Cut off tops of two garlic bulbs and place on a piece of foil. Drizzle with olive oil; wrap garlic in foil. Roast 35 to 40 minutes. Squeeze garlic from cloves; mash with a fork. Prepare potatoes as directed in Step 2, mashing or beating in roasted garlic and 4 oz. cubed cream cheese with the butter. Stir in warm milk, ⅓ cup chopped green onions and, if desired, ⅓ cup roasted red peppers, drained and chopped. Serves 10.
***Tip** If you leave peels on the potatoes, use a potato masher rather than a mixer to mash the potatoes.

CELERY ROOT PUREE

HANDS-ON TIME 15 min.
TOTAL TIME 30 min.

3   lb. celery root, peeled and cut into ½-inch cubes (8 cups)
4   cloves garlic
2   tsp. kosher salt
1   cup heavy cream,
½   cup unsalted butter

1. In a large saucepan combine celery root, garlic, and salt. Add water to cover. Bring to boiling; reduce heat. Simmer, covered, 12 to 15 minutes or until tender; drain.
2. Transfer celery root to a food processor; add cream and butter. Cover and process until smooth. Season to taste with additional salt and pepper. If desired, top with additional butter. Serves 8.
EACH SERVING *277 cal, 23 g fat (14 g sat fat), 64 mg chol, 672 mg sodium, 17 g carb, 3 g fiber, 4 g sugars, 4 g pro*

MASHED CAULIFLOWER

HANDS-ON TIME 5 min.
TOTAL TIME 10 min.

4   cups cauliflower florets
¼   cup sour cream
2   Tbsp. olive oil
½   tsp. kosher salt

In a large covered saucepan steam cauliflower in a steamer basket over a small amount of boiling water 4 minutes or until fork-tender. Transfer cauliflower to a food processor; add sour cream, oil, and salt. Process until smooth. Season with salt and black pepper. Serves 4.
EACH SERVING *108 cal, 9 g fat (2 g sat fat), 7 mg chol, 174 mg sodium, 6 g carb, 2 g fiber, 2 g sugars, 2 g pro*

GARLIC MASHED
POTATOES

ROASTED SQUASH WITH MACADAMIA NUT GREMOLATA

ROASTED SQUASH

For holiday flair, finish caramelized acorn or butternut squash or sweet potatoes with one of three toppings. To roast nuts or seeds, see tip, page 50.

HANDS-ON TIME 20 min.
TOTAL TIME 40 min.

3 medium acorn squash, seeded and cut into 1-inch wedges or chunks; 4 lbs. butternut squash, peeled, seeded, and cut into 1½-inch chunks; or 3 lbs. red garnet or jewel sweet potatoes, peeled, if desired, and cut into 1-inch chunks
3 Tbsp. olive oil
   Macadamia Nut Gremolata, Almond-Maple Drizzle, or Ginger-Sesame Drizzle

Preheat oven to 425°F. Line a large shallow baking pan with foil. Place in oven and heat at least 5 minutes. Place squash and/or sweet potatoes in an extra-large bowl; add oil, 1 tsp. salt, and ½ tsp. black pepper; toss to coat. Carefully spread evenly on hot pan. Roast 20 to 25 minutes or just until tender and beginning to brown, turning once halfway through roasting. To serve, top with gremolata or drizzle. Serves 6.

Macadamia Nut Gremolata In a small bowl stir together ¼ cup finely chopped toasted macadamia nuts; 3 Tbsp. finely chopped fresh flat-leaf parsley; 3 Tbsp. unsweetened shredded or chip coconut, toasted; 2 Tbsp. chopped chives; 1½ Tbsp. coconut oil, melted; 2 tsp. orange zest; 1 clove minced garlic; and ½ tsp. salt. Top roasted vegetables with gremolata.
EACH SERVING *230 cal, 16 g fat (6 g sat fat), 589 mg sodium, 23 g carb, 4 g fiber, 1 g sugars, 2 g pro*

Almond-Maple Drizzle In a small bowl whisk together ¼ cup almond butter, 2 Tbsp. maple syrup, 3 Tbsp. cider vinegar, 1 tsp. paprika, and ⅛ tsp. cayenne. Add water, 1 tsp. at a time, until drizzling consistency. Top roasted vegetables with drizzle; sprinkle with ¼ cup toasted sliced almonds.
EACH SERVING: *248 cal, 29 g carb, 15 g fat (2 g sat fat), 29 g carb, 5 g fiber, 5 g sugars, 5 g pro*

Ginger-Sesame Drizzle In a small bowl whisk together 2 Tbsp. rice vinegar, 1½ tsp. peanut oil or vegetable oil, 1 Tbsp.

GREENS, CABBAGE, & GREEN BEAN SALAD WITH HONEYED APRICOT-LIME VINAIGRETTE

lemongrass paste, 2 to 3 tsp. gochujang paste, 2 tsp. grated fresh ginger, and 1 tsp. toasted sesame oil. Drizzle mixture over roasted squash; toss gently to coat. To serve, transfer to a platter and top with 3 Tbsp. chopped green onions and 1 Tbsp. toasted sesame seeds.
EACH SERVING: *184 cal, 23 g carb, 10 g fat (1 g sat fat), 3 g fiber, 1 g sugars, 2 g pro*

GREENS, CABBAGE & GREEN BEAN SALAD HONEYED APRICOT-LIME VINAIGRETTE

Green vegetables balance rich side dishes. This citrus-forward, slightly sweet vinaigrette is versatile.

HANDS-ON TIME 30 min.
TOTAL TIME 1 hr. 30 min.

½ cup dry white wine
3 dried apricots, finely chopped
3 Tbsp. honey
3 Tbsp. rice vinegar
2 tsp. lime zest
2 garlic cloves, minced
1 serrano chile pepper, stemmed, seeded, and finely chopped (tip, page 28)
16 oz. green beans or haricots verts, trimmed and cut into 2- to 3-inch pieces
3 Tbsp. olive oil
2 Tbsp. lime juice
½ tsp. sea salt
¼ cup chopped flat-leaf parsley

2 green onions, chopped
12 oz. napa cabbage, shredded, or Brussels sprouts, shaved
8 cups torn greens, such as green leaf, romaine, and/or Bibb
¼ cup shaved Pecorino Romano

1. In a small saucepan combine white wine, apricots, honey, rice vinegar, lime zest, garlic, and serrano. Bring to boiling over medium-high; gently boil 10 minutes or until reduced by one-third, stirring occasionally. Remove from heat; let cool.*

2. Bring a large saucepan of salted water to boil. Add green beans; return to boil and cook 4 minutes. Drain and immediately submerge in ice water. Drain well.*

3. Whisk oil, lime juice, and salt into white wine reduction. Stir in parsley and green onions. In a medium bowl toss cabbage with about ¼ cup vinaigrette; set aside up to 1 hour.

4. To serve, arrange greens on a platter. Top with cabbage and green beans. Spoon remaining vinaigrette over. Top with cheese. Serves 6.

EACH SERVING: *172 cal, 8 g fat (2 g sat fat), 3 mg chol, 288 mg sodium, 21 g carb, 4 g fiber, 13 g sugars, 4 g pro*

*Tip White wine reduction can be made, cooled, and refrigerated up to 3 days. Blanch beans up to 24 hours before serving.

TURKEY HALL OF FAME

The *Better Homes & Gardens* Test Kitchen shares a mouthwatering turkey recipe perfected over 90 years of roasting, testing, and tasting.

GLAZED ROAST TURKEY

HANDS-ON TIME 20 min.
TOTAL TIME 4 hr. 35 min.

1 14- to 16-lb. turkey
2 Tbsp. butter, softened
   Double Mustard-Brown Sugar Glaze or Hot Honey-Sesame Glaze

1. Preheat oven to 325°F.
2. Skewer neck skin of turkey to back. Tuck ends of drumsticks under band of skin across the tail. If there's no band of skin, tie drumsticks securely to tail with 100%-cotton kitchen string. Twist wing tips under back. Rub turkey all over with softened butter.
3. Place turkey, breast side down, on a rack in a roasting pan. If desired, insert an oven-going thermometer into the center of an inside thigh muscle. It should not touch bone. Cover loosely with foil.
4. Roast 2¼ hours. Remove foil; turn turkey, breast side up, using turkey lifters. Cut band of skin or string between drumsticks so thighs cook evenly. Continue roasting for 1¾ to 2¼ hours or until thermometer registers 175°F. Juices should run clear, and drumsticks should move easily in their sockets. Brush turkey occasionally with desired glaze the last 45 minutes of roasting.
5. Remove turkey from oven. Cover with foil; let stand 15 to 20 minutes before carving. Serves 14.
EACH SERVING *522 cal, 29 g fat (6 g sat fat), 214 mg chol, 680 mg sodium, 6 g carb, 6 g sugars, 57 g pro*

Double Mustard-Brown Sugar Glaze In a small saucepan combine ¼ cup cider vinegar, ¼ cup packed brown sugar, 2 Tbsp. Dijon mustard, and 2 Tbsp. whole grain mustard. Cook and stir until bubbly. Boil gently, uncovered, 3 minutes, stirring occasionally. Remove from heat; stir in 2 Tbsp. chopped fresh thyme. Makes ⅔ cup.
Hot Honey-Sesame Glaze In a small saucepan combine ¼ cup honey, 2 Tbsp. reduced-sodium soy sauce, 2 Tbsp. unseasoned rice vinegar, 2 to 3 Tbsp. Korean chili paste (gochujang), 1 Tbsp. grated fresh ginger, and 3 minced cloves garlic. Cook and stir until bubbly. Boil gently, uncovered, 3 minutes, stirring occasionally. Remove from heat; stir in 1 Tbsp. sesame seeds and, if desired, 1 tsp. toasted sesame oil. Cool to thicken slightly. Makes ¾ cup.

HOW TO CARVE

This step-by-step how-to-carve-a-turkey series is efficient and straightforward. It requires only a sharp knife and simple cuts.

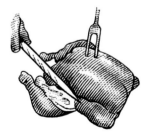

REMOVE THE LEGS Cut the joints that attach thighs to body. Cut joints between thighs and drumsticks. Remove the thigh meat from bone.

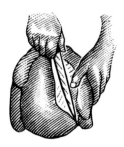

REMOVE BREAST Cut along one side of the breast bone, moving downward while pulling the breast away from the bone with your hand. Repeat on opposite side.

SLICE THE BREAST Slice each breast portion crosswise. Cut the wings away from the body.

SWEET SURPRISES

Fall is baking season, and cookbook author Jerrelle Guy is here to help fill ovens with inventive treats—all special enough for a holiday feast and easy enough for any day.

Craving desserts that have a dash of nostalgia mixed with something new? These are the treats Jerrelle Guy describes as "charming." They fall somewhere on the spectrum between comforting and surprising. Like brioche bread pudding rendered as a muffin, or sweet potato pie dressed up with a chocolate-hazelnut crust and waves of marshmallow meringue. Jerrelle's combo of rich flavors and simple techniques will make any moment this season a special occasion.

MEET JERRELLE GUY

"I'm obsessed with the feelings of comfort and nostalgia the holidays bring." For the cookbook author of *Black Girl Baking*, photographer, and blogger of *Chocolate for Basil*, tapping into the tastes and aromas that evoke emotions is what she's after, in any season. "Brown sugar, lots of spice, vanilla, toasted nuts, and rich, dark liquors are the hallmarks of my baking all year round," she says.

ORANGE-ALMOND CAKE WITH CRANBERRY CURD

This one-bowl whisk-together almond cake has a delicious trick up: puddles of vibrant, tart cranberry curd. "This one is exceptional," Jerrelle says.

HANDS-ON TIME 20 min.
TOTAL TIME 50 min.

    Butter, softened
¼   cup plus ⅓ cup sliced almonds
1   cup homemade or canned whole berry cranberry sauce
1   Tbsp. cornstarch or tapioca flour
    Kosher salt
1   cup all-purpose flour
½   cup almond flour
1   tsp. baking powder
1   cup plus 2 tsp. granulated sugar
2   eggs plus 1 egg yolk
2   oranges (2 tsp. zest, ½ cup juice)
½   tsp. almond extract
5   Tbsp. unsalted butter, melted and cooled
    Powdered sugar

1. Preheat oven to 350°F. Butter a 9-inch springform pan. Line bottom of pan with parchment paper. Butter the paper. Pat ¼ cup sliced almonds about 1½ inches up sides of pan.

2. In a food processor or blender combine cranberry sauce, cornstarch, and pinch kosher salt. Process until smooth. Press mixture through a fine-mesh sieve into a small bowl. Discard solids.

3. In a second small bowl whisk together flours, baking powder, and ½ tsp. salt.

4. In a large bowl whisk together 1 cup granulated sugar, eggs, egg yolk, orange zest, and almond extract until well combined. Whisk in orange juice and melted butter. Add flour mixture; whisk just until combined.

5. Spread batter in prepared pan. Drop spoonfuls of cranberry mixture on batter. Sprinkle ⅓ cup sliced almonds on top. Sprinkle with remaining 2 tsp. granulated sugar.

6. Bake 30 to 35 minutes or until golden brown and a toothpick inserted near center comes out clean. Let cool completely in pan on wire rack. Using a small sharp knife, loosen and remove sides of pan. Just before serving, dust cake with powdered sugar. Serves 8.

EACH SERVING *398 cal, 15 g fat (5 g sat fat), 89 mg chol, 153 mg sodium, 60 g carb, 2 g fiber, 29 g sugars, 7 g pro*

JERRELLE TRIPLED THE ALMOND— ALMOND FLOUR, EXTRACT, AND TOASTED SLIVERS—IN THIS NOT-SO-SWEET CAKE.

JERRELLE PILES BILLOWING MERINGUE ON THE SWEET POTATO FILLING. THE HAZELNUT FLOUR AND CHOCOLATE CRUST ARE ADDITIONAL CHARMERS.

SWEET POTATO MARSHMALLOW MERINGUE PIE

Jerrelle skips the labor-intensive task of toasting and skinning whole hazelnuts for this crisp nut crust. Instead she uses hazelnut flour that she toasts in a skillet until it gives off a popcorn scent.

HANDS-ON TIME 30 min.
TOTAL TIME 6 hr., includes chilling

1½	lb. medium sweet potatoes
4	cups hazelnut meal/flour*
1	cup semisweet chocolate chips
¼	cup coconut oil or butter
¾	cup packed brown sugar
½	cup milk
3	eggs
2	tsp. vanilla
1	orange (1 tsp. zest, 2 Tbsp. juice)
½	tsp. ground cinnamon
⅛	tsp. freshly ground nutmeg
	Marshmallow Meringue

1. Preheat oven to 400°F. Line a baking sheet with foil. Pierce sweet potatoes with a fork. Place on prepared baking sheet. Bake 45 to 50 minutes or until tender; let cool. Halve sweet potatoes and scoop out flesh; discard skins.

2. For crust: In an extra-large skillet heat hazelnut meal over medium-low 5 to 7 minutes or until toasted, stirring constantly to prevent burning. Turn off heat and stir in chocolate chips, coconut oil, and ½ tsp. salt. Stir until chocolate is melted and incorporated. Press mixture onto bottom and 1 inch up sides of a 13×9-inch foil-lined pan. Bake 12 to 15 minutes or until lightly browned. Let cool on a wire rack.

3. Reduce oven temperature to 300°F and position a rack in upper third of oven. For filling: In a food processor or blender combine sweet potatoes, brown sugar, milk, eggs, vanilla, orange zest, orange juice, cinnamon, nutmeg, and ¼ tsp. salt. Process just until smooth. Pour into crust.

4. Bake 40 minutes or until center is set; let cool on a wire rack 1 hour. Chill at least 3 hours or overnight.

5. To serve, spoon Marshmallow Meringue on filling. Use a culinary torch to brown the meringue, or broil about 5 inches from heat until golden brown. Serves 12.

*Tip If you can't find hazelnut meal, pulse 4 cups toasted hazelnuts in a food processor until finely ground.

**Tip To make in a springform pan: Halve the crust recipe and press into an unlined 9-inch springform pan. Bake crust 12 to 15 minutes or until lightly browned. Let cool on a wire rack. Add filling and bake 50 to 60 minutes or until center is set; let cool on a wire rack 1 hour. Chill at least 3 hours or overnight. Continue with Step 5.

Marshmallow Meringue In a large bowl combine 4 egg whites (from pasteurized eggs), 1 tsp. cream of tartar, and ⅛ tsp. salt. Beat with a mixer on medium to high until foamy. Add ¼ cup granulated sugar, 1 Tbsp. at a time, beating until soft, glossy peaks form (tips curl). Add one 7-oz. jar marshmallow creme in large spoonfuls while beating on medium. Beat until smooth and just shy of stiff peaks (tips won't quite stand straight).

EACH SERVING *517 cal, 26 g fat (7 g sat fat), 47 mg chol, 251 mg sodium, 61 g carb, 7 g fiber, 41 g sugars, 10 g pro*

WHEN IT'S TIME TO ROLL OUT THE RED CARPET, THIS IS THE TART TO SERVE. WHISKEY IN THE FILLING IS SUBTLE, WHICH IS EXACTLY WHAT JERRELLE IS AFTER. "FOR AN EXTRA FLAVOR LAYER, I OPT FOR ALCOHOL OVER EXTRACTS, WHICH MIGHT OVERPOWER IF YOU ADD TOO MUCH."

WHISKEY & CREAM PUMPKIN TART WITH PECAN BUTTER SHORTBREAD CRUST

This tart, best served within a few hours after it has cooled, keeps well in the refrigerator overnight. Decorate the tart with cookies cut from the same dough as the crust. If you prefer to skip the cookies, reduce ingredients for the crust by half.

HANDS-ON TIME 30 min.
TOTAL TIME 4 hr. 30 min., includes chilling

- ½ cup unsweetened pecan butter, stirred before measuring*
- ⅔ cup unsalted butter, softened
- ¾ tsp. kosher salt
- 2 cups all-purpose flour
- 1 cup plus 1 Tbsp. powdered sugar
- 1 15-oz. can pumpkin
- 1½ cups heavy cream
- ½ cup granulated sugar
- 2 eggs
- 2 Tbsp. bourbon whiskey or apple cider or juice
- 2 tsp. vanilla
- 1 tsp. ground ginger
- ½ tsp. ground cinnamon
- ¼ tsp. freshly grated nutmeg
  Cookies (optional)
  Glaze (optional)

1. Preheat oven to 375°F. For crust: In a medium bowl combine pecan butter, butter, and ½ tsp. kosher salt. Beat with a mixer on high until smooth. Add flour and 1 cup powdered sugar; beat on low until a crumbly dough forms. Lightly knead dough until it forms a ball. Divide dough in half.

2. Press one dough portion into bottom and up sides of a 9-inch tart pan with removable bottom. Bake 15 minutes or until browned. Let cool completely on a wire rack.

3. Reduce oven temperature to 300°F. For filling: In a medium bowl whisk together pumpkin, ½ cup cream, the granulated sugar, eggs, bourbon, 1 tsp. vanilla, the ginger, cinnamon, nutmeg, and ¼ tsp. kosher salt until combined. Pour filling into crust.

4. Bake 50 to 55 minutes or until set. Let cool completely. Cover and chill at least 2 hours or until ready to serve.

5. To serve, in a medium bowl beat the remaining 1 cup cream, 1 Tbsp. powdered sugar, and 1 tsp. vanilla with a mixer on high until stiff peaks form (tips stand straight). Pipe or spoon whipped cream onto tart. Serves 8.

*Tip You can purchase pecan butter to save time, though homemade is easy to make and often tastes better than store-bought. Preheat oven to 350°F. Spread 1 lb. pecan halves or pieces in a shallow pan. Bake 10 to 12 minutes or until deep golden brown, stirring once. Let cool. Process in a food processor or blender 5 minutes or until smooth and creamy, scraping down sides of bowl as needed. Season to taste with kosher salt.

EACH SERVING (WITHOUT COOKIES)
458 cal, 31 g fat (16 g sat fat), 118 mg chol, 139 mg sodium, 40 g carb, 3 g fiber, 24 g sugars, 6 g pro

Cookies On a lightly floured surface, roll out remaining dough portion to ¼-inch thickness. Jerrelle Guy cuts leaf-shape cookies freehand using a sharp knife to top her pie, although any shape 1½- to 2-inch cookie cutter can substitute. Place cutouts 1 inch apart on an ungreased cookie sheet. Bake at 375°F for 10 to 12 minutes or until lightly browned. Let cool on a wire rack.

Cookie Glaze In a small bowl combine 1 cup powdered sugar and 1 to 2 Tbsp. bourbon whiskey or apple cider or juice to make dipping consistency. If desired, sprinkle a little edible gold luster dust on glaze. Dip tops of cookies in glaze. Let stand until set. If cookies are added to top of pie before chilling, they will soften as the pie chills and cut evenly for serving. If you prefer crisp cookies, top pie with cookies just before serving. Store extra cookies in an airtight container up to 5 days.

"I GET EXCITED WATCHING THESE PUFF IN THE OVEN. PREPARE FOR A SLIGHT FALL; THEY AREN'T AS PRIDEFUL WHEN THEY COOL. THEY ARE SO DELICIOUS."

BRIOCHE BREAD
PUDDING MUFFINS
WITH MAPLE CARAMEL

BANANAS FOSTER CRISP

BRIOCHE BREAD PUDDING MUFFINS WITH MAPLE CARAMEL

For one large bread pudding, place bread and custard in a 1¹/₂-qt. baking dish; bake 45 minutes or until puffed, golden brown, and set.

HANDS-ON TIME 10 min.
TOTAL TIME 2 hr. 30 min.

8   oz. brioche bread, cut into ¾-inch cubes (about 6 cups)
    Butter, softened
2   cups buttermilk
5   Tbsp. unsalted butter, melted
⅓   cup plus 2 Tbsp. packed light brown sugar
2   eggs
2¼ tsp. vanilla
¾   tsp. kosher salt
¼   cup pure maple syrup
2   Tbsp. heavy cream

1. Preheat oven to 300°F. Spread bread cubes evenly in a shallow baking pan. Bake 20 minutes or until crisp, stirring once. Let cool. Increase oven temperature to 350°F.
2. Butter six 3- to 3½-inch muffin cups or twelve 2½-inch muffin cups. Fill each cup with toasted bread.
3. In a large bowl whisk together buttermilk, melted butter, ⅓ cup brown sugar, the eggs, 2 tsp. vanilla, and ¼ tsp. salt. Slowly pour mixture over bread in each cup. Cover and let stand 30 minutes or chill up to 4 hours.
4. Meanwhile, for maple caramel: In a small saucepan combine maple syrup and remaining 2 Tbsp. brown sugar. Bring to boiling; reduce heat. Boil gently 2 minutes, stirring occasionally. Remove from heat; carefully add cream, the remaining ¼ tsp. vanilla, and remaining ½ tsp. salt. Return to heat; boil gently 1 minute more, stirring constantly. Remove from heat. Maple caramel will thicken as it cools. Rewarm, if necessary, for drizzling.
5. Bake muffins 30 to 35 minutes or until puffed, golden brown, and set. Let cool 10 minutes. Remove muffins from cups. Serve warm, drizzled with maple caramel. Makes 6 muffins.

EACH MUFFIN *432 cal, 26 g fat (15 g sat fat), 161 mg chol, 474 mg sodium, 44 g carb, 31 g sugars, 8 g pro*

BANANAS FOSTER CRISP

With a few basic ingredients, you can make Jerrelle's take on bananas Foster. She recommends using firm bananas for the best texture. The sauce bubbles as the bananas bake, for a warm, melty dessert without the torch.

HANDS-ON TIME 20 min.
TOTAL TIME 1 hr.

    Butter, softened
4   medium firm ripe bananas, halved lengthwise, then cut in half crosswise
½   cup crushed gingersnap cookies
2   Tbsp. all-purpose flour
1   Tbsp. plus ¼ cup packed brown sugar
½   tsp. kosher salt
5   Tbsp. unsalted butter, softened
2   Tbsp. dark rum or apple cider or juice
½   tsp. vanilla
    Vanilla ice cream

1. Preheat oven to 350°F. Butter four 10-oz. shallow ramekins and place on a rimmed baking sheet. Divide bananas among ramekins.
2. In a small bowl combine crushed cookies, flour, 1 Tbsp. brown sugar, and ¼ tsp. salt. Add 2 Tbsp. unsalted butter; stir together until crumbly.
3. In a small saucepan melt remaining 3 Tbsp. unsalted butter over medium. Stir in remaining ¼ cup brown sugar. Bring to boiling; reduce heat. Boil gently 3 minutes, stirring frequently. Remove from heat. Carefully whisk in rum, vanilla, and remaining ¼ tsp. salt; mixture will foam up. Return to boiling. Boil gently 1 minute more, stirring constantly. Spoon hot syrup over bananas. Sprinkle cookie mixture over each.
4. Bake 25 to 30 minutes or until bubbly and browned. Let cool 15 minutes. Serve warm with ice cream. Serves 4.

EACH CRISP *489 cal, 23 g fat (14 g sat fat), 62 mg chol, 429 mg sodium, 66 g carb, 4 g fiber, 42 g sugars, 4 g pro*

in praise of
PEARS

If you've been gifted a box of pears this season, savor your good fortune. You've received a blank canvas to create elegant recipes or the simplest of dishes. Let this beautifully versatile fruit inspire you.

HOW TO BUY PEARS

Pears are one of only a few common fruits that don't ripen on the tree. Instead, they reach peak texture and flavor at room temperature. Buy them firm, smooth, and bruise-free, then check them daily for ripeness. The fruit is ready to eat when its neck yields to gentle pressure. At that point, refrigerate the pears up to 5 days—if you can resist devouring them immediately.

PEPPERY PEAR-VANILLA SCONES

Sharp bursts of tart cranberries and warm black pepper will wake up taste buds.

HANDS-ON TIME 25 min.
TOTAL TIME 40 min.

2¾ cups all-purpose flour
½ cup sugar
1   Tbsp. baking powder
1   tsp. freshly ground black pepper
½ cup cold butter, cut up
1   cup fresh or frozen cranberries
½ cup finely chopped fresh pear
½ cup chopped walnuts
2   eggs
¾ cup plus 1 Tbsp. heavy cream
1   tsp. vanilla bean paste
1   egg yolk
1   small pear, halved, cored, and very thinly sliced
    Vanilla Bean and Pepper Butter

1. Preheat oven to 400°F. Line an extra-large baking sheet with parchment paper. In a large bowl stir together flour, sugar, baking powder, pepper, and ½ tsp. salt. Using a pastry blender, cut in butter until mixture resembles coarse crumbs. Stir in cranberries, finely chopped pear, and walnuts. Make a well in center of flour mixture.

2. In a small bowl whisk together the 2 eggs, ¾ cup cream, and vanilla bean paste. Add egg mixture to flour mixture. Using a fork, stir just until moistened. Turn dough out onto a lightly floured surface, knead dough by gently folding and pressing 10 to 12 strokes or until dough holds together.

3. Divide dough in half. Pat each half into a 6-inch circle. Cut each circle into six wedges. Place wedges on prepared baking sheet. In a small bowl combine the egg yolk and remaining 1 Tbsp. cream. Brush some yolk mixture over wedges. Arrange pear slices and, if desired, additional cranberries on wedges. Brush with remaining yolk mixture. Sprinkle with additional pepper.

4. Bake 15 minutes or until golden. Remove from baking sheet; let cool slightly on wire rack. Serve with Vanilla Bean and Pepper Butter. Makes 12 scones.

Vanilla Bean and Pepper Butter
In a small bowl beat together ½ cup softened butter, ½ tsp. freshly ground black pepper, and ¼ tsp. vanilla bean paste until smooth.

EACH SCONE *326 cal, 18 g fat (9 g sat fat), 86 mg chol, 299 mg sodium, 36 g carb, 2 g fiber, 11 g sugars, 6 g pro*

BOSC PEARS—DEEP AND DENSELY SWEET—ARE THE CLASSIC CHOICE FOR BAKING.

**SOUFFLÉ PANCAKES WITH
MAPLE-PEAR SYRUP**
Recipe on page 253

SAVORY PEARS
& SQUASH WITH
GRANOLA TUMBLE
Recipe on page 253

WINTER PEAR
SALAD

WINTER PEAR SALAD

Combine red and green Anjou pears, Brussels sprouts, citrus, and grapes in this seasonal salad.

TOTAL TIME 40 min.

- 4 cups thinly sliced stemmed kale
- 2 cups thinly shaved Brussels sprouts
- 3 pears, halved, cored, and sliced
- 1 orange, peeled and sliced
- 1 cup kumquats, halved
- 1 cup red seedless grapes, halved
- ½ cup olive oil
- ⅓ cup Prosecco or dry white wine
- ¼ cup white wine vinegar
- 2 Tbsp. finely chopped shallot
- 1 Tbsp. chopped fresh chives
- 2 tsp. Dijon mustard
- ¼ cup pomegranate seeds (optional)

1. Mix together kale and Brussels sprouts. Arrange pears, orange slices, kumquats, and grapes over greens.
2. For dressing: In a screw-top jar shake well to combine the olive oil, Prosecco, vinegar, shallot, chives, mustard, ½ tsp. salt, and ¼ tsp. black pepper. Drizzle dressing over salad. If desired, sprinkle with pomegranate seeds. Serves 12.

EACH SERVING *156 cal, 10 g fat (1 g sat fat), 30 mg sodium, 16 g carb, 4 g fiber, 10 g sugars, 2 g pro*

SAVORY PEARS & SQUASH WITH GRANOLA TUMBLE

Photo on page 251
HANDS-ON TIME 25 min.
TOTAL TIME 55 min.

- 4 medium pears
- 1 1½-lb. butternut squash, peeled, seeded, and cubed (about 4 cups)
- ½ cup chopped onion
- 2 cloves garlic
- ½ cup butter
- 2 to 4 Tbsp. heavy cream
- ¼ cup regular rolled oats
- 2 Tbsp. chopped pecans
- 2 Tbsp. raw pepitas (pumpkin seeds)
- 2 large shallots, peeled and quartered
- ⅓ cup sage leaves (about 15 leaves)

1. Peel, halve, and core two pears and cut into large pieces. Halve and core the remaining two pears; cut into ½-inch thick wedges; set aside.

2. In a 4- to 5-qt. pot combine pear pieces, squash, onion, and garlic. Add salted water to cover. Bring to boiling; reduce heat. Cover and simmer 15 to 20 minutes or until very tender. Drain well; return to pot. Add half the butter, ½ tsp. salt, and ¼ tsp. black pepper. Cover and let stand 5 minutes to soften. Mash with a potato masher. Stir in enough cream for desired consistency.
3. Meanwhile, for granola: In a large skillet melt 1 Tbsp. butter over medium. Add oats, pecans, and pepitas. Cook and stir 3 to 5 minutes or until toasted. Transfer to foil to cool.
4. In the same skillet heat the remaining 3 Tbsp. butter over medium-high. Add pear wedges; cook 3 to 5 minutes or until lightly browned and tender, turning occasionally. Using a slotted spoon, transfer pears to a large bowl. Add shallots to skillet; cook 5 minutes or until tender and browned, turning occasionally. (Reduce temperature if necessary to prevent overbrowning.) Using a slotted spoon, transfer shallots to bowl with pears. Add sage to skillet; cook 1 to 2 minutes or until browned and crisp, stirring occasionally. Transfer to bowl with pears and shallots.
5. To serve, spread mashed squash mixture in a serving dish. Top with shallot-pear mixture. Sprinkle with granola. Serves 6.

EACH SERVING *327 cal, 21 g fat (11 g sat fat), 46 mg chol, 340 mg sodium, 37 g carb, 7 g fiber, 16 g sugars, 4 g pro*

SOUFFLÉ PANCAKES WITH MAPLE-PEAR SYRUP

Photo on page 250

Each puffy pancake has plenty of tiny air pockets to absorb every drop of maple-pear syrup.

HANDS-ON TIME 15 min.
TOTAL TIME 40 min.

- Nonstick cooking spray
- 2 eggs, separated
- ½ cup milk
- 2 Tbsp. butter, melted
- ½ tsp. vanilla
- ¾ cup cake flour
- 1 tsp. baking powder
- ¼ tsp. apple pie spice or ground cinnamon

- ½ tsp. lemon juice
- 2 Tbsp. sugar
- Maple-Pear Syrup

1. Make six foil rings* or use 4-inch cake rings or 3×1-inch round cookie cutters. Coat insides of rings or round cutters with nonstick cooking spray.
2. In a large bowl whisk together egg yolks, milk, butter, vanilla, and ¼ tsp. salt. Holding a sieve over the bowl, sift cake flour, baking powder, and spice into yolk mixture. Whisk to combine.
3. Place egg whites in a large mixing bowl; add lemon juice. Beat egg whites with a mixer on medium to high until frothy. Gradually beat in sugar until stiff peaks form (tips stand straight). Fold half the beaten egg whites into the yolk mixture. Repeat with remaining beaten egg whites.
4. Arrange three rings in an extra-large lightly oiled skillet. Heat over medium-low. Spoon batter into rings, filling each about two-thirds full. (Fill 4-inch rings half full; fill cookie cutter to the top.) Add 1 Tbsp. water to skillet around cakes. Cook, covered, 8 minutes or until bottoms are browned. Use kitchen scissors to cut away foil from cakes. (Or loosen cakes from rings, then lift rings away. Leave cookie cutters on cakes.) Carefully turn cakes. Add 1 Tbsp. water to skillet. Cook, covered, 5 minutes more or until set and browned on bottom. Remove to a plate. Repeat with remaining rings and batter. (If using cookie cutters, let them cool a few minutes, then loosen and remove cake.) Serve pancakes with Maple-Pear Syrup. Serves 6.

*Foil Rings Soufflé pancakes need support as they cook. To make rings, fold a 12×6-inch piece of foil lengthwise in thirds to make a 12×2-inch strip. Bring short ends together to form a ring 3 to 3½ inches in diameter; tape to secure.
Maple-Pear Syrup In a small saucepan combine 1 cup finely chopped pears, ¾ cup pure maple syrup, and, if desired, 2 to 3 tsp. pear liqueur or pear nectar. Warm over low heat.

EACH PANCAKE *265 cal, 6 g fat (3 g sat fat), 74 mg chol, 247 mg sodium, 49 g carb, 1 g fiber, 31 g sugars, 4 g pro*

EACH FLAVORFUL POACHING LIQUID CHANGES THE PERSONALITY OF THIS CLASSIC DESSERT. THE FIRM TEXTURE OF BOSC PEARS IS IDEAL FOR POACHING, ALTHOUGH ANJOU OR BARTLETT ALSO POACH WELL.

POACHED PEARS

HANDS-ON TIME 15 min.
TOTAL TIME 2 hr. 25 min., includes cooling

Poaching Liquid
6 **Bosc pears, peeled, halved, and cored**
   Blackberries, chopped pistachios, and/or mascarpone cheese (optional)

In a 5- to 6-qt. pot bring Poaching Liquid to boiling; reduce heat. Simmer, uncovered, 10 minutes. Add pears. Return to boiling; reduce heat. Simmer, covered, 10 to 15 minutes or until pears are tender. Let cool in syrup. If desired, serve with blackberries, pistachios, and/or mascarpone cheese. Serves 6.

White Wine Poaching Liquid Combine 2 cups water, 2 cups dry white wine, 1 cup sugar, and 2 whole star anise.
EACH SERVING *313 cal, 4 mg sodium, 64 g carb, 6 g fiber, 52 g sugars, 1 g pro*

Red Wine-Pomegranate Poaching Liquid Combine 2 cups dry red wine, 1 cup pomegranate juice, 1 cup water, ¼ cup packed brown sugar, two 3-inch cinnamon sticks, 8 whole cloves, and 4 whole allspice.
EACH SERVING *242 cal, 9 mg sodium, 45 g carb, 6 g fiber, 33 g sugars, 1 g pro*

Citrus-Maple Poaching Liquid Combine 2 cups water, 2 cups orange juice, ½ cup pure maple syrup, two 3-inch cinnamon sticks, and ½ tsp. ground turmeric.
EACH SERVING *226 cal, 4 mg sodium, 55 g carb, 6 g fiber, 41 g sugars, 1 g pro*

PEAR TARTS WITH CARAMELIZED PASTRY CREAM

Photo on page 257

HANDS-ON TIME 40 min.
TOTAL TIME 3 hr. 10 min., includes chilling

1¼ **cups granulated sugar**
2   **cups milk**
4   **egg yolks**
⅓   **cup cornstarch**
¼   **cup butter**
1   **tsp. vanilla**
2   **cups all-purpose flour**
½   **cup powdered sugar**
½   **tsp. ground ginger**
¼   **tsp. ground cinnamon**
⅛   **tsp. ground cloves**
1   **cup plus 3 Tbsp. butter**
2   **Tbsp. molasses**
4   **medium pears, cored and halved**
3   **Tbsp. packed brown sugar**
    Pomegranate seeds

1. For pastry cream: Line a 15×10-inch baking pan with parchment paper. In an extra-large skillet heat granulated sugar over medium-high until sugar starts to melt. Reduce heat to medium-low. Stir unmelted sugar into melted sugar. When all sugar is melted and amber colored, pour into prepared baking pan; let cool. Break caramelized sugar into pieces. Set aside some shards for garnish. Place remaining caramelized sugar in a food processor. Process until fine (you should have about 1 cup). In a medium saucepan combine the milk and half the caramelized sugar. Cook over medium just until edges are bubbly. Meanwhile, in a large bowl stir together egg yolks, remaining caramelized sugar, cornstarch, and ½ tsp. salt until combined. Gradually stir about half the hot milk mixture into yolk mixture. Return all to saucepan. Cook and stir over medium until very thick and bubbly. You may need to whisk as it thickens. Remove from heat. Stir in the ¼ cup butter and the vanilla. Transfer pastry cream to a bowl; cover surface with plastic wrap. Let cool 30 minutes. Chill 2 hours.

2. Meanwhile, preheat oven to 350°F. In a large bowl stir together flour, powdered sugar, ginger, cinnamon, and cloves. Using a pastry blender, cut in 1 cup butter until pieces are pea-size. Drizzle with molasses and toss gently with a fork. Knead gently until dough holds together. Divide into eight equal pieces.

3. Pat each dough portion into a 4-inch tart pan with or without removable bottom. Prick pastry all over with fork. Arrange on a baking sheet. Bake 17 to 20 minutes or until golden. Let cool; gently remove from pans.

4. Increase oven to 400°F. Arrange pear halves cut sides down in a 2-qt. rectangular baking dish. In a small saucepan combine ¼ cup water, the brown sugar, and remaining 3 Tbsp. butter. Stir over medium until sugar is dissolved and butter is melted. Pour over pears in baking dish. Roast, uncovered, 30 minutes or until tender, basting with liquid twice. Let cool slightly. Remove and slice pears, reserving liquid.

5. To assemble: Divide pastry cream evenly among crusts. Arrange pears on cream then drizzle with some of the cooking liquid. Top each with pomegranate seeds and reserved caramelized sugar shards. Serves 8.
EACH TART *724 cal, 37 g fat (23 g sat fat), 185 mg chol, 447 mg sodium, 94 g carb, 4 g fiber, 60 g sugars, 7 g pro*

POACHED
PEARS

PEAR-ROSEMARY
POTATO GRATIN
Recipe on page 258

PEAR TARTS WITH CARAMELIZED PASTRY CREAM
Recipe on page 254

257

PEAR-ROSEMARY POTATO GRATIN

Photo on page 256

Pears lighten the carb-heavy reputation of this traditional dish, while contributing sweetness to the herbed cheese sauce. For baking, bosc pears hold the best shape.

HANDS-ON TIME 25 min.
TOTAL TIME 1 hr. 15 min.

- 12   oz. yellow potatoes, sliced ⅛ inch thick
- 2   Bosc pears, peeled, halved, cored, and sliced lengthwise ⅛ inch thick
- 1   5.2-oz. pkg. semisoft cheese with garlic and fine herbs (such as Boursin)
- ¾   cup half-and-half
- 4   Tbsp. grated Parmesan cheese
- 1   Tbsp. chopped fresh rosemary
- ½   tsp. lemon zest

1. Preheat oven to 375°F. In a medium saucepan bring salted water to boiling. Add potato slices. Simmer, uncovered, 3 minutes; drain. Let cool slightly, about 10 minutes. In a 1½-qt. gratin dish alternate potato and pear slices.

2. In a small saucepan combine semisoft cheese, half-and-half, 2 Tbsp. Parmesan, and ¼ tsp. salt. Whisk over medium-low just until cheese is melted. Add rosemary and zest. Pour over potato and pear slices. Sprinkle with remaining 2 Tbsp. Parmesan. If desired, top with additional rosemary and lemon zest strips.

3. Bake, uncovered, 40 minutes or until potatoes are tender and browned. Let stand 10 minutes. Remove rosemary and lemon zest strips, if used. Serves 4.

EACH SERVING *353 cal, 22 g fat (14 g sat fat), 58 mg chol, 498 mg sodium, 32 g carb, 4 g fiber, 12 g sugars, 7 g pro*

PICK YOUR PEARS

At about 100 calories each, pears are a good source of vitamins C and K, fiber, and antioxidants. Pictured above, left to right, top to bottom:

RED ANJOU Aromatic, juicy, and sweeter than its green variety.

GREEN ANJOU Best all-purpose pear. Subtly sweet with hints of lemon and lime. Skin stays green even when ripe.

BARTLETT Signature pear flavor with abundant juice. Ideal for canning.

BOSC Crisp, firm flesh with notes of woodsy spice and honey.

STARKRIMSON Aromatic with a floral essence. Red skin changes to bright crimson as it ripens.

CONCORDE Crunchy, earthy all-purpose pear with hints of vanilla.

COMICE Aka the Christmas pear. It's buttery, extra sweet, and an ideal partner to cheese.

SECKEL Bite-size, crunchy, and ultrasweet, it's known as the dessert pear.

FORELLE Green skin with red freckles that turns golden as it ripens. Crisp and tangy. Eat fresh.

EGG BAKE REMIX

This strata takes its cue from North African shakshuka, a popular brunch menu item of eggs poached in a bold smoky tomato sauce.

FIRE-ROASTED TOMATO STRATA

HANDS-ON TIME 25 min.
TOTAL TIME 2 hr. 40 min.

7	to 8 cups crusty bread cubes
1	to 1½ tsp. ground cumin
1	tsp. sweet paprika
⅛	to ¼ tsp. cayenne pepper
1	Tbsp. olive oil
1	cup chopped onion
1	cup chopped red bell pepper
3	cloves garlic, minced
1	14.5-oz. can diced fire-roasted tomatoes, drained, reserve 2 Tbsp. liquid
¾	cup grape tomatoes, quartered
4	to 6 oz. crumbled feta cheese
16	eggs
3	cups milk
¼	cup fresh cilantro

1. Spread half the bread cubes in a greased 3-qt. baking dish. In a small bowl stir together cumin, paprika, cayenne, and ½ tsp. salt.
2. In a large skillet heat oil over medium. Add onion, bell pepper, and garlic; cook 3 minutes or until tender. Stir in tomatoes, reserved tomato liquid, and half the spice mixture. Spoon half the tomato mixture over bread. Sprinkle with half the feta. Repeat layers.
3. In a bowl whisk together 6 eggs, milk, and remaining spice mixture. Pour over ingredients in dish; press to moisten bread. Chill, covered, 1 hour or up to 24 hours.
4. Preheat oven to 325°F. Bake, uncovered, 30 minutes. Using the back of a spoon, press 10 indents in strata top. Slip an egg into each indentation. Bake 25 to 30 minutes more or until a thermometer registers 170°F. Let stand 15 minutes. Top with cilantro and freshly ground black pepper. Serves 10.
EACH SERVING *327 cal, 14 g fat (5 g sat fat), 314 mg chol, 639 mg sodium, 32 g carb, 3 g fiber, 7 g sugars, 19 g pro*

ALMOND SUGAR COOKIES & MASCARPONE-COCOA CUTOUTS
Recipes on page 280

december

Expectations for traditional holiday foods run deep—and include a vast variety of cookies and bars, warm and tender breads, hearty soups, enticing main dishes, and luscious desserts.

265   268   287

GINGERBREAD
CINNAMON STAR
Recipe on page 265

breakfast
BRUNCH STAR

Even the aroma of cinnamon rolls cues a comforting, inviting atmosphere. These gingerbread-inspired brunch treats are extra luscious, with warm spices and a scoop of mashed potatoes stirred into the dough.

GINGERBREAD CINNAMON ROLLS
Recipe on page 264

THIS SIMPLE BUT IMPRESSIVE STAR SHAPE GIVES A FAVORITE PASTRY A SPECIAL HOLIDAY TWIST. FOR TRADITIONALISTS, A CLASSIC ROLL SHAPE IS ALWAYS WELCOME— AND JUST AS DELICIOUS.

GINGERBREAD CINNAMON ROLLS

Photo on page 263

Shaped traditionally or in a festive holiday centerpiece, this brunch bread will star only briefly. Expect each delicious bite to be savored—and the bread to disappear quickly.

HANDS-ON TIME 30 min.
TOTAL TIME 2 hr. 30 min.

3¾ to 4¼ cups all-purpose flour
4   tsp. ground ginger
4   tsp. ground cinnamon
½   tsp. ground cloves
1   pkg. active dry yeast
¾   cup milk
1   cup mashed potatoes
⅓   cup butter
⅓   cup molasses
2   eggs
½   cup packed brown sugar
¼   cup butter, softened
    Spiced Brown Butter Frosting

1. In a large bowl stir together 1½ cups flour, 3 tsp. ginger, 1 tsp. cinnamon, ¼ tsp. cloves, and the yeast. In a 2-qt. saucepan heat and stir milk, mashed potatoes, ⅓ cup butter, the molasses, and 1 tsp. salt just until warm (120°F to 130°F) and butter is almost melted. Add milk mixture and eggs to flour mixture. Mix until smooth. Add about 2 cups flour and stir in as much as you can.

2. Turn dough out onto a lightly floured surface. Knead in enough of the remaining flour to make a moderately soft dough that is smooth and elastic (3 to 5 minutes total). Shape dough into a ball. Place in a lightly greased bowl, turning to grease surface of dough. Cover; let rise until double in size (45 to 60 minutes).

3. Punch dough down. Turn out onto a lightly floured surface.* For traditional rolls, cover; let rest 10 minutes. Lightly grease a 13×9-inch baking pan.

4. For filling: In a small bowl stir together brown sugar and remaining ginger, cinnamon, and cloves.

5. Roll dough into an 18×12-inch rectangle. Spread with softened butter and sprinkle with filling, leaving 1 inch unfilled along one long side. Roll up tightly, starting from filled long side and pinching seam to seal. Cut into 12 slices; arrange in pan. Cover; let rise until nearly double in size (30 minutes).

6. Preheat oven to 375°F. Bake 25 to 30 minutes or until golden. Cool in pan on a wire rack 10 minutes; invert to remove from pan. Invert again. Spread with Spiced Brown Butter Frosting. Makes 12 rolls.

***Tip** To make a star shape instead of rolls, follow the step-by-step directions on page 265.

Spiced Brown Butter Frosting In a 1- to 1½-qt. saucepan melt ¾ cup butter over low until butter turns a delicate light brown, stirring occasionally. Let cool slightly. In a large bowl combine 3⅔ cups powdered sugar, 1 tsp. ground ginger, ½ tsp. ground cinnamon, dash ground cloves, 2 Tbsp. milk, and 1 tsp. vanilla. Stir in the brown butter until combined. Add additional milk, 1 tsp. at a time, to reach spreading consistency. Makes 1¾ cups.

EACH ROLL *567 cal, 22 g fat (14 g sat fat), 87 mg chol, 385 mg sodium, 87 g carb, 2 g fiber, 53 g sugars, 7 g pro*

1 After punching down dough in Step 3, divide into eight portions. Let rest 10 minutes. Roll each to a 10-inch round. Melt the ¼ cup butter. For each star: On a parchment-lined baking sheet, brush one round with melted butter then sprinkle with filling.

2 Repeat with two more layers of dough, butter, and filling. Top with fourth dough round; brush with melted butter. Gently press a 2½-inch round cutter into the center to create an indent. Cut 16 wedges, leaving center circle intact.

GINGERBREAD CINNAMON STAR: A DUSTING OF POWDERED SUGAR IS A SWEET FINISHING TOUCH. AFTER THE STAR COOLS, PLACE A SMALL PAPER STAR IN THE CENTER THEN SPRINKLE THE ROLLS WITH POWDERED SUGAR. ROLL FROZEN CRANBERRIES IN GRANULATED SUGAR TO SCATTER ON TOP FOR FESTIVE SPARKLE.

3 Twist each wedge twice, pinching outer edges to secure. Alternate direction of each twisted wedge. Let rise 30 minutes; brush with melted butter and bake 20 minutes at 375°F.

BIG ON TRADITIONS

Holiday menus vary widely among traditions—with heritage, culture, and customs contributing to the proverbial buffet. Here, noted food personalities attest to a range of delicious choices.

REVERSE-SEAR PRIME RIB WITH SOY-GINGER GRAVY

A less-expensive top round roast may be substituted for prime rib with good results. Roast a 5-lb. top round roast approximately 3 hours at 250°F for medium rare.

HANDS-ON TIME 30 min.
TOTAL TIME 4 hr. 15 min.

- 1 Tbsp. vegetable oil
- 1½ cups roughly chopped carrots
- 1½ cups roughly chopped onion
- 8 garlic cloves, smashed
- 1 3-inch knob of ginger, cut into ½-inch disks
- 2 cups sake or dry white wine
- 1 qt. homemade or purchased low-sodium chicken stock
- 1 8-lb. standing rib roast (prime rib) or one 5-lb. top round roast (see above)
  Kosher salt
- 4 Tbsp. unsalted butter
- 2 Tbsp. all-purpose flour
- 2 Tbsp. soy sauce

1. Adjust oven rack to lowest position. Preheat oven to 250°F. Heat oil in a large Dutch oven over high until lightly smoking. Add carrots, onion, garlic, and ginger. Cook, stirring occasionally, until deeply browned and charred in spots, 8 to 10 minutes. Add sake. Using a wooden spoon, scrape up any browned bits from bottom of pan. Allow sake to reduce by half, about 10 minutes. Add stock and remove from heat.
2. Pour vegetables and stock mixture into a large roasting pan. Place a V rack on top, arranging vegetables so rack rests on bottom of pan.

3. Generously season rib roast with kosher salt and black pepper on all sides, then place on rack, fat cap facing up. Roast until center of rib roast registers 125°F on an instant-read thermometer for medium-rare or 135°F for medium, 3½ to 4 hours.
4. Remove roast from oven, transfer to a large platter, and tent loosely with foil. Place in a warm spot in the kitchen and allow to rest while making gravy. Meanwhile, increase oven temperature to highest possible setting, 500°F to 550°F.
5. Strain vegetables and drippings through a fine-mesh strainer into a medium saucepan, pressing on the vegetables with the back of a ladle to extract as much liquid as possible. Discard vegetables. Using a ladle, skim and discard excess fat off the top of the liquid. Bring liquid to a boil, reduce to a simmer, and cook until reduced to about 2 cups, 25 to 30 minutes.
6. To make the Soy-Ginger Gravy: Heat butter and flour in a small saucepan over medium heat; cook, whisking frequently, until mixture is golden blond and has a nutty aroma, about 3 minutes. Whisking constantly, slowly drizzle in the reduced liquid. Bring to a simmer, then whisk in the soy sauce. Season to taste.
7. Wipe out the roasting pan and replace the V rack. Place the foil-tented rib roast on the rack. Ten minutes before serving, remove foil and place roast back in hot oven until well-browned and crisp on the exterior, 6 to 10 minutes. Remove from oven, carve rib roast and serve immediately. Pass the Soy-Ginger Gravy. Serves 8 to 10.
EACH SERVING *593 cal, 27 g fat (11 g sat fat), 155 mg chol, 802 mg sodium, 6 g carb, 62 g pro*

J. KENJI LÓPEZ-ALT

Kenji is the chief culinary adviser for seriouseats.com and author of the award-winning *The Food Lab: Better Home Cooking Through Science.* He lives in San Mateo, CA, and recently released a children's book called *Every Night Is Pizza Night.*

"We go all out at Christmas," Kenji says. "Ever since I was a kid, we've done a whole roasted prime rib." The cookbook author, chef, and restaurateur is known for his thoroughly tested and explained recipes. This one is no different. His go-to technique uses a low-and-slow cook with a final blast of heat to caramelize the roast. Inspired by his mother's Japanese heritage, the finishing jus gets rich flavor from a dose of soy sauce. "Despite me being a professional chef for years, it wasn't until the last 10 [years] that my mom let me cook the prime rib. I used this recipe, and I've been in charge ever since."

"KWANZAA IS ANOTHER WAY TO CONNECT DURING THE HOLIDAYS."

RICHE HOLMES GRANT

Riche is a designer and the creator behind the web series *The Riche Life*. She splits her time between the Washington, D.C., area and Los Angeles with her husband and daughter.

For Riche, December is all about holidays. The blogger (*The Riche Life*) celebrates both Christmas and Kwanzaa with her family. "Kwanzaa is an African American cultural holiday," Riche says. "It's all about family, community, and being together." The weeklong holiday starts December 26 and usually culminates in a celebratory dinner. Riche puts a Caribbean spin on the menu: Her Jerk Chicken takes on maximum flavor as it marinates overnight in a mixture of chiles, brown sugar, and spices. She makes enough pepper jelly to serve with the corn bread and to gift a few jars.

JERK CHICKEN

HANDS-ON TIME 20 min.
TOTAL TIME 1 hr. 20 min., plus overnight marinating

- 1 large onion, cut up
- 5 scallions, trimmed and cut up
- 2 to 3 Scotch bonnet or habanero peppers, stemmed, seeded, and cut up (tip, page 28)
- 1 Tbsp. chopped fresh ginger
- 2 garlic cloves
- 1 oz. fresh thyme
- ¼ cup packed brown sugar
- 1 Tbsp. kosher salt
- 1 tsp. coarsely ground black pepper
- 1 tsp. dried thyme
- 1 tsp. ground cinnamon
- 1 tsp. ground allspice
- ½ tsp. ground nutmeg
- ½ tsp. ground cloves
- 2 Tbsp. fresh lime juice
- 2 Tbsp. olive oil
- 2 Tbsp. reduced-sodium soy sauce
- 4 lb. meaty chicken pieces (preferably dark meat)

1. In a food processor combine all ingredients except chicken. Process until marinade is uniform but not pureed.
2. Place the chicken in a resealable plastic bag then pour marinade over chicken. Seal bag. Turn bag to coat all pieces and place in a shallow dish. Refrigerate chicken 18 to 24 hours.
3. Preheat oven to 375°F. Remove chicken from marinade, discarding any remaining marinade. Arrange chicken pieces, skin side up, in a foil-lined 13×9-inch baking pan. Bake, uncovered, about 50 minutes or until an instant-read thermometer inserted in chicken registers at least 175°F (165°F for light meat).
4. Once chicken is fully cooked, broil 5 inches from the heat for 2 to 3 minutes until browned and crisp. Let stand under tented foil for approximately 10 to 15 minutes before serving. Serves 8.
EACH SERVING *345 cal, 16 g fat (4 g sat fat), 104 mg chol, 626 mg sodium, 14 g carb, 2 g fiber, 9 g sugars, 35 g pro*

SKILLET CORN BREAD

HANDS-ON TIME 15 min.
TOTAL TIME 35 min.

- 1 cup yellow cornmeal
- 1 cup all-purpose flour
- ¼ cup sugar
- 2 tsp. baking powder
- 1 tsp. baking soda
- 1 tsp. kosher salt
- 2 eggs
- 1½ cups buttermilk
- 8 Tbsp. unsalted butter, melted Whipped Honey Butter (optional) Hot Pepper Jelly optional)

1. Place a 10-inch cast-iron skillet in oven and preheat to 400°F. In a large bowl whisk together cornmeal, flour, sugar, baking powder, baking soda, and salt.
2. In a medium bowl lightly whisk eggs. Stir in buttermilk and 6 Tbsp. of the butter. Pour egg mixture into cornmeal mixture. Stir just until combined.
3. Carefully remove skillet from the oven and add 1 Tbsp. remaining melted butter to coat the bottom and sides of the pan. (Be careful; it will pop.) Pour batter into skillet.
4. Bake 18 to 20 minutes or until corn bread is golden brown and a toothpick inserted in the center comes out clean. Drizzle the remaining melted butter over the top of the hot corn bread. If desired, serve with Whipped Honey Butter and/or Hot Pepper Jelly. Serves 8.
EACH SERVING *275 cal, 14 g fat (8 g sat fat), 79 mg chol, 602 mg sodium, 33 g carb, 2 g fiber, 9 g sugars, 6 g pro*
Whipped Honey Butter In a small bowl combine ⅓ cup softened unsalted butter, ¼ cup honey, and, if desired, a pinch of sea salt. Using a hand mixer, beat until fluffy. Store in the refrigerator up to 1 week. Serve at room temperature. Makes ½ cup.
Hot Pepper Jelly In a large pot combine 2 cups finely chopped and seeded red bell pepper, 1 cup finely chopped and seeded jalapeño pepper, 2 cups apple cider vinegar, and 6 Tbsp. powdered pectin for lower-sugar recipes. Bring mixture to a full boil. Add 4 cups sugar to pot. Return to full rolling boil. Cook and stir 1 minute. Remove from heat; skim off foam as needed. Ladle hot mixture into clean, hot 4-oz. or half-pint jars, leaving ¼-inch headspace. Process immediately in water bath canner for 10 minutes. Remove and cool on a wire rack; let stand at least 24 hours. Makes twelve 4-oz. or 6 half-pint jars.

ALEX ADDS A SPLASH OF THE FRENCH LIQUEURS PERNOD OR PASTIS FOR A FENNEL-LIKE FLAVOR. "SIP A GLASS OF IT WHILE COOKING THIS TO GET INTO THE MOOD," ALEX SAYS.

SHRIMP BISQUE

Alex serves her creamy soup in caraway-studded bread bowls (recipe, page 272).

HANDS-ON TIME 55 min.
TOTAL TIME 1 hr. 30 min.

- 6 Tbsp. unsalted butter
- 1½ lb. medium (28–30 count) shrimp, peeled (reserve shells)
- ¼ cup Pernod or pastis
  Kosher salt
- 1 dried bay leaf
  Leaves from 4 sprigs fresh basil
- 2 small yellow onions, minced
- 2 celery stalks, thinly sliced
- 2 small carrots, peeled and thinly sliced
- 2 Tbsp. dry long grain white rice
- ½ tsp. cayenne pepper
- 1 28-oz. can peeled whole tomatoes, drained
- 2 cups heavy cream
- 1 Tbsp. Worcestershire sauce
- 1 tsp. Tabasco sauce
  Juice of 1 large lemon
- 6 sprigs fresh tarragon, chopped (stems and all)
  Bread Bowls (recipe, page 272) (optional)

1. To make the shrimp stock: In a large heavy-bottom pot melt 2 Tbsp. butter over medium, then add the reserved shrimp shells. Cook, stirring, until the shells brown slightly, 5 to 8 minutes. Add Pernod and cook until it has evaporated, 5 to 8 minutes (do not rush this step). Add 8 cups water, a pinch kosher salt, and the bay leaf. Bring to a boil, reduce heat to medium, and simmer 20 minutes. Taste the stock. If it seems watery, cook another 5 to 8 minutes. Strain the stock through a fine-mesh sieve into a large bowl. Press on the shells as you strain the stock to maximize the flavor. Discard the shells (don't clean the pot; you'll use it again). Set the stock aside.

2. To cook the shrimp: In a large sauté pan heat 1 Tbsp. butter over low and stir in the shrimp along with a generous pinch of salt. Cook, stirring, just until shrimp turns pink, 2 to 3 minutes. Transfer shrimp to a medium bowl and stir in the basil; refrigerate.

3. To make the soup: In the same heavy-bottom pot combine remaining 3 Tbsp. butter with the onions, celery, carrots, rice, cayenne, and a pinch of salt. Cook over medium until the vegetables are tender, 10 to 12 minutes. Add tomatoes and shrimp stock. Simmer until the vegetables are soft, 15 to 20 minutes. Stir in the cream, Worcestershire sauce, and Tabasco, and simmer until all the ingredients meld together, 2 to 3 minutes. Taste; adjust seasoning.

4. To finish the soup: Add about one-fourth of the soup to a blender; puree. Pour the puree back into the soup pot, then puree another one-fourth of the soup. Return it to the pot (this way the soup has body, but also some texture from the unpureed vegetables). Bring soup to a simmer. Taste for seasoning. Stir in the shrimp, lemon juice, and tarragon. If desired, serve soup in Bread Bowls. Serve immediately. Serves 8.
EACH SERVING *404 cal, 31 g fat (19 g sat fat), 210 mg chol, 347 mg sodium, 11 g carb, 2 g fiber, 6 g sugars, 18 g pro*

ALEX GUARNASCHELLI

When she's not cooking at Butter, her Manhattan restaurant, you can find Alex on numerous *Food Network* shows. She lives in New York City with her daughter and has a new book, *Cook with Me*, which explores how her family relationships have shaped her as a chef.

"Growing up we'd eat shrimp at home once a year," Alex says. The chef, cookbook author, and restaurateur remembers eating both shrimp scampi and shrimp bisque with her parents during the holiday. "I knew it was Christmas if we were eating shrimp." Like most French bisques, Alex's starts with a homemade stock and is thickened with rice, but her recipe has some serious Italian influence. That, according to Alex, says everything about her heritage and childhood. "My father was Italian, but also a history teacher who loved everything about Napoleon Bonaparte. He could never choose between Italy and France, and that has impacted the way I cook and my traditions."

Reprinted with permission from *Cook with Me: 150 Recipes for the Home Cook* by Alex Guarnaschelli, copyright © 2020. Published by Clarkson Potter Publishers, an imprint of Penguin Random House.

WE ADJUSTED ALEX'S BREAD BOWL RECIPE TO MAKE FOUR LARGE BOWLS—VERSUS THE EIGHT IN HER ORIGINAL RECIPE—TO HOLD DINNER-SIZE PORTIONS OF BISQUE.

BREAD BOWLS

HANDS-ON TIME 25 min.
TOTAL TIME 3 hr. 25 min., includes rising

2¼	tsp. active dry yeast
2	Tbsp. extra virgin olive oil
3	cups bread flour
3	Tbsp. honey
1	Tbsp. blackstrap or full-flavor molasses
2	tsp. caraway seeds
1	Tbsp. kosher salt
1	cup whole-milk cottage cheese
1	egg

1. To prepare the yeast: In a medium bowl dissolve yeast in ½ cup warm water (110°F to 120°F). Set the bowl aside until yeast bubbles and froths a little, 5 to 10 minutes.

2. To make the dough: Oil a medium bowl with 1 Tbsp. olive oil. In the bowl of a stand mixer fitted with the paddle attachment, combine flour, honey, molasses, caraway seeds, and salt on low until blended. Blend in cottage cheese and egg. With the mixer on low, add yeast mixture and mix until dough becomes cohesive and starts to form a ball. Transfer dough to oiled bowl, cover with a kitchen towel, and set in a warm place to double in volume, 1½ to 2 hours.

3. Shape the dough: Grease a large sheet pan with the remaining 1 Tbsp. olive oil. Gently push the air out of the dough, and divide dough into four equal pieces. Shape them into balls, and place on the sheet pan. Flatten the balls gently with your hand. Cover loosely and let rise at room temperature 30 minutes.

4. Bake the bread: Preheat the oven to 400°F. Place the sheet pan in the oven, immediately reduce the heat to 350°F, and bake until the roll tops are light to medium brown, 20 to 25 minutes. The interior of the bread should register 185°F to 190°F on an instant-read thermometer. Remove from the oven. Allow the rolls to rest at least 30 minutes before turning them into bread bowls.

5. Finish the bread bowls: Slice off the tops of the rolls and set them aside. Carefully hollow out the center of each roll to make a bowl. (Reserve the interior of the rolls to dry for bread crumbs.) Place the bowls and tops on the sheet pans and bake for 5 to 10 minutes to firm the texture. Fill bowls with soup. Top each bowl with the roll top and serve. Makes 4 bread bowls.

EACH BREAD BOWL *571 cal, 12 g fat (3 g sat fat), 55 mg chol, 1,030 mg sodium, 94 g carb, 4 g fiber, 17 g sugars, 21 g pro*

TAMALES COLORADITOS

Substitute other meat for the pork tenderloin, or combine different meats as does Pati's mom, who uses a combo of ground beef and diced pork.

HANDS-ON TIME 2 hr. 15 min.
TOTAL TIME 3 hr. 25 min.

- 1 cup lard or vegetable shortening
- 1¼ tsp. kosher salt
- 3½ cups chicken broth, plus more as needed
- 1½ tsp. baking powder
- 1 lb. instant corn masa flour, preferably masa for tamales (about 3¼ cups)
- 3 guajillo peppers, stemmed, halved, and seeded (tip, page 28)
- 3 ancho peppers, stemmed, halved, and seeded (tip, page 28)
- 1 roma tomato
- 1 Tbsp. white distilled vinegar
- ½ tsp. dried oregano, preferably Mexican
- 2 whole cloves
- ½ tsp. ground Ceylon cinnamon or canella
  Pinch ground cumin
- 2 Tbsp. vegetable oil
- ⅓ cup chopped white onion
- 2 garlic cloves, finely chopped
- 1 lb. pork tenderloin, diced
  Freshly ground black pepper
- 1½ cups chicken broth
- ⅓ cup raisins
- ⅓ cup slivered almonds
- ⅓ cup Manzanilla olives stuffed with pimientos, chopped
- ½ tsp. brown sugar
- 25 dried corn husks

1. To make the masa (tamal dough): Place lard in a mixer and beat until very light, about 1 minute. Add salt and 1 Tbsp. of the broth, and continue to beat until white and fluffy, about 2 minutes. Add baking powder and beat in. Take turns adding corn masa flour and remaining 3½ cups broth in three or four additions. Continue beating about 10 minutes on medium until dough is homogeneous, very fluffy, and aerated. To test to see if the masa is ready, drop ½ tsp. into a cup of cold water. It should float. If it doesn't, beat 4 or 5 minutes more; test again.
2. To make the filling: Heat a comal or skillet over medium and toast guajillo and ancho peppers about 1 minute,

flipping a few times, until they become more pliable, lightly toasted, fragrant, and their inner skin turns opaque. Transfer to a medium saucepan. Add tomato, cover with water, and bring to a simmer over medium. Simmer 10 to 12 minutes until tomato is very soft and the peppers are plumped and soft.

3. Place peppers, tomato, and ½ cup of the chile pepper water in a blender or food processor. Add vinegar, oregano, cloves, cinnamon, and a pinch cumin; puree until smooth.

4. Heat 2 Tbsp. vegetable oil over medium-high in a large skillet. Add onion and cook, stirring occasionally, until tender and edges begin to brown, 3 to 4 minutes. Add garlic and cook, stirring, until fragrant, about 1 minute. Add meat, season with ¾ tsp. kosher salt and freshly ground black pepper, and cook, stirring occasionally, until lightly browned, 8 to 10 minutes.

5. Reduce heat to medium, pour chile puree over meat, and stir in the 1½ cups broth. Add raisins, almonds, olives, and brown sugar; stir together. Reduce heat to medium-low, cover, and cook 12 to 15 minutes, stirring occasionally. The mixture should cook down to the consistency of chile con carne.

6. To assemble the tamales: Soak dried corn husks in hot water for a few minutes or until they are pliable; drain. Lay out a corn husk with the tapered end toward you. Spread about 3 Tbsp. masa mixture into a 3- to 4-inch square on the husk.

The layer should be about ¼ inch thick, leaving a border of at least ½ inch on the sides. Spoon 1 to 2 Tbsp. filling in the middle of the masa.

7. Pick up the two long sides of the corn husk and bring them together (masa starts to swaddle the filling). Holding long sides together, roll them in the same direction around the tamal. Fold up bottom half of the husk. (The top will be left open.) Assemble all the tamales; place them as vertically as you can in a container as you go.

8. Place water in the bottom pan of a steamer (so water is under the basket); bring it to a simmer. Line the steamer basket with one or two layers of soaked corn husks. Place the tamales vertically in the prepared steamer with the open ends up. (If there is space left in the steamer, tuck in some corn husks, so the tamales won't dance around.) Cover with more corn husks and steam, covered, 50 minutes to 1 hour. The tamales are ready when they easily come free from the husks.

9. Tamales in the steamer stay warm about 2 hours. They can be made ahead and refrigerated, well wrapped, several days. They can also be frozen for months. In either case, reheat tamales in a steamer. Refrigerated tamales take about 20 minutes; frozen tamales take about 45 minutes. Makes 25 tamales.

EACH TAMALE *217 cal, 12 g fat (4 g sat fat), 20 mg chol, 201 mg sodium, 21 g carb, 3 g fiber, 2 g sugars, 7 g pro*

PATI JINICH

Pati is a chef, cookbook author, and the host and co-producer of PBS' *Pati's Mexican Table*. Her third cookbook is slated for fall 2021. She lives in the Washington, D.C., area with her husband and three sons.

In Mexican traditions, Pati says, "tamales are practically required on so many holidays." She says that "of course, tamales are also an everyday food for Mexicans. But I can eat tamales every day of the year and still feel the desperate need to have them for Christmas." Typically she, her husband, and her boys spend the holidays with family in Mexico. "We all stay together, and we're all making this food that we love." For tamales that feel extra special for the holidays, Pati suggests Tamales Coloraditos. The pork tenderloin filling simmers in a rich Oaxacan-style mole with chiles, olives, almonds, and raisins.

TECHNIQUE: TAMALES

Tamales are labor-intensive but, oh so worth it. Make the tamale assembly line a family affair (la tamalada) to lighten the load. The wrapping basics:

1 Spread each husk with a 3- to 4-inch square of masa dough and a couple tablespoons of filling.

2 Bring long edges together and fold to one side, rolling as if you're closing a paper bag.

3 Fold the tapered end of the husk from the bottom up, leaving the top open.

SERI STICKS TO THE SAME LATKE RECIPE EVERY YEAR. HER FAVE TOPPERS? SOUR CREAM AND SMOKED SALMON.

SERI KERTZNER

Seri is the brains behind Little Miss Party, an event planning and styling company based out of New York City. "My grandmother makes her latkes with leavening; hers are more fluffy," Seri says. "But I like mine really thin and crispy. If you don't celebrate Hanukkah, these make a great side dish for breakfast or brunch."

Seri knows how to party. The event planner, content creator, and self-proclaimed "chief party officer" behind Little Miss Party looks forward to throwing her annual latke party every Hanukkah. Seri cranks out a big batch of potato pancakes, provides a spread of topper options, and lets her guests take it from there. (This year Seri's guest list will be her husband and sons, but she still plans to have her latke bar.) She decks out the table with her menorah collection, mix-and-match serveware, and a modern interpretation of Hanukkah's traditional palette. "I like black, white, metallics, and a pop of color. Pantone's 2020 Color of the Year is a rich cobalt blue. It's trendy but still nods to the blue tradition."

TOPPINGS BAR

A few flavor combos:

HONEY-NUT sliced apples or pears, honey, chopped pistachios

SALMON-DILL smoked salmon or lox, crème fraîche, fresh dill

APPLE-POM applesauce, pomegranate arils, cinnamon

SOUR CREAM AND ONION sour cream, labneh, or Greek yogurt, plus fresh chives or scallions

CRISPY LATKES

HANDS-ON TIME 30 min.
TOTAL TIME 50 min.

- 4 large russet potatoes (9 to 11 oz. each)
- 1 small white onion
- 2 eggs, lightly beaten
- 3 Tbsp. all-purpose flour
- 1 Tbsp. kosher salt
- ¼ tsp. freshly ground black pepper
  Corn oil for frying
  Desired toppers

1. Preheat oven to 200°F. Place a wire rack in a shallow baking pan.
2. Peel potatoes. Use the coarse blade of a box grater to shred potatoes into a large bowl of ice water. Grate onion on the fine blade of a box grater. (You should have approximately ½ cup of grated onion.)
3. Drain potatoes; transfer them to a bowl lined with a clean flour sack towel or a fine-mesh 100-percent-cotton cheesecloth. Gently wrap and squeeze dish towel, getting out as much liquid as humanly possible. In a large bowl combine potatoes, onion, eggs, flour, salt, and pepper; stir.
4. In a heavy nonstick skillet heat ¼ inch of oil over medium-high until the oil shimmers. For each latke, scoop a small handful (¼ cup) of potato mixture and squeeze gently over the bowl. Flatten mixture and add to skillet. Repeat, adding a few at a time so you don't overcrowd the pan. Fry both sides until golden brown, 2 to 3 minutes per side.
5. Transfer to rack in shallow baking pan to drain and keep warm in oven while preparing the rest of your latkes. Serve warm with toppers. Makes 16 latkes.
EACH LATKE *145 cal, 11 g fat (2 g sat fat), 23 mg chol, 221 mg sodium, 10 g carb, 1 g fiber, 2 g pro*

what's your COOKIE PERSONALITY?

Cookie recipes exist for every holiday baking preference—from simple and homey to elaborately decorated and everything in between. In this collection of recipes, your true cookie identity may be revealed.

TRIPLE-GINGER COOKIES

Choose your level of spiciness—from mild to snappy—for these soft and chewy treats rolled in gingered sugar.

HANDS-ON TIME 30 min.
TOTAL TIME 2 hr., includes chilling

2	cups all-purpose flour
1½ to 2 tsp.	ground ginger
1	tsp. baking soda
1	tsp. ground cinnamon
½ to 1 tsp.	ground cloves
½ to ¾ cup	finely snipped crystallized ginger
½	cup shortening
¼	cup butter, softened
1	cup packed light brown sugar
1	egg
¼	cup dark molasses
¾	cup Ginger Sugar or granulated sugar

1. In a medium bowl stir together flour, ground ginger, baking soda, cinnamon, cloves, and ¾ tsp. salt. Stir in crystallized ginger.
2. In a large bowl beat shortening and butter with a mixer on medium 30 seconds. Add brown sugar and beat until combined, scraping bowl as needed. Beat in egg and molasses. Beat in flour mixture. Chill, covered, 1 hour or until dough is easy to handle.
3. Preheat oven to 350°F. Lightly grease two cookie sheets. Place Ginger Sugar in a small bowl. Shape dough into 1-inch balls. Roll balls in Ginger Sugar to coat. Place 1½ inches apart on prepared cookie sheets.
4. Bake 10 to 12 minutes or until edges are set. Let cool on cookie sheets 1 minute. Let cool on wire racks. Makes 48 cookies.

Ginger Sugar In a small bowl stir together ¾ cup granulated sugar and ¼ cup coarsely chopped fresh ginger. Let stand 1 hour; sugar will clump slightly from moisture in ginger. Place mixture in a fine-mesh sieve set over a bowl; stir gently so sugar separates from ginger. Discard chopped ginger.
EACH COOKIE *88 cal, 3 g fat (1 g sat fat), 6 mg chol, 76 mg sodium, 14 g carb, 10 g sugars, 1 g pro*

TRADITIONALISTS: THESE BAKERS KNOW THAT BAKING COOKIES SIGNALS THE BEGINNING OF THE HOLIDAYS. ESPECIALLY SO WHEN RELYING ON TRIED-AND-TRUE RECIPES THAT ARE ALWAYS WELL RECEIVED, SUCH AS THIS OLD-FASHIONED GINGER CRINKLE COOKIE.

ARTISTS: THESE CREATIVE TYPES LOOK AT A PLAIN SUGAR COOKIE AS A BLANK CANVAS, THEN EAGERLY TAKE PIPING BAG IN HAND. LIKELY A DRAWER HOLDS SPRINKLES AND DECORATING TIPS, INSPIRATION COMES FROM MANY SOURCES, AND GETTING STARTED ON THESE CUTE SANTAS IS ALREADY UNDER WAY.

ALMOND SUGAR COOKIES

Transform simple shapes into a jolly array of Santa cookies. Use smooth Royal Icing for flooding and detail work, then add beards and poms with Buttercream Frosting.

HANDS-ON TIME 20 min.
TOTAL TIME 2 hr. 30 min., includes chilling

¾   **cup slivered almonds, toasted (tip, page 50)**
2¼ **cups all-purpose flour**
1   **cup butter, softened**
¾   **cup sugar**
1   **egg**
1   **tsp. vanilla**
½   **tsp. lemon zest**
     Royal Icing
     Buttercream Frosting

1. In a food processor pulse toasted almonds until finely ground. In a medium bowl combine ground almonds, flour, and ¼ tsp. salt.
2. In a large bowl beat butter and sugar with a mixer on medium until light and fluffy. Add egg, vanilla, and lemon zest. Beat until combined. Beat in as much of the flour mixture as you can with the mixer. Stir in any remaining flour mixture. Divide dough in half. Cover and chill 2 hours or until dough is easy to handle.
3. Preheat oven to 350°F. On a lightly floured surface, roll one portion of dough at a time to ¼-inch thickness. Using 2½- to 3-inch cookie cutters, cut dough into desired shapes. Place 1 inch apart on an ungreased cookie sheet. Reroll scraps as needed.
4. Bake 8 to 12 minutes or until edges are light brown and centers are set. Let cool on cookie sheet 1 minute. Let cool on a wire rack. Decorate with Royal Icing and Buttercream Frosting. Makes 22 (3-inch) cookies.
EACH COOKIE 169 cal, 10 g fat (6 g sat fat), 31 mg chol, 96 mg sodium, 17 g carb, 7 g sugars, 2 g pro

MASCARPONE-COCOA CUTOUTS

HANDS-ON TIME 20 min.
TOTAL TIME 2 hr. 30 min., includes chilling

½   **cup butter, softened**
½   **cup mascarpone cheese**
1   **cup sugar**
¼   **tsp. baking powder**
½   **tsp. baking soda**
1½ **tsp. vanilla**
1   **egg**
¼   **cup unsweetened cocoa powder**
2¼ **cups all-purpose flour**
     Royal Icing
     Buttercream Frosting

1. In a large bowl beat butter and mascarpone cheese with a mixer on medium 30 seconds. Add sugar, baking powder, baking soda, and ¼ tsp. salt; beat until combined. Beat in vanilla and egg. Beat in cocoa powder and as much flour as you can with mixer. Stir in any remaining flour. Divide dough in half. Chill, covered, 30 to 60 minutes or until dough is easy to handle.
2. Preheat oven to 350°F. On a lightly floured surface, roll one portion of dough at a time to ¼-inch thickness. Using 2½- to 3-inch cookie cutters, cut dough into shapes. Place 1 inch apart on an ungreased cookie sheet. Reroll scraps.
3. Bake 8 to 12 minutes or until edges are light brown and centers are set. Let cool on cookie sheet 1 minute; cool completely on a wire rack. Decorate with Royal Icing and Buttercream Frosting.
EACH COOKIE 102 cal, 5 g fat (3 g sat fat), 18 mg chol, 71 mg sodium, 14 g carb, 6 g sugars, 2 g pro

ROYAL ICING

TOTAL TIME 15 min.

In a large bowl stir together one 16-oz. pkg. (4 cups) powdered sugar, 3 Tbsp. meringue powder, and ½ tsp. cream of tartar. Add ½ cup warm water and 1 tsp. vanilla. Beat with a mixer on low until combined. Beat on high 7 to 10 minutes or until icing is very stiff (for piping outlines and details). For flooding, divide out some of the icing and beat in additional warm water (4 to 5 tsp. per 1 cup icing) to reach desired consistency. When not using icing, keep it covered with plastic wrap or a damp paper towel to prevent drying out. If desired, chill up to 48 hours; stir before using. Makes about 3 cups.
EACH 1 TBSP. 37 cal, 9 g carb, 9 g sugars

BUTTERCREAM FROSTING

TOTAL TIME 15 min.

In a large bowl beat ½ cup softened butter with a mixer on medium 1 to 2 minutes or until creamy. Beat in ½ cup powdered sugar. Add 1 Tbsp. heavy cream and ½ tsp. vanilla; beat on low until combined. Gradually beat in an additional 1½ cups powdered sugar just until combined. Beat on medium 5 minutes or until fluffy, scraping bowl as needed. Add an additional 2 tsp. heavy cream; beat on high 1 minute more. Makes 1¾ cups.
EACH 2 TBSP. 131 cal, 7 g fat (5 g sat fat), 19 mg chol, 58 mg sodium, 17 g carb, 17 g sugars

ALMOND SUGAR
COOKIES &
MASCARPONE-
COCOA CUTOUTS

SHAPE SHIFTERS: EAGER TO EXPERIMENT AND UPDATE THE ORDINARY, THESE HOLIDAY BAKERS ARE EXPERTS WITH COOKIE PRESSES AND IN TURNING OUT DELICATE GERMAN SPRITZ COOKIES. HAVING CHOICES OF SHAPES AND FLAVORS MAKES THE DESIGN WORK OF BAKING EVEN MORE FUN.

LATTE SPRITZES

Choose a shape, then give this updated coffee version a spin. With espresso flavoring the dough and milk in the icing, it's a latte to nibble.

HANDS-ON TIME 30 min.
TOTAL TIME 55 min., includes cooling

- 2 Tbsp. instant espresso coffee powder
- 1½ cups butter, softened
- 1 cup sugar
- 1 tsp. baking powder
- 1 egg
- 1 tsp. vanilla
- 3½ cups all-purpose flour
  Coffee Cream Icing
  Edible gold glitter, fine sugar, luster dust, and/or instant espresso coffee powder

1. In a small bowl stir together espresso powder and 1 Tbsp. hot water. Set aside.
2. Preheat oven to 375°F. In a large bowl beat butter with a mixer on medium to high 30 seconds. Add sugar, baking powder, and ¼ tsp. salt. Beat until combined, scraping bowl as needed. Beat in egg, vanilla, and espresso mixture. Beat in flour until thoroughly combined.
3. Force unchilled dough through a cookie press onto an ungreased cookie sheet. Bake 6 minutes or until edges are firm. Let cool on a wire rack. Dip tops in or spread tops with Coffee Cream Icing; sprinkle as desired with glitter, sugar, luster dust, and/or instant espresso coffee powder. Makes 96 cookies.

Coffee Cream Icing In a large bowl beat ½ cup softened butter with a mixer on medium 30 seconds. Beat in one 7-oz. jar marshmallow creme and ½ tsp. vanilla just until combined. Beat in 2 Tbsp. unsweetened cocoa powder and 1 Tbsp. instant espresso coffee powder. Beat in ½ cup powdered sugar and enough milk (2 to 3 Tbsp.) for a dippable or spreadable consistency.

EACH COOKIE *73 cal, 4 g fat (3 g sat fat), 12 mg chol, 44 mg sodium, 8 g carb, 4 g sugars, 1 g pro*

PRESSING MATTERS

To make spritz cookies, you'll need a cookie press. If you have a hand-twist model, consider upgrading to a press with a squeeze-and-release mechanism. All models are equipped with a variety of discs to shape cookies and savory canapés.

SPIRITED BAKERS: THOSE WHO HOPPED ON THE CRAFT COCKTAIL TREND FROM THE BEGINNING—AND WHO MAINTAIN A COLLECTION OF FLAVORED LIQUEURS—BELIEVE THAT A LITTLE SPLASH OF SPIRIT BELONGS IN THE OVEN AS WELL AS IN A GLASS.

LIMONCELLO CHEESECAKE BARS

This festive pairing—refreshingly light citrus-spiked cheesecake bars and citrusy, bubbly cocktail—features limoncello. Sounds like the makings for a delivery to friends, along with an invitation to a virtual holiday happy hour.

HANDS-ON TIME 20 min.
TOTAL TIME 3 hr. 45 min., includes cooling and chilling

2	cups graham cracker crumbs
¼	cup sugar
2	tsp. lemon zest
½	cup butter, melted
2	8-oz. pkg. cream cheese, softened
⅔	cup sugar
2	tsp. vanilla
½	cup limoncello (Italian lemon liqueur)
2	eggs
	Candied Lemon Slices

1. Preheat oven to 350°F. Line a 13×9-inch baking pan with foil, extending foil over edges. In a medium bowl stir together graham cracker crumbs, the ¼ cup sugar, and the lemon zest. Add melted butter; stir until combined. Spread in prepared pan; press firmly. Bake 8 minutes or until lightly browned. Let cool on a wire rack.
2. For filling: In a large bowl beat cream cheese, the ⅔ cup sugar, and the vanilla with a mixer on medium until combined. Beat in limoncello until smooth. Beat in eggs just until combined. Pour filling over baked crust. Bake 20 minutes or until set. Let cool in pan on a wire rack 1 hour. Chill at least 2 hours.

3. Using foil, lift out uncut bars. Cut into bars. Top with Candied Lemon Slices. If desired, dust with powdered sugar. Refrigerate up to 3 days. Makes 24 bars.
Candied Lemon Slices Cut 2 lemons into ¼-inch slices; remove seeds. Roll slices in sugar to coat (about 3 Tbsp.). Heat an extra-large skillet over medium-high. Add lemon slices in a single layer. Cook 3 to 4 minutes per side or until glazed and starting to brown. Let cool on foil or parchment paper. Roll in additional sugar to coat. If desired, cut slices into halves or quarters.

EACH BAR *201 cal, 12 g fat (7 g sat fat), 45 mg chol, 147 mg sodium, 20 g carb, 15 g sugars, 3 g pro*

CITRUS SHIMMER

Tangerine juice and limoncello give this companion cocktail its pucker; a pour of bubbly Prosecco makes it glimmer.

TOTAL TIME 10 min.

In a cocktail glass combine 1 oz. (2 Tbsp.) fresh tangerine or orange juice and ½ oz. (1 Tbsp.) limoncello (Italian lemon liqueur). Add 3 oz. chilled Prosecco or other sparkling wine. Add ice cubes and garnish with a tangerine or lemon twist. Makes 1 cocktail.

EACH COCKTAIL *109 cal, 12 mg sodium, 3 g carb, 7 g sugars*

CURIOUS BAKERS: INTRIGUED COOKS OFTEN SEE AN UNUSUAL OR UNFAMILIAR INGREDIENT AND JUST CAN'T WAIT TO TEST IT FOR THEMSELVES. FREEZE-DRIED RASPBERRIES COULD BE A LIKELY MUSE. IT'S THE INGREDIENT IN THESE MARBLED COOKIES THAT PROVIDES PRETTY PINK ALONG WITH DELICATE FLAVOR.

RASPBERRY MARBLED SHORTBREAD

With no frosting to squish, these pretty cookies stack well in a jar or layer in a box for gifting.

HANDS-ON TIME 30 min.
TOTAL TIME 50 min., includes cooling

½   a 1.2- to 1.5-oz. pkg. freeze-dried raspberries
1¼ cups all-purpose flour
3   Tbsp. sugar
½   cup butter, cut up
    Pink or red food coloring (optional)

1. Place freeze-dried raspberries in a small food processor or blender. Process to a fine powder. Place powder in a fine-mesh sieve over a small bowl. Use a spoon to press powder through sieve; discard seeds. (You should have a scant ¼ cup raspberry powder.)

2. Preheat oven to 350°F. In a large bowl combine flour and sugar. Using a pastry blender, cut in butter until mixture resembles fine crumbs and starts to cling. Transfer half the mixture to a medium bowl and stir in raspberry powder; if desired, add pink or red food coloring. Form both dough portions into balls and gently knead until smooth. Divide each dough portion in half. Gently knead a raspberry dough portion with a plain dough portion to marble. Repeat with remaining two portions of dough.

3. On a lightly floured surface, roll each marbled dough piece to ¼-inch thickness. Using 2- to 2½-inch cookie cutters, cut dough into desired shapes. Place shapes approximately 2 inches apart on an ungreased cookie sheet.

4. Bake 6 to 8 minutes or until bottoms start to brown and cookies are set. Let cookies cool on a wire rack. Makes 24 cookies.

EACH COOKIE *66 cal, 4 g fat (2 g sat fat), 10 mg chol, 31 mg sodium, 7 g carb, 2 g sugars, 1 g pro*

REVERSE ENGINEERS: THESE FOODIES REVEL IN DECIPHERING INGREDIENTS AND RE-CREATING ELABORATE RESTAURANT DESSERTS, POPULAR GIRL SCOUT COOKIES, AND ETHNIC DISHES—SURE IN THEIR BELIEF THAT IMITATION IS THE SINCEREST FORM OF FLATTERY.

CHOCOLATE-ORANGE SANDWICH COOKIES

This version has orange zest folded into the cookie and a tender, rather than crisp, texture. Madeleine meets soft sugar cookie.

HANDS-ON TIME 45 min.

TOTAL TIME 1 hr. 30 min., includes cooling

- 1½ cups butter, softened
- 1⅓ cups powdered sugar
- ¾ cup granulated sugar
- 4 eggs
- 2 tsp. orange zest
- 1 tsp. vanilla
- 2⅔ cups all-purpose flour
- 2 cups dark chocolate chips
- 1 cup heavy cream

1. Preheat oven to 400°F. Line two cookie sheets with parchment paper.

2. In a large bowl beat butter, powdered sugar, granulated sugar, and ¼ tsp. salt with a mixer on medium until very light and fluffy. Beat in eggs, one at a time, until combined. Beat in orange zest and vanilla. Beat in flour.

3. Transfer dough to a large pastry bag fitted with a ½-inch round tip or a gallon-size resealable bag with the corner snipped off. For each batch, slide cookie template* under the parchment on prepared cookie sheet. Pipe dough onto parchment to fill template outlines. Remove template.

4. Bake 8 to 10 minutes or until edges are just beginning to turn golden. Let cool on a wire rack.

5. For ganache: Place chocolate chips in a medium bowl. Heat cream in a small saucepan over medium until it begins to simmer (do not boil). Pour hot cream over chocolate; let stand 5 minutes. Gently stir until smooth. Let cool 20 to 30 minutes or until ganache is room temperature and of spreading consistency, stirring frequently.

6. Spread bottoms of half the cookies with ganache. Top with remaining cookies. Let stand until ganache is set. Makes 22 sandwich cookies.

***Tip** A template makes it easier to pipe uniform ovals. Create the template by drawing 2½×1¼-inch ovals 2 inches apart onto a sheet of parchment paper.

EACH SANDWICH COOKIE *374 cal, 24 g fat (15 g sat fat), 79 mg chol, 150 mg sodium, 39 g carb, 2 g fiber, 26 g sugars, 4 g pro*

MASH-UP BAKERS: YOU'RE SMITTEN WITH THE CRONUT, THINK CHOCOLATE TACOS ARE GENIUS, AND ALWAYS ANSWER "BOTH!" WHEN ASKED TO CHOOSE BETWEEN DESSERTS. THESE TWO-IN-ONE FUSION BARS ARE FOR YOU. MOUNDS OF PEPPERMINT-SUGAR COOKIE DOUGH BAKE INTO A RICH BROWNIE BATTER.

PEPPERMINT-CHOCOLATE BROOKIES

HANDS-ON TIME 25 min.
TOTAL TIME 50 min.

- ½ cup butter, cut up
- 3 oz. unsweetened chocolate, coarsely chopped
- 1⅔ cups all-purpose flour
- ½ tsp. baking soda
- 2 cups sugar
- 3 eggs
- 1¼ tsp. vanilla
- ¼ cup butter, softened
- ¼ cup shortening
- ½ tsp. cream of tartar
- ¼ tsp. peppermint extract
- 14 layered chocolate-mint candies, chopped (½ cup)

1. For brownie batter: In a medium saucepan heat and stir cut-up butter and unsweetened chocolate over low until melted. Let cool 10 minutes.

2. Preheat oven to 350°F. Line a 9-inch square baking pan with foil, extending foil over edges. Grease foil. In a small bowl combine ⅔ cup flour and ¼ tsp. baking soda.

3. Stir 1 cup sugar into cooled chocolate mixture. Add 2 eggs, one at a time, beating with a spoon until combined. Stir in 1 tsp. vanilla. Stir in flour mixture just until combined. Spread batter in prepared pan.

4. For cookie dough: In a large bowl beat softened butter and shortening with a mixer on medium to high 30 seconds. Add remaining 1 cup sugar, the cream of tartar, remaining ¼ tsp. baking soda, and a pinch of salt. Beat in remaining egg, remaining ¼ tsp. vanilla, and the peppermint extract. Beat in as much of the remaining 1 cup flour as you can with the mixer. Stir in any remaining flour and the chopped mint candies.

5. Drop mounds of cookie dough over brownie batter. Bake about 30 minutes or until lightly browned and set. Cool in pan on a wire rack. Use foil to lift out uncut bars. Cut into bars. Makes 20 bars.

EACH BAR *256 cal, 14 g fat (8 g sat fat), 46 mg chol, 107 mg sodium, 32 g carb, 2 g fiber, 22 g sugars, 3 g pro*

RAISE A GLASS

Rising star sommelier Cha McCoy shares how to pair wines with holiday meals and encourages you to enjoy the adventure.

"Wine is meant to be connected to food. You need to be able to see the magic in the pairing," says certified sommelier and wine consultant Cha McCoy. It's a balancing act many of us struggle with when tables are packed with a dizzying selection of flavors. Cha suggests wines with minerality to offset rich holiday foods and first considers the main dish. "It tends to have the most dominant flavor and typically takes up most of your plate," she says. Browse her picks.

TURKEY

Cha pairs traditional turkey with light reds from Oregon or California that have earthy, floral flavors. Try **Raft Wines 2019 Love Ranch Counoise** ($28). Made by a woman-owned winery in Madera, CA, this pale red features ripe, dusty raspberry flavors and a lavender finish. **Maison Noir's 2018 P-Oui Pinot Noir** ($28, 375 ml) is an earthy, smoky red produced by a Black-owned winery in Willamette Valley, OR.

RED MEAT

If roast beef is taking center stage, Cha recommends tannic reds with fresh and ripe fruitiness to stand up to fat in meat. "And if there is cranberry sauce nearby, either of these wines is a trifecta with the beef." The **2018 Sheldrake Point Gamay Noir** ($18), from New York's Finger Lakes region, has what Cha describes as bruised red apple and wild berry flavors with spice notes from partial oak aging. **2013 Domaine Rolet Pere et Fils Arbois Trousseau**, Jura, France ($22), comes from a family-owned winery in a lesser-known region. Notes of strawberry, blackberry, and baking spices pair well with beef.

IF YOU CAN'T FIND THESE SPECIFIC WINES, CHA RECOMMENDS ASKING YOUR LOCAL WINE SHOP TO HELP YOU FIND WINES WITH SIMILAR CHARACTERISTICS OR FROM THE SAME REGION.

VEGETABLES

When pairing with vegetable dishes, Cha focuses on fruit-driven wines high in minerality. With fresh salads and chilled dishes, Cha recommends a Sauvignon Blanc like the **2019 McBride Sisters Collection** ($17) from a winery owned by Black women in Marlborough, New Zealand. It has Meyer lemon and pineapple notes with white peppercorn and floral aromas. For heavy dishes or ones with a rich sauce, Cha looks for white wines that had skin contact (sometimes called orange wines), which results in round texture and lowers the acidity. The **2017 Monastero Suore Cistercensi Coenobium** ($25), made by nuns in Lazio, Italy, tastes of ripe fruit with notes of orange oil and baked green apple.

RECIPE INDEX

METRIC INFORMATION

PRODUCT DIFFERENCES

Most of the ingredients called for in the recipes in this book are available in most countries. However, some are known by different names. Here are some common American ingredients and their possible counterparts:

SUGAR (white) is granulated, fine granulated, or castor sugar.

POWDERED SUGAR is icing sugar.

ALL-PURPOSE FLOUR is enriched, bleached or unbleached white household flour. When self-rising flour is used in place of all-purpose flour in a recipe that calls for leavening, omit the leavening agent (baking soda or baking powder) and salt.

LIGHT-COLOR CORN SYRUP is golden syrup.

CORNSTARCH is cornflour.

BAKING SODA is bicarbonate of soda.

VANILLA OR VANILLA EXTRACT is vanilla essence.

GREEN, RED, OR YELLOW SWEET PEPPERS are capsicums or bell peppers.

GOLDEN RAISINS are sultanas.

SHORTENING is solid vegetable oil (substitute Copha or lard).

MEASUREMENT ABBREVIATIONS

MEASUREMENT	ABBREVIATIONS
fluid ounce	fl. oz.
gallon	gal.
gram	g
liter	L
milliliter	ml
ounce	oz.
package	pkg.
pint	pt.

COMMON WEIGHT EQUIVALENTS

IMPERIAL / U.S.	METRIC
½ ounce	14.18 g
1 ounce	28.35 g
4 ounces (¼ pound)	113.4 g
8 ounces (½ pound)	226.8 g
16 ounces (1 pound)	453.6 g
1¼ pounds	567 g
1½ pounds	680.4 g
2 pounds	907.2 g

OVEN TEMPERATURE EQUIVALENTS*

FAHRENHEIT SETTING	CELSIUS SETTING
300°F	150°C
325°F	160°C
350°F	180°C
375°F	190°C
400°F	200°C
425°F	220°C
450°F	230°C
475°F	240°C
500°F	260°C
Broil	Broil

*For convection or forced air ovens (gas or electric), lower the temperature setting 25°F/10°C when cooking at all heat levels.

APPROXIMATE STANDARD METRIC EQUIVALENTS

MEASUREMENT	OUNCES	METRIC
⅛ tsp.		0.5 ml
¼ tsp.		1 ml
½ tsp.		2.5 ml
1 tsp.		5 ml
1 Tbsp.		15 ml
2 Tbsp.	1 fl. oz.	30 ml
¼ cup	2 fl. oz.	60 ml
⅓ cup	3 fl. oz.	80 ml
½ cup	4 fl. oz.	120 ml
⅔ cup	5 fl. oz.	160 ml
¾ cup	6 fl. oz.	180 ml
1 cup	8 fl. oz.	240 ml
2 cups	16 fl. oz. (1 pt.)	480 ml
1 qt.	64 fl. oz. (2 pt.)	0.95 L

CONVERTING TO METRIC

centimeters to inches	divide centimeters by 2.54
cups to liters	multiply cups by 0.236
cups to milliliters	multiply cups by 236.59
gallons to liters	multiply gallons by 3.785
grams to ounces	divide grams by 28.35
inches to centimeters	multiply inches by 2.54
kilograms to pounds	divide kilograms by 0.454
liters to cups	divide liters by 0.236
liters to gallons	divide liters by 3.785
liters to pints	divide liters by 0.473
liters to quarts	divide liters by 0.946
milliliters to cups	divide milliliters by 236.59
milliliters to fluid ounces	divide milliliters by 29.57
milliliters to tablespoons	divide milliliters by 14.79
milliliters to teaspoons	divide milliliters by 4.93
ounces to grams	multiply ounces by 28.35
ounces to milliliters	multiply ounces by 29.57
pints to liters	multiply pints by 0.473
pounds to kilograms	multiply pounds by 0.454
quarts to liters	multiply quarts by 0.946
tablespoons to milliliters	multiply tablespoons by 14.79
teaspoons to milliliters	multiply teaspoons by 4.93